EUROPE'S ECONOMIC RESPONSE TO THE COVID-19 PANDEMIC

EDITED BY
ZOË KATHARINA STRAUSS AND ERIK JONES

European and Eurasian Studies Program
Johns Hopkins SAIS
Bologna, Italy

Perch

First published in 2020 by Perch Press
405 Western Ave., Suite 302
South Portland, ME 04106
USA

ISBN 978-1-7359722-1-3 (ePdf)
ISBN 978-1-7359722-0-6 (ePub)

Typeset by JS Typesetting Ltd, Porthcawl, Mid Glamorgan

CONTENTS

PROLOGUE: FINDING THE RIGHT LEVEL

A coronavirus attacks individuals, who live in communities that tend to be organized as towns, cities, provinces, and regions. When an outbreak starts, it is rarely a national problem and almost never understood as something larger than that. Nevertheless, effective control over an outbreak or pandemic works the other way around, particularly when people are free to move from one place to the next. Isolation and containment depend upon coordination. Ideally the scale of that coordination would be the same as the scale of movement. If you have a big area where people can travel freely, then you need an equally high level of coordination to prevent a localized outbreak from spreading.

The European Union (EU) has a large internal market that places strong emphasis on freedom of movement. Indeed, even those countries that never joined the EU, like Norway, or that chose to leave, like the United Kingdom, remain integrated via the movement of people across national boundaries. The governments of these countries will necessarily need to consider what governments elsewhere are doing in crafting an effective response.

The problem of coordination applies in the economic domain as well. The movement of people takes place alongside the flow of goods and services. This is not accidental; that linkage is fundamental to the European project. To see why, it is only necessary to run that process in reverse – and start by closing down the movement of people to see what the economic consequences are. Even those countries that choose a more liberal response to the coronavirus, like Sweden, find themselves powerfully affected by the economic impact.

The challenge for policymakers is that what may be optimal in public health terms or in economic terms, is not optimal politically. Whatever the arguments for a higher level of coordination, people place a high value on their independence – as individuals, communities, regions, and nations. By implication, policymakers have to trade off effectiveness for legitimacy. At one extreme, individuals, regions, or countries may try to go it alone; at the other extreme, political leaders may try to centralize responsibility despite local, regional, or national opposition.

This tension is not unique to policy responses to a global pandemic, but a global pandemic does bring this tension into sharp relief. The question is how well policymakers are able to respond.

We put that question to a group of students studying European Financial Markets at the Johns Hopkins School of Advanced International Studies (SAIS) in Bologna, Italy. In doing so, we gave them a choice to focus on either a national case or a European institution. The goal is not to provide a comprehensive overview. Rather it is to highlight a variety of perspectives on the same problematic – how much do policymakers need to look across countries to respond effectively, and how much do they need to focus their attention within countries to generate adequate support for the extraordinary measures they have to undertake.

The result is an interesting mix of insights focusing primarily on the economic dimension of the problem – the Johns Hopkins School of Public Health can take up the epidemiological considerations. The collection starts with the experience of Italy, Spain, and France. These are the three countries that caught the leading edge of the pandemic. We then introduce the macroeconomic response – starting with the ECB both before and after the crisis became truly European in its dimensions, and then moving to national fiscal responses through the debate about fiscal mutualization, and into the proposals put forward by the European Commission. As we publish this collection, those proposals have been agreed upon but much of the implementation remains to be done. We realize this means our narrative will be overtaken by events. That would be inevitable for any such project; what matters is the overlapping perspectives. This story is not going to end quickly.

The contrasts emerge in the last three chapters. That is where we look at the Dutch, British, and Norwegian cases. The Dutch case is important because the government of that country has a very clear position on the requirements for greater European solidarity. The British case matters because that government arose out of an effort to leave the European Union. The Norwegian case sheds light on the possibilities for national autonomy under the best possible circumstances – defined not only in terms of relative geographic isolation, but also in terms of financial preparedness.

Finally, we should add a word of acknowledgment. This volume would not have been possible without the generous support of our colleagues at Agenda Publishing. Although this book is not produced under their imprint, the editors at Agenda gave us invaluable advice on how to assemble the manuscript and convert it into publishable format. Our friend and colleague Tony Ramunni came up with the logo for Perch Press many years ago. This is the first time we have been able to put it to use. The financing for this project came from colleagues at *Government & Opposition* as part of a wider project on the future of democracy in the transatlantic community. Contributors were very generous in responding to comments and queries. Finally, the European Council came up with an agreement for which this entire analysis is merely prologue, given that we asked our contributors to use 19 June as a common end date for their analysis. Hopefully, Europe will recover strongly from this crisis. If and when it does, this collection will play a useful role in explaining how.

Zoë Katharina Strauss
Amsterdam, The Netherlands

Erik Jones
Bologna, Italy

CONTRIBUTORS

Charles Lawrie is studying Environmental Policy and International Economics at the Johns Hopkins School of Advanced International Studies.

Erik Jones is Professor of European Studies and International Political Economy at the Johns Hopkins School of Advanced International Studies.

Hayden Hubbard is studying International Development and International Economics at the Johns Hopkins School of Advanced International Studies.

Niklas Hintermayer studied European and Eurasian Studies at the Johns Hopkins School of Advanced International Studies.

Isabeau Mensing studied International Affairs at the Johns Hopkins School of Advanced International Studies.

Moritz Osterhuber is studying International Political Economy and International Economics at the Johns Hopkins School of Advanced International Studies.

Rebecca Neri is studying International Relations at the University of Bologna and the Johns Hopkins School of Advanced International Studies.

Thomas Rave is studying International Affairs at the Johns Hopkins School of Advanced International Studies and Sciences Po Lille.

Volodymyr Nesplyak is studying International Political Economy and specializing in International Finance at the Johns Hopkins School of Advanced International Studies.

William Marshall is studying International Political Economy and International Economics at the Johns Hopkins School of Advanced International Studies.

Zixuan Feng is studying International Political Economy and International Economics at the Johns Hopkins School of Advanced International Studies.

Zoë Katharina Strauss is studying International Political Economy and International Economics at the Johns Hopkins School of Advanced International Studies.

ACRONYMS

ABSPP	Asset-backed Securities Purchase Program
ACPR	French Prudential Control and Resolution Authority
AfD	Alternative for Germany
AMECO	Annual macro-economic database of the European Commission
APP	Asset Purchase Program
BNP	BNP Paribas
BoS	Bank of Spain
bpd	barrels per day
BVerfG	German Federal Constitutional Court
CA	Crédit Agricole
CBPP3	Covered Bond Purchase Program
CBS	Dutch national statistics agency (Centraal Bureau voor de Statistiek)
CET1	Common Equity Tier 1
CRR	Capital Requirements Regulation
CSPP	Corporate Sector Purchase Programme
DNB	De Nederlandsche Bank
EBA	European Banking Authority
ECB	European Central Bank
ECCL	Enhanced Conditions Credit Line
ECJ	European Court of Justice
ECSC	European Coal and Steel Community
EEC	European Economic Community
EFSI	European Fund for Strategic Investment
EFSF	European Financial Stability Facility
EFSM	European Financial Stabilization Mechanism
EIB	European Investment Bank
ESM	European Stability Mechanism
EU	European Union
EURIBOR	Euro Interbank Best Offered Rates
FCA	Financial Conduct Authority

FDP	German Free Democratic Party
FSA	Financial Services Authority
FOBR	Fund for Orderly Bank Restructuring
FvD	Forum for Democracy (Forum voor Democratie) (Dutch political party)
GDP	Gross Domestic Product
GFC	Global financial crisis
GNI	Gross National Income
IMF	International Monetary Fund
INSEE	French national statistics agency (Institut national de la statistique et des études économiques)
Istat	Italian national statistics agency (Istituto Nazionale di Statistica)
IoT	Internet of Things
LIBOR	London Interbank Best Offered Rate
LPF	Pim Fortuyn List (Lijst Pim Fortuyn) (Dutch political party)
LTD	Loan-to-deposit (ratio)
LTROs	Longer-term refinancing operations
MFF	Multiannual Financial Framework
MRO	Main refinancing operations
MTO	Medium-Term Budgetary Objective
M5S	Five Star Movement
NFCs	Non-financial firms
NOK	Norwegian Kroner
NPL	Non-performing loans
OECD	Organization for Economic Co-operation and Development
OMT	Outright Monetary Transactions
OIS	Overnight indexed swaps
PCSCL	Pandemic Crisis Support Credit Line
PELTROs	longer-term refinancing operations
PEPP	Pandemic Emergency Purchase Program
PD	Italian Democratic Party
PRA	Prudential Regulatory Authority
PSOE	Spanish Socialist party
PSPP	Public Sector Purchase Program
PVV	Dutch Party for Freedom (Partij voor de Vrijheid)
RFI	Rapid Financing Instrument
RRF	Recovery and Resilience Facility
SFEF	Association for financing the French Economy (Société de Financement de l'Economie Française)
SGP	Stability and Growth Pact
SMEs	Small and medium-sized enterprises

SMP	Securities Markets Program
SocGen	Société Générale
SP	Dutch socialist party (Socialistische Partij)
SPPE	State Shareholding Corporation (Société de Prise de Participation de l'État)
SRM	Single Resolution Mechanism
SRR	Special Resolution Regime
SURE	Support to mitigate Unemployment Risks in an Emergency
Svimez	Associazione per lo sviluppo dell'industria nel Mezzogiorno (Association for the Development of Southern Italy)
S&P	Standard & Poor's
TARGET2	Trans-European Automated Real-time Gross Settlement Express Transfer System
TLTRO	Targeted longer-term refinancing operations
VVD	People's Party for Freedom and Democracy (Volkspartij voor Vrijheid en Democratie)
YCC	Yield curve control

FIGURES AND TABLES

1

ITALY'S CONSTRAINTS IN THE FIGHT AGAINST THE CORONAVIRUS

Niklas Hintermayer

The economic challenges facing Italy due to the outbreak of the novel coronavirus highlight the country's long-standing structural problems. This is due to the high level of public debt, almost non-existent economic growth rates, and the fragile banking system. Furthermore, although Italy has a new government since August 2019, the country is not more stable politically. Prime Minister Giuseppe Conte confronts strong political headwinds from the opposition parties. In addition, the governing parties disagree on which financial resources are best suited at the EU level. Italy will need money from the EU to master the challenge of economic reconstruction as the country is in its deepest economic recession of the post-Second World War period. This, in turn, is having an impact on the budget deficit. And if Italy does not get this under control, the next debt crisis could already be on the horizon – with possible consequences for the entire eurozone.

This overview of the Italian response to the coronavirus begins by describing the initial outbreak of the pandemic in February followed by the nationwide shutdown. It then explores the economic consequences of this lockdown, and outlines the decrees introduced by the government. The analysis focuses on the constraints facing the Italian government and draws comparisons with the sovereign debt crisis of 2011–2012. The chapter concludes with the EU dimension including Italy's approach toward the European Stability Mechanism (ESM).

Lockdown

Italy reported its first coronavirus infections on January 31 in Rome (Amante 2020), with 16 further cases on 21 February in Lombardy and Veneto, and its first death due to COVID-19 on 22 February in Padua in the Veneto region (Badkar et al. 2020). From that time on, the spread of the virus concentrated on the northern regions Lombardy, Veneto, and Piedmont, and then also on the central regions, Emilia-Romagna, and Lazio. By the beginning of March, the coronavirus had reached all Italian regions. In less than a month, between 21 February and 21 March, some 53,578 were infected (Statista 2020a). Soon, Italy became the worldwide epicenter of the new pandemic. On 21 March, Italy reported its highest rate increase in cases with 6,557 new infections within one day. By that time Italy had more than 4,800 deaths, and thus had surpassed China in terms of mortality from the coronavirus (Statista 2020b).

Prime Minister Giuseppe Conte reacted relatively swiftly to the outbreak. The leader of the government, comprised of the anti-establishment Five Star Movement (M5S) and the center-left Democratic Party (PD), gradually tightened the restrictions on the movement of people and business activities to contain the spread of the virus. On 9 March, Italy became the first country in Europe to order a nationwide lockdown to slow the spread of the coronavirus. From that point on, the only reasons to go outside were for groceries, medical appointments, or exercise. Traveling abroad and across regions was only allowed for specific work purposes.

In view of the rapid spread of the virus and the excessive demands on the Italian healthcare sector, it was unsurprising that even the opposition parties agreed with Conte. At that time, Italy showed a certain degree of political unity. Even the right-wing Lega leader Matteo Salvini gave the Prime Minister some credit. He went even further when stating earlier the day of the announcement of the nationwide shutdown, that it had been necessary 'to close everything and immediately, without leaving space for doubts or interpretations' (Horowitz 2020). Matteo Renzi, the center-left former prime minister and now leader of the newly Viva Italia party, stated that the government should have acted faster in expanding the measures to whole Italy in order to prevent the spread of the coronavirus to other regions.

On 11 March, Conte forbade almost all retail activities in Italy. The government also announced the closure of all non-essential businesses and industries. Only banks, supermarkets, pharmacies, and post offices could stay open. By that time, Italy accounted for more than one-third of the around 13,000 deaths worldwide.

Soon the serious consequences of the lockdown for the Italian economy became clear. The private non-profit organization Svimez (Associazione per lo sviluppo dell'industria nel Mezzogiorno) published a report on the economic and social impact of COVID-19. According to their estimates, the Italian economy lost €48 billion in value added (or 3.1 percent of Italian Gross domestic product, GDP) each month that the restrictions remain in place. About €37 billion was lost in the center and north of the country, while the remaining €10–11 billion came from the regions to the south (Svimez 2020: 5–6).

The medical situation improved slowly, with the number of people positively infected falling on 20 April for the first time since the coronavirus outbreak. On 4 May, Prime Minister Conte announced the beginning of 'Phase Two'. In order to lift the lockdown gradually, several measures were introduced. The most important were that: people could travel again within their regions but not to other ones; bars and restaurants could offer takeaway services, and bars, restaurants and hairdressers and beauty salons could open by 1 June. On 3 June, Italy opened its borders and stopped the regional travel restrictions. Twelve days later, on 15 June, the country went into 'Phase Three' of the relaxation, which included the re-opening of cinemas and theatres, the allowance of amateur contact sports, and the re-opening of nightclubs by certain dates.

Even though Conte reacted relatively quickly to the outbreak of the coronavirus pandemic, there was criticism of the gradual implementation of measures to prevent the spread of the virus. This has to do with the fact that the government was constrained by regional conditions. Health issues in Italy are not managed centrally as regions are legally responsible for hospital and health assistance. This decentralization process has started at the end of the 1990s (Di Quirico 2010). Business experts criticized, among other things, Italy's political management, as Lombardy and Veneto had different approaches in combating the pandemic. In their opinion, it would have been more efficient using the successful 'Veneto approach' earlier to adapt other regional and central responses adequately.

Veneto, one of the leading industrial regional economies in Italy, followed a more proactive strategy than the richest region, Lombardy. Veneto especially made early use of extensive testing to contain the coronavirus. When a person tested positive for coronavirus infection, his or her household members and neighbors had to undergo testing as well (Pisano, Sadun and Zanini 2020). As a result, Veneto had significantly lower coronavirus cases and deaths than Lombardy.

Financial stimulus packages

The Conte government introduced three decrees to provide liquidity for households, workers, and companies during the lockdown and to facilitate economic recovery. The first decree, called 'Cure Italy', was issued on 17 March and provided support measures worth €25 billion euros (Canino et al. 2020). This decree represented 'a very strong injection of liquidity into the credit system that can mobilise around €340 billion in loans to the real economy, with suspension of loan and mortgage repayments,' said Economy Minister Roberto Gualtieri (The Local 2020). As part of the program, €3.5 billion were immediately deployable for the health system and €10 billion in order to support families and workers (CNBC 2020). The decree was approved in the Senate on 9 April and in the Chamber of Deputies on 24 April. The opposition opposed the decree, with Matteo Salvini at the forefront: The Lega leader stated that the package was insufficient 'and bedeviled by bureaucracy which made it hard for people to access the funds available' (Jones 2020). The political unity that prevailed in the country at the beginning of the coronavirus outbreak dissipated.

The core of this package is the suspension of loan and mortgage repayments for hard-hit companies and families through the creation of guarantees for banks by the states. Additionally, the decree sets up increasing funds in order for companies to be able to pay workers who had been temporarily laid off due to the lockdown (Jones 2020). This support to stabilize employment is important. According to Svimez (2020: 11), 34.4 percent of the workers and 41.5 percent of the self-employed in Italy were affected by the nationwide lockdown. In March 2020, unemployment in Italy stood at 8.4 percent, the forecast for the whole year is at 11.2 percent due to the consequences of the coronavirus crisis (Statista 2020c). However, Svimez (2020: 6) also states that the decree does not reach all working people. Some 1.8 private employees are still defenseless, including 800,000 domestic workers and about one million temporary workers. In addition, there are about two million irregularly employed.

'Restore Liquidity' was the second decree, and was introduced by the government on 8 April, coming into effect the next day. This fiscal stimulus package include provisions to strengthen the government's power to block foreign, hostile takeovers in sectors such as finance, energy, transport, together with state guarantees of €400 billion – in order to provide loans and investments to support companies. All firms with a registered office in Italy can apply for these guarantees. Companies that are too big to apply for the Central Guarantee Fund, operate in specific sectors and have lost revenues due to the coronavirus pandemic can apply for a separate state guarantee. The 'Restore Liquidity' decree also contains tax cuts and investments to support exports.

A third decree, called the 'Relaunch Decree' by the Italian government, had to wait until mid-May. According to Conte, the 'Relaunch Decree' worth of €55 billion is to help the economic and social recovery after the re-opening of the country. The package again consists of grants and tax breaks to support firms in their recovery. In addition, the decree introduces subsidies to families and financial help for the tourism sector.

Economic impacts of the coronavirus crisis

While these three decrees are a first step to reboot the economy, they will not be enough. The pandemic-induced shock has hit Italy's economy massively, disrupting supply chains and straining manufacturing. The nationwide lockdown accelerated the shutdown of production and service facilities. Comparing March to February, seasonally adjusted industrial production (without construction) fell by 28.4 percent, retail trade decreased by 20.5 percent in terms of value 21.3 percent in terms of volume. The Italian National Institute of Statistics (Istat) estimates that real GDP contracted by 4.7 percent in the first quarter of 2020 over the previous quarter (Istat 2020).

The difficulty for Italy also lies in the fact that the economy was already struggling at the end of last year. At the end of the fourth quarter of 2019 Italy's GDP shrank by 0.3 percent. For over a decade, Italy experienced almost no economic growth (Lachmann 2020). The European Commission forecasts real output to contract by 18 percent in the first two quarters of 2020 and 9.5 percent over the year as a whole – which means any recovery in the second half will be modest (European Commission 2020a: 94).

The coronavirus crisis also constrains public finances due to the slump in economic activity and the costs of the automatic stabilizers and fiscal responses. Last year, the government deficit ranked at a historic low (with 1.6 percent of GDP, due to policy measures and a resilient labor market that helped government revenues). However, this year government expenditures will rise and could put the government deficit up to 11 percent of GDP (European Commission 2020a: 95). As mentioned, the Italian government has already put into effect three fiscal stimulus packages to help workers, families, and firms. At the same time, due to the long-lasting halt in economic activity, the government is confronted with declining revenues: as firms stopped producing or had to shut down, thus making lower profits, revenues from corporate taxes will decrease. And as private consumption has already fallen, this will result in the decline of indirect taxes (European Commission 2020a: 95).

Moreover, Italy has a long history with a high public debt burden: The government debt-to-GDP ratio has increased constantly since the 1970s (De Cecco 2007). In 2010 Italian public stood at 119.2 percent of GDP; after the sovereign debt crisis the amount was up to 132.4 percent in 2014 (Banca d'Italia 2020: 6). At the end of last year, the government debt-to-GDP ratio was at 134.8 percent. The strongly increasing costs in order to keep the economy alive do not play well for Italy's high public debt either. The government debt-to-GDP ratio is expected by the EU to climb up to 159 percent this year. Such high levels of debt mean high financing requirements. Italy's maturing debt in 2020 is expected to be 19.93 percent of GDP in 2020 (International Monetary Fund 2020a). Any new debt will come on top of that.

Prior to the pandemic, Italy attempted to reduce the soaring public debt burden. In September 2019, Prime Minister Conte and the Minister for Economy and Finance, Roberto Gualtieri, announced several economic policies that should be developed by the government along a multiannual horizon. This was seen to be necessary:

> in the light of the need to place the public debt ratio to GDP on a clear downward path.... The decline in the debt ratio will be pursued in the first place through the gradual convergence of the deficit towards the MTO (Medium-Term Budgetary Objective of the EU which should ensure sound fiscal policies), economic recovery, the reduction of the cost of debt financing and a realistic privatisation programme (Ministero dell'economia e delle finanze 2019: 5).

However, against the background of the current crisis, and the government's budget constraints, these objectives are unrealistic. The high public indebtedness could also change the perception of market investors to rate Italy as riskier. As a consequence, this doubt over its financial stability could lead to a rise in the yield of Italy's government bonds (as it was already seen in recent months, see below) (European Commission 2020a: 95). This makes it just more difficult for Italy to borrow money on the capital markets in order to fight adequately the economic consequences of the coronavirus crisis.

In turn, the high debt ratio might also impact the health of the Italian banking sector. According to the OECD, the stability of the Italian bank system is intertwined with public finance and the impacts on government bond yields. The lower government bond yields fall, the better it is for the banking system (OECD 2019a: 26). Already during the financial crisis, EU member states in the periphery saw the effects of a 'sovereign debt–domestic bank loop'. As government expenditures rose, and the debt burden grew, the sovereign risk of the countries concerned increased. This led to a threat of distorting the collateral function of sovereign debt. In turn, the funding conditions of banks were harmed (Howarth and Quaglia 2013). Today, Italian banks hold large amounts of government bonds (Gros 2019). If yields on Italy's government bonds rise further, banks who hold them could suffer from balance sheet losses – because a rise in the yield corresponds with a fall in the price (and value) of the underlying asset. In turn, this could lead banks to decrease lending and seek recapitalization (OECD 2019a: 23).

Bond markets

The political atmosphere in the country plays an important role in the extent to which the market investors trust Italy. This can be seen by the fact that political changes and controversies in recent years put pressure on market trust in Italy. In June 2018, the far-right Lega and the anti-establishment Five Star Movement formed a new government coalition. In Europe, this coalition was received with uncertainty due to the high degree of political volatility as well as the Euroscepticism of the Lega. The Lega makes no secret of the fact that they would leave the eurozone if necessary. As a result, the holders of government bonds were confronted with paper losses as the yield on 10-year government bonds climbed up to more than 0.5 percent at the end of May 2018. The 10-years bond yield was up to 2.32 percent on May 22, 2018 – a record high since 2014 (Allen and Johnson 2018).

On August 9, 2019, then Interior Minister Matteo Salvini pushed forward a vote of no confidence in Prime Minister Conte in the Parliament (in the end, Conte won the no-confidence vote) (Momigliano and Povoledo 2019). In doing so, Salvini saw the only chance to force new elections as political tensions had become unbearable in the coalition. This political instability, with the underlying uncertainty of new elections, put Italian debt once more under pressure. The 10-years bond yield grew by 0.23 percentage points up to 1.76 percent (Stubbington 2019).

International events matter too. After European Central Bank (ECB) president Christine Lagarde's statement that it is not the duty of the European Central Bank to 'close the spread' between the bonds of the EU member states, Italian borrowing costs rose to more than 2.3 percent on 17 March 2020 – the highest number within nine months (Stubbington 2020b). The 10-year government bonds of Italy and Germany are best used to estimate the yield spreads. As German bond yields representing assets with the fewest risk, the yield spread between Italian and German bonds represent how markets perceive risk (Jones 2012).

But there were also good reactions on the bond markets: on 18 March the Bank of Italy announced that it would buy Italian bonds on behalf of the ECB to stabilize the highly volatile markets. As a result, Italy's 10-year bond yield pulled back from its highs at 2.78 percent (Ranasinghe 2020). However, that recovery proved short lived. After the Eurogroup announced its agreement on a European stabilization package of €540 billion, the Italian bond markets reacted negatively. The Prime Minister's criticism was directed in particular against the credit lines of the European Stability Mechanism (ESM). Conte stated that Italy would not make use of the cheap loans from the bailout fund as he referred to it as a 'totally inadequate tool'.

The rating agencies highlighted Italy's increasing problems in the financial markets when they downgraded the country's creditworthiness. Standard & Poor's (S&P) announced on April 24 that it holds Italy's credit rating at BBB, which means two notches above 'junk'. This rating was made despite the already high Italian debt levels; however, a future downgrade was not excluded. 'We could lower the ratings if government debt to GDP fails to shift on to a clearly discernible downward path over the next three years, or if there is a marked deterioration in borrowing conditions that jeopardizes the sovereign's public finance sustainability,' the rating agency said in a statement (Stubbington 2020a). Fitch Ratings stated on 29 April that is had cut Italy's creditworthiness to a single notch above 'junk' (Fitch Ratings 2020). Fitch raised concerns over the increasing debt levels, resulting from the economic response to the coronavirus crisis, and in this context how sustainable the country's financial borrowings will be (Stubbington and Johnson 2020).

Lessons from the sovereign debt crisis in Italy

In this context, it is important to look at the sovereign debt crisis 2011–2012 to see what lessons can be drawn from that time. At first, things did not look too bad for Italy in the midst of the financial crisis that started off in some European countries in 2008. According to the Organization for Economic Cooperation and Development (OECD), Italy experienced the smallest reduction in its fiscal balance between 2009 and 2011 of any of the eurozone countries. The austerity measures, imposed by then Prime Minister Silvio Berlusconi (The People of Freedom Party), at first took pressure off the public debt burden. The government knew that a weakening of its fiscal position could lead to an increase in the spread between Italian and German bonds.

This positive situation did not last long. More countries in the eurozone could not find an appropriate way to hold the interest rates down at the new issuances of debt. As a consequence, markets became fearful of spill-over effects in the eurozone. This was reinforced by the fact that the European Central Bank could not find an appropriate way to tackle the soaring debt problems, and also the dividing's between the governments of the eurozone became more and more apparent. Investors got fearful of investing in Italy with its high public debt burden. Italy soon became the new problem child of the eurozone and started to slip into a debt crisis that fully hit the country in summer 2011 (Hopkin 2012).

At the same time, Italy had to fight with its long-lasting structural problems. Some of them have not been resolved. First, Italy's economic growth was the weakest between 1990 and 2012 in the eurozone. This weak growth has been a continuing cause for concern – and even after the crisis, Italy still had difficulties in stimulating economic performance. With a debt burden larger than the country's annual output, economic growth would have to be higher than the cost of debt service if the debt were to be reduced, and any spike in borrowing costs would destroy any hope of this. In the absence of recovery, markets would have to believe that the Italian government would deliver harsh austerity measures in order to protect its budget position. Here, the poor credibility of Italy's political leadership during the country's sovereign debt crisis became a major burden (Hopkin 2012).

Italy continues to struggle to boost economic growth, and with the massive supply shock due to the coronavirus outbreak, it will be difficult to introduce austerity measures. However, Prime Minister Conte is not as badly perceived abroad in the EU as it was the case with Berlusconi in 2011. This could be an advantage in terms of how the market assesses Italy's creditworthiness. Moreover, unlike in 2011, the rating agencies did not cite political leadership as one of the reasons for the credit rating downgrade.

The growing domestic political disputes between the parties are another challenge that Conte faces. At times of the sovereign debt crisis, Berlusconi proved to be the wrong person to lead Italy through the sovereign debt crisis. Not only did the struggle with the Lega Nord, his principal coalition partner in the government, but also his focus on business interests and tax-cutting rhetoric turned out to be a source of vulnerability for the country as a whole. Berlusconi's government finally presented a fiscal-consolidation package in autumn 2011, but that was too late to reassure investors.

Markets had already turned against Italy, with Italy's sovereign debt yields overtook those from Spain. Also, the credit agencies anticipated this changing perception towards Italy and downgraded Italy's creditworthiness in September 2011 (Hopkin 2012). Finally, on 9 November 2011, the spread between Italian and German 10-years bonds climbed to its highest-ever level with over 500 basis points. Only a few days later, Berlusconi stepped down as Prime Minister (Cencig 2012). He was replaced by the former EU-Commissioner Mario Monti who was nominated as Prime Minister on 13 November 2011 (Messia and Chance 2011).

Italy and the EU

The stabilization package accepted by the Eurogroup in early April was adopted by the European Council later that month. That package consists of three sources of funding: the EU's short-time work program SURE (provides loans to member states of up to €100 billion in order to mitigate unemployment), a pan-European guarantee fund of the European Investment Bank (it gives loans up to €200 billion for companies) and the European Stability Mechanism (ESM) worth up to €240 billion (see chapters from Lawrie and Rave in this volume). The credit lines of the ESM are based on already existing ones but were adapted to the coronavirus crisis. Each member state of the eurozone can draw on these loans up to a limit of 2 percent of its GDP – in Italy's case this is around €36 billion (Marro 2020). A precondition is that the sum is directly or indirectly spent into the health system (European Council 2020a). The advantage of this ESM fund is that it would involve loans with very long maturity for the recovery of Italy's health care system, and the interest rates would be lower than those that Italy faces on the markets (Paqué 2020).

The Conte government reluctantly supported this package. However, whether Italy will make use of the ESM fund is uncertain. First, the country has never used this mechanism. Second, Italy is traditionally reluctant towards the ESM as in the last financial crisis loans were given only under the provision of structural reforms and fiscal conditionality. But at the meeting of the Eurogroup this topic of strict conditionality was off the table. What was agreed upon is a 'light conditionality' with the money being used to 'support domestic financing of direct and indirect healthcare costs.'

Even this light conditionality put Prime Minister Conte under pressure. That is why Conte said that the ESM mechanism was inadequate. On 9 May, Conte made a slight twist in his approach: 'In any case, even if we consider the rules that will govern the new credit line to be adequate, the Italian Parliament will decide whether or not it is appropriate for Italy to activate it' (Castaldi 2020). The Democratic Party supports loans from the ESM in order to prevent the risk of a financial collapse. Its coalition partner Five Star Movement is divided on the usage of credit lines from the ESM. Right-wing populist Matteo Salvini strongly opposes any ESM involvement – with both party's fear that further conditions could be imposed on Italy (Ladurner 2020).

The ESM is where Salvini sees his chance to cause divisions in Italian politics and discontent among the population – in favor of his party Lega. In the opinion polls, Salvini's party is still at the top. However, support for the Lega has been declining since March. Salvini's personal reputation was damaged in the coronavirus crisis. His anti-immigration and populist policies fit poorly with the politics of the times. By contrast, the right-wing 'Brothers of Italy' or Fratelli d'Italia have gained in the polls (Politico 2020).

Conclusion

The European recovery fund – announced on 27 May by the European Commission – offered a way out. Such a fund would not only bring more money to Italy, but it would also bring that money in the form of grants as well as loans. Nevertheless, Italy is not in an easy position. The worst economic recession since the end of the Second World War will not only lead to a sharp reduction in GDP this year but will also cause government spending to rise. The three government decrees of a total of €80 billion are a first step to revive the economy after the lockdown. However, this will not be enough to make Italy fully economically viable again. This is because, in addition to the problems of Italy's high debt rate, public finances cannot be overstretched on the expenditure side. So, Italy has only the possibility to look for financial help within the EU. Here, the first signs of an economic relief are in sight. At first glance, however, these should not be overestimated. First, the EU recovery fund still has to be ratified. Second, the grants and loans under the recovery package will only be paid out gradually over the next few years. This could create a financing gap for Italy, which is expected to lose 9.5 percent of its GDP this year. And third, this could lead to Italy having to rely on the disbursement of the credit lines under the ESM after all. Here, Italy is struggling with party-political squabbles, which will not be easy to overcome. Prime Minister Conte faces the big task of either risking that the governing coalition will not remain stable in the long term (as the parties are divided over the ESM) or that Italy will not get the urgently needed money.

2

SPAIN AND THE LOCKDOWN CRISIS

Volodymyr Nesplyak

The COVID-19 crisis engulfed the world arguably at a faster pace than any other global crisis in modern history. Among other European countries, Spain was barely recovering from the global financial crisis as it faced the challenge of unprecedented proportions. In addition to the economic and political calamities, this crisis added another dimension – a loss of human life and public health crisis. According to the Spanish Health Ministry, by early June there were more than 230,000 cases of COVID-19 and more than 25,000 died as a result. Spain imposed draconian measures to curb the spread of the disease in mid-March, enacting measures to support the economy and keep the virus in check. Only in early May 2020, the country began to relax some of the restrictions through the four-phase process, which is supposed to tentatively end by late June, with what Prime Minister Pedro Sanchez named as return to a 'new normality'. The economic impact is likely to be one of the most severe due to the structure of the Spanish economy which relies heavily on tourism. This industry faces significant losses from the steep drop in tourist activity over a prolonged period of time. Spain is experiencing a liquidity shock and demand shock, whereby a perfectly functioning businesses and sectors of the economy suddenly ran out of income due to workers inability to go to work and lower demand from the population due to the pandemic. As Spain moves to adjust to a 'new normal', Spaniards go out to the streets in an atmosphere of a looming recession, social anxiety, and uncertainty about future prospects.

Spain's delayed response to the pandemic in combination with political and economic factors make it the most affected country in Europe in absolute terms. It would therefore need a significant support from the European Union. The European Council adopted measures to mitigate the impact across countries in the short term on 23 April. These include a loan program from the Commission for unemployment benefits in member states as well as about €200 billion in investments in small and medium-size enterprises through the European Investment Bank; and €240 billion in loans from the ESM for health care systems.

More importantly, pandemic emergency longer term-refinancing operations are set to provide liquidity through short-term maturities (Stevis-Grindneff 2020, European Central Bank 2020a). The numbers seem large, but these funds can quickly be used by two of the most affected countries, namely Italy and Spain. Alas, neither government is eager to draw down on these resources. Both are waiting for the European recovery fund to start up instead. The open question is whether that support will be sufficient.

The chapter proceeds in four sections. The first looks at the impact of the last crisis on Spain and investigates the Spanish government's responses. Most of those responses centered on the banking system, and yet government austerity also impacted on health care. The second section outlines the events that led to the rapid spread of the coronavirus in Spain and explains the incoherent pattern of responses from the Spanish government. The weakness of the health system became one of the main problems. The third section considers possible consequences of the crisis for the Spanish economy and political environment. There the focus is on the tourism, retail, and hospitality industry. The final section stresses the role of banks in buying time. For Spain to emerge from the pandemic, European support and structural reforms are crucial.

The financial crisis in Spain and its aftermath 2008–2014

The consequences of the international financial crisis in Spain that started more than a decade ago were particularly dire. Economic indicators like public debt, unemployment, budget deficit, and real growth in gross domestic product (GDP) all deteriorated as a result of the recession. To understand the dramatic downfall of the Spanish economy during that crisis, it is necessary to examine the structure of the Spanish financial system.

Spain's banking system is unique in that it is divided among commercial banks, cajas, and cooperative banks. A caja is a savings bank that is also a not-for-profit entity that channels people's savings into investment ventures and performs social tasks in their respective territories (Cardenas 2013: 8). Cajas make up half of the financial sector's assets. Over time they became locally-oriented savings banks that became politicized to the extent that political parties and unions participated in their governance (Cardenas 2013: 9, Royo 2013a: 179). They expanded heavily into the real estate market, lending large amount of loans to construction companies and individuals and fueling in this way real estate bubble that burst in 2007. Billions of euros in loans were at risk of default. Consequently, a clear distinction between cajas and large banks emerged. The large banks like Santander and BBVA were less affected than the cajas because they diversified heavily abroad, especially in the Latin America and other European countries.

According to the Santander's (2011) financial report as much as 80 percent of profits came from outside of Spain.

According to the Bank of Spain (2017), the distance between the commercial and savings banks increased during the period in terms of their coverage ratio, non-performing loans (NPL), and ability to generate profits. For instance, the percentage of year-on-year change in 2011 was 17 percent for commercial banks and 44 percent for savings banks (BoS 2017: 85). Interestingly, among other factors like changes in regulation, Sebastian Royo (2013b: 11) cites the dynamic 'counter-cyclical' capital requirements of the Bank of Spain as the single most important element to account for the performance of the financial system in the period 2008–2011. The Bank of Spain required banks to allocate a portion of their provisions equal to the amount of the portfolio considered at risk of loss during the good times and inject those reserves during downturns. Unfortunately, those funds provided only a lean buffer to shield the banks from the deteriorating assets and limited access to market funding.

In the end, the financial crisis in Spain revealed the deep structural problems of the Spanish economy and the banking sector and the need for a balanced growth in the future. While the financial reforms enacted along the way presented a sign of failure in the policy and regulatory framework of Spain (see Royo 2013a: 206), it did set the stage for further restructuring of the banking sector in 2012–2013 improving the operations that would prevent any similar dilemmas from happening in the future. Chief among them were the creation of the Fund for Orderly Bank Restructuring (FOBR) and a 'bad bank' called Sareb, from its Spanish acronym, tasked with taking non-performing loans off bank balance sheets and pushing for repayments. Both institutions include the involvement of the Bank of Spain either in supervisory or governance roles (European Stability Mechanism Report 2019: 223). In this way, the crisis triggered revitalizing reforms aimed at remodeling the economy, which soon after boosted the growth of the Spanish economy improving solvency ratios and profitability indicators. The numbers speak for themselves, Spain only used 41 billion for the banking sector out of 100 billion available, exited the ESM program after 18 months and began making payments on the loan already in 2014 (European Stability Mechanism 2019: 224–226).

In the period 2010–2012, a financial crisis turned into a sovereign debt crisis. The adverse recessionary conditions related to the real estate collapse severely increased the country's debt which at the beginning of 2007 stood at 36 percent of GDP and reached 86 percent by the end of 2012. Nonfinancial private debt surged to 134 percent of GDP over the same period (one of the highest in the EU), a considerable portion of which was tied in the real estate assets thus posing significant challenges for the Spanish economy (Bank of Spain 2017). As a result, investors lost confidence in the credit worthiness of the national government the risk premium on Spanish bonds sky-rocketed. The premium that the Spanish government paid to borrow over ten years relative to Germany reached 485 basis points and yields on Spanish ten-year bonds increased to over 7 percent in June 2012. More importantly, the banking system suffered high delinquency rates because of real estate loans, reaching 8 percent in February 2012 (Bjork and Roman 2012).

To cope with the crisis, the Spanish government responded by implementing a series of reforms aimed at restructuring the cajas by merging them. This strategy was unsuccessful. Victor Mallet and Miles Johnson (2012) point out the case of Bankia – a merger of the large Caja Madrid and Bancaja and other smaller cajas, which proved to be disastrous. The two giant ones faced serious financial difficulties, forcing the government to nationalize a newly formed Bankia in 2012 which had an astonishing 3.3 billion loss. By that time, the Spanish government was in no position to raise funds in markets and international capital fled the country. The Spanish banking system needed a bailout from the European Union (EU) as a result. When the EU agreed to the bailout, European leaders implicitly recognized that Spain was 'too big to fail'. It was not until Mario Draghi made it clear that ECB would do whatever it takes to save the euro that investor confidence was revived and the risk premium fell.

Spanish citizens would feel the effects of the crisis down to the local and community level. According to Eurostat, the percentage of people living at risk of poverty increased from 15 to 20 percent between 2007 and 2014, and the unemployment rate soared from 8 to 24 percent (Eurostat 2008, Eurostat 2014). More important, austerity measures had far-reaching effects on the provision of health care. Public spending on healthcare was reduced to respond to the costs of borrowing related to the costs of bailing out and merging cajas. The report from Amnesty International (2018) indicated that in post-crisis Spain, the cost of healthcare has been shifted onto the patient, spending on health workers decreased, resulting in lower salaries, poor working conditions, insecure contracts and deteriorating quality of the medical equipment. Put simply, Spain was increasingly suffering the consequences of the austerity policies in one of the sectors that becomes crucial in overcoming the global pandemic that befell Spain in 2020. Having established the background of developments in 2008–14, we now turn our discussion to whether the lessons from the financial crisis might give us a clue on how to deal with the crisis that Spain currently faces.

The time when Spain stood still

At the beginning of 2020, the future seemed bright. Forecasts for Spanish economic growth were positive and unemployment was on the decline. According to the European Commission (February 2020a), Spain was on a path of moderate expansion: real GDP growth was set at 1.6 percent for 2020 and 1.5 percent for 2020, the unemployment rate was expected to decline to 12 percent in 2021, and the government deficit was going to continue to decline to 2.1 percent in 2020, and 2.0 percent in 2021, reducing the external liabilities and making progress toward decreasing public and private debt and curbing government deficit.

Those forecasts broke down once the pandemic struck. That said, it would be erroneous to state that the crisis took Spain completely by surprise. The indicators were already visible in late February and early March; they were ignored. The first case of coronavirus registered in Spain was in La Gomera, Canary Islands where a German tourist tested positive, however, on February 9, the head of Medical emergencies in Madrid exclaimed that 'Spain will only have a handful of cases' (Tremlett 2020). The first confirmed death was a few days later on 13 February. The rapidly evolving situation in Italy had not proven to be a cause for concern for the Spanish government. Even with the first registered cases of the virus on the peninsular Spain, the authorities failed to take precautionary measures of implementing social distancing, health control checks at the train stations and the airports or prepare the health system for the possible surge in cases. At that point, travel was unrestricted, and a mix of tourists and football fans went back and forth between Italy and Spain as late as the end of February.

By the first of March, Spain had registered more than 100 confirmed cases. Furthermore, as William Chislett (2020) points out, Spain is a particularly gregarious and tactile nation: self-isolation and social distancing are not part of Spaniards' DNA. In other words, Spain is known for its sociable lifestyle. Certain cultural norms like hugging and kissing and being in close proximity to someone else contributed to the rapid spread of the virus among the population. More consequential were the mass demonstrations during International Women's Day on 8 March. At that point, the government of Spain announced that there had been a change for the worse in the evolution of the disease in Spain (Ramos and Castro 2020). Nevertheless, it continued to allow groups to gather; political party conferences were held during that same weekend. Tens of thousands of people assembled in Madrid while the number of cases increased by nearly two thousand on 13 March. In essence, the government ignored the looming threat of the coronavirus, downplaying the risk. The mass demonstrations were a political outlet for parties like the Spanish Socialist Party (PSOE) and Podemos. Public gatherings were allowed to happen on the basis of political considerations, setting aside the concerns for public health.

When Prime Minister Pedro Sanchez announced measures to stop the spread of the virus on 14 March the number stood at 6,271 confirmed cases and 189 deaths. The response of the Spanish government was slow when compared to Italy, the first country in Europe that went into a lockdown. More importantly, the Spanish government's decisions did not seem to be coordinated with health experts and scientific committees, contributing to the unorganized responses. While the Italian Prime Minister Giuseppe Conte established such a committee on coronavirus at the beginning of the crisis, Spain only created a similar advisory body a week after the lockdown was already in force (Sánchez Nicolás 2020a). Indeed, when considering the number of days that passed between the first case and when universities and schools closed, Spain ranks poorly: 34 days had passed in Italy and 44 days in Spain. Similarly, when looking at the number of days between the first death and school closures, one finds that Spain closed schools 18 days later than Italy. However, nonessential movement was restricted 4 days later in Spain than in Italy. Interestingly, the responses by the French and German were equivalently late, yet they have registered around 30 percent less of the cases of the virus than Spain or Italy.

This points to a number of differences between European countries, including cultural and structural, but more importantly to the quality of the public health sector. Among the affected countries Germany has the highest number of nurses and hospital beds with 13.2 and 8.2 per 1000 inhabitants, respectively. Spain lags behind with 5 nurses and 3 hospital beds per 1000 inhabitants. These numbers are relevant as they highlight the potential link between the strict austerity measures that Spain had to implement in the last decade in the form of diminished funding for hospitals and decreased spending on health workers, impacting its ability to effectively manage the inflow of patients and turnout in the hospitals during the current crisis.

Furthermore, when investigating the reasons behind the government's delayed response, it is important to assess the political environment of the country. In January 2020, the government formed as a coalition of political parties for the first time since the country's transition to democracy in 1975. Pedro Sanchez, the leader of the Socialist Party (PSOE), without a parliamentary majority, agreed to form a coalition with Pablo Iglesias, the leader of the more radical left-wing Unidas Podemos party, after Spain held two national elections in April and November 2019 (Minder 2020). Podemos flourishes on polarization campaigns often condemning government institutions for not serving the people's interests. Strictly speaking, the Spanish political environment can be summed up as fragmented and volatile. As a result, when it came to the need to implement national measures to combat the virus, the government was far from united in its response.

The Council of Ministers meeting on 14 March lasted seven hours and failed to produce concrete decisions regarding the measures that needed to be undertaken. One point of disagreement was how to respond to the economic consequences of the lockdown. Iglesias argued that any response should include payments of rents and mortgages for the poor, yet the Minister of Finance rejected them because of the high cost it entailed. Another debate had a more political character, as Iglesias objected to the fact that emergency powers were delegated to the members of the PSOE party, demanding that his party members were given a greater role in handling the crisis (Hernàndez-Morales 2020). To make things worse, the political antagonisms led to the cancelling of the teleconference between the Prime Minister and heads of regional governments on the same day, fueling regional disdain for the central government's actions, especially in Catalonia.

The unity of the government is essential to respond efficiently and effectively to the virus, setting aside political differences in an uncharted situation that the country has faced. Instead, Spain's coalition partners started pointing fingers at each other rather than working on the management of the pandemic (Sánchez Nicolás 2020b). Sometimes minimal regional cooperation (such as the Basque autonomous community refusing to close down all non-essential business) is another example of the lack of contact between the Sanchez's team and the opposition in the weeks after the imposed lockdown. All of this points to an often-chaotic Spanish political environment. Such confusion is part of the long-term trend in Spanish politics. The current situation is different from ten years ago, however, as the right-wing populist Vox party has grown to become the third largest in the Spanish parliament (Grevori 2020).

The implications for the economy and politics of Spain

The fragile coalition formed as a result of the past elections is too valuable to lose for the Spanish government. This explains why Sanchez has been so eager to secure European support. As in Italy, however, the Sanchez government is likely to oppose any conditionality attached to the support that comes from the EU. It is difficult to imagine that Podemos, a party that emerged in 2014 on a platform of opposition to the conditions imposed by Europe, would accept European supervision of Spanish economic and fiscal policy. Moreover, the dilemma of the Catalan independence movement is unlikely to calm, and it complicates the delicate political balance. Although, Sanchez benefited from a 'rally around the flag' moment that increased the popularity of his government, there is a high probability that things will go back to business as usual once the lockdown is over. In fact, one of the most discussed issues in Spain in 2019 were the dilemmas associated with Spanish unity and Catalan independence (Valvidia 2019). In the end, Spain might be at risk of new elections and internal turmoil as a result of the crisis.

The rapid spread of the virus meant that the stock markets in Spain fell sharply (unprecedented 14 percent drop in a single day) and the economic outlook worsened. Hence, soon after the lockdown went into force, Sanchez announced a €200 billion package that includes a combination of loans, direct aid, credit guarantees and unlimited liquidity lines for companies in order to alleviate economic pressures (Landauro et al. 2020). The package represents about 16 percent of the country's gross domestic product. Nevertheless, whether this will be enough will only be answered as the crisis progresses. In terms of macroeconomic implications, Spain faces another debt problem with an increasing debt-to-GDP ratio, and external debt-to-GDP, which is around 170 percent as of February 2020. This could gradually erode Spain's fiscal standing and place fiscal consolidation as the government's priority which would reduce the opportunity to enact bold spending measures embedded in its policy agenda (Davies 2020). An extreme worst-case scenario that might befall the Spanish economy involves a spiraling debt, meaning that Spain will have a hard time borrowing in the markets if bond spreads widen, as we saw during the last crisis.

Additionally, raising funds for a hefty package would be an additional challenge for the Spanish Treasury. As this is a response of the national government without the support of the European Union, it would require high financing needs. More important, Spain cannot afford to stay under lockdown. The Spanish economy depends heavily on tourism, retail, hotels, and transport which comprise 24 percent of the economy (Roldan et al. 2020). According to the Institute of National Statistics (2020), for 11 months of 2019, Spain received around 80 million tourists and 4.7 million in November 2019 alone in a country of 45 million people.

Another challenge is that the Spanish labor market usually sees a dramatic surge in unemployment during recessions due to a high number of temporary job contracts as companies tend to dismiss workers instead of reducing the work hours. Unemployment figures were already around 14 percent before the crisis hit, and it is expected that they will get as high as 25–30 percent, partly because more than a quarter of the workforce is on temporary contracts (Dombey 2020a). By the end of April, around seven million people were either unemployed or laid off (McMurtry 2020). According to the European Commission (2018), Spanish small and medium-sized enterprises account for 72 percent of employment in Spain, well above the EU average of 64 percent. To add to the strain, Spain has one of the highest percentages of elderly people, and with the virus affecting the older population in particular, the impact will be considerable.

The banking sector to the rescue

One of the main tools available to Spain to deal with economic consequences of the pandemic is the banking system. As the coronavirus crisis escalated, it led to a sudden drop in income of businesses that otherwise had been perfectly functioning. Employees were not able to go to work in the same capacity due to restrictions and demand from the population abruptly plummeted as people are uncertain about future prospects or a stable income. Subsequently, it is vital to ensure that liquidity is available to those that need it the most and business begin hiring again.

After its restructuring from the last crisis, the banking system in Spain is well capitalized and able to extend liquidity into the economy. For instance, Bankia, the main culprit of the banking meltdown in 2012, had a stable common equity Tier 1 (CET1) ratio of 13 percent. According to European Central Bank (ECB) data, CET1 ratio of Spanish banks increased by 40 basis points year-on-year, to 12 percent at the end of June 2019, higher than the required levels for all credit institutions but still below the EU average of 15 percent (European Commission 2020d, European Central Bank 2020b). To put this number in the perspective, the Bank of Spain indicates that the Tier 1 capital ratio was 8 percent at the end of 2007 (BoS 2017: 47). In other words, Spain developed the capacity to absorb the levels of NPLs that are expected to surge in the current crisis. To add to the support net, Sareb, 'the bad bank', that is set to be liquidated in 2027, could take in NPLs should the banks become overwhelmed with non-performing assets which currently stand at 3.5 percent slightly above the EU average of 3 percent (European Commission 2020d: 38). In the end, the recovery will be faster if the financial machine operates properly and its wheels are well-oiled with liquidity.

Spanish banks are more favorably positioned than a decade ago. They are more resilient as the significant diversification in the foreign markets led by two of Spain's major banks Banco Santander and BBVA means that the risk of failing is mitigated to an extent. They are capable of weathering a temporary shock and due to their strong interconnectedness with small and medium-sized enterprises in terms of credit access, they are able to mitigate the income shocks of small business owners.

As firms face temporary shortages of liquidity, it is critical that these do not turn into solvency problems, putting their capabilities to finance the economy at risk. To mitigate this risk, the Spanish government passed a regulation on the loan debt moratorium to help resume the economic activity. The three-months moratorium allows debtors, especially those in the situation of economic vulnerability, to postpone their payments to guarantee liquidity thereby preventing the accumulation of bad loans by simply suspending the loans (Zunzunegui 2020). This moratorium offers an opportunity for banks to alleviate the pressures of the surge in NPLs and for debtors to ensure the continuity of the business life. It thus increases the likelihood of jump-starting the economy. Nonetheless, it seems that the moratorium policy is not covering everyone affected due to the complicated requirements.

Finally, in the eurozone context, discussions about the establishment of a eurozone bad bank have been futile on the grounds of opposition from the European Commission while some ECB officials like Andrea Enria adamantly push for it (Arnold and Espinoza 2020). Indeed, such a bank would remove toxic assets from balance sheets of lenders on a European level. If the bad bank were to be established, it would be a move in the right direction toward a proposed banking union that has been in the works since the financial crisis with the SSM as a first step in its construction.

Conclusion

Spain is set to be one of the worst impacted countries in the world due to COVID-19 while still suffering the consequences of depressed income and growth from the last crisis. The austerity measures imposed at the beginning of the previous decade poorly prepared the public healthcare system and decreased its ability to efficiently overcome the global pandemic that befell Spain in 2020. As Spain struggles to relax its lockdown measures, much uncertainty remains about the looming recession and the possibility of the second wave of coronavirus cases. Part of the reason for the drastic impact of this crisis is the shock to the tourism, retail, hotel, and transport industries that make up about a quarter of Spanish GDP. The political situation is more tenuous than it was ten years ago with more populist movements across Europe and Spain as well as reignited campaigns of Catalan independence. The Spanish government and the current coalition are more fragile than they have ever been. In the current situation, it is the time for national and European unanimity on the most essential topics.

Fortunately, banks, unlike the past crisis, may well be part of the rescue efforts of the Spanish economy although they are also exposed, as are all major sectors. Spain has the ability to withstand the temporary shock with the capital and liquidity buffers, however, those will not last long. Once again, Spain requires substantial support from the EU just as the summer is around the corner. Since summer is the tourist peak of the year, Spain is likely to see the lowest number of visitors on record. As we saw in this chapter, the implications for the Spanish economy will be severe with an uncertain and strained future of the recovery. The coronavirus crisis is pushing Europe and the world into the worst economic recession, and the consequences will be felt throughout the 20s, setting back economic growth and possibly labeling the 20s as the lost decade. In addition, this crisis tests the unity not only of the European project but of individual nations. The downturn and social distress will change the economic and political trends throughout Europe.

3

LA PESTE: THE FRENCH FINANCIAL SYSTEM CONFRONTS CORONAVIRUS

William Marshall

The European Union's collective response to the COVID-19 pandemic, French President Emmanuel Macron declared April 16, is its 'moment of truth'. In his view, the pandemic presents an existential threat to the EU project and the euro, that can be overcome only with economic and political solidarity, rather than a patchwork of go-it-alone national approaches. Specifically, Macron framed the debate about funding the economic recovery as one in which the Northern countries, such as Germany and the Netherlands, should make sacrifices to prop up cratering economies in the pandemic-stricken nations of Southern Europe. If the EU fails to cooperate on this front, Macron said, the ensuing economic trauma would be a boon for populists and Eurosceptics.

Though Macron's plea for unity could be dismissed as self-serving, the scale and scope of the economic crisis are putting unprecedented pressure on the EU to deliver tangible benefits to member states. In the latest negotiations among European diplomats, a Franco-German consensus has ushered in an unprecedented deal on the Next Generation EU, in which the frugal euro area members have abandoned their hardened economic orthodoxies in favor of solidarity – though major structural reforms remain unlikely. While the Macron administration would prefer to see progress on broader banking union reforms that would enhance risk-sharing in the bloc, the urgency of the crisis has forced Paris to prioritize near-term objectives. In doing so, it has carved out a role as a mediator between the debtor countries of the South and the creditor countries of the North.

A key objective for French policymakers is to arrive at a consensus for an EU solution that would prevent the wider European banking system from collapsing. The deal reached in the July negotiations over the Recovery and Resilience Fund (RFF) is a monumental step towards reaching this objective, but the EU is only part of the story. France's ability to shape fiscal and financial policies in intergovernmental negotiations is contingent on the resilience of its own banking sector which is instrumental to its economic recovery. This chapter examines contemporary and historic data on the French banking sector to argue that, barring a major escalation in the COVID-19 pandemic, France's financial system should prove resilient and indeed will be a source of stability that can power the recovery of the wider economy. It also examines how the French banking system was able to endure the 2008 financial crisis without serious upheaval and whether any lessons from that experience can be applied to the current crisis. Finally, this paper analyzes how underlying financial conditions in France have made its lobbying in Brussels for greater risk-sharing more urgent. It also explains why France is calling for new funding solutions to shore up the Union's fiscal capacity rather than settling for retooling existing institutions.

The analysis begins with an assessment of the damage inflicted on the French economy and the government's national policy response to the crisis so far. According to the French Finance Ministry, gross domestic product (GDP) plummeted 5.8 percentage points in the first quarter of 2020, the economy's worst performance since 1949. The Ministry also projects GDP will fall by a total of 8.0 percentage points in 2020, though figures released by the OECD in June project an 11 percent decrease in the event of no resurgence (Agence France Trésor 2020, OECD 2020a).

France entered the lockdown with a budget deficit of 3 percent and a debt-to-GDP ratio approaching 100 percent. Projections from French economist Marc Touati show the deficit could grow to 9 percent and national debt could reach nearly 130 percent by the time the crisis passes (Laurent 2020). Unemployment in May fell to 7.8 from 8.1 percent in the fourth quarter of 2019 – a statistical aberration caused by how France counts labor force participation (Ministère du Travail 2020). This latest figure does not account for the nearly two in three private sector workers – or about 12.4 million people – whose salaries the state is paying as part of a national wage support scheme (Thomas 2020). Even with wage support, unemployment claims jumped by a combined 500,000 in March and April (Manceaux 2020). This means the economy is heavily dependent on state spending to continue operating at its current capacity, which the national statistics agency (INSEE) estimates to be only 65 percent of normal volume (INSEE 2020). Though most quarantine restrictions were lifted by June 15, it is not clear yet how quickly economic activity will return to pre-crisis levels. In the meantime, there is growing pressure on the government for additional fiscal stimulus, which to date add up to €56.7 billion and could reach €110 billion in the coming weeks (Anderson et al. 2020).

Will the French banking sector prove resilient?

Amid the widespread suspension of economic activity, French non-financial firms (NFCs) were drawing on cash deposits to stay afloat. The lockdown has precipitated both a solvency problem and a liquidity crunch that will weigh on French banks' asset quality and dent their profitability in the near term. Compounding the liquidity and solvency issues, banks must grapple with a weaker lending climate, fewer fees from advisory services, and increased cost of risk associated with the pandemic (Nikolaeva 2020). French banks are particularly exposed to certain types of equities and commodities.

In early April, BNP Paribas (BNP), considered a French 'national champion', reported a €184 million loss in its equity-derivatives business due to turbulence in the dividend futures market as corporations halted dividend payments to save cash and appease regulators (Griffin 2020). Another national champion, Société Générale (SocGen), also has large investments in the equity-derivatives market. It posted a first-quarter net loss of €326 million and warned that its Tier 1 capital ratio, now at 12.6 percent would continue to deteriorate this year (Patrick and Lombardi 2020). Meanwhile, other major French banks, including Natixis and Crédit Agricole (CA), have faced headwinds as the price of crude oil plummeted in April (Comfort and Griffin 2020), but they have largely avoided the equity-related losses of their larger competitors (Crofts 2020).

The latest earnings reports from top French banks have not inspired confidence among investors, especially as the number of bad loans on their balance sheets mount. Since the onset of the crisis, the top three French banks (BNP, SocGen, and CA) have underperformed compared to their counterparts in Europe, according to Bloomberg's index of 500 largest European banks (Griffin 2020). Poor performance in their first-quarter earnings reports is not the only source for concern. Research from the German investment bank Berenberg reveals CA and SocGen increased their share of Tier 3 assets (custom derivatives and asset-backed securities that are often illiquid and difficult to price) since the last financial crisis. In doing so, they have bucked the trend by large financial institutions, such as Deutsche Bank, which have aggressively offloaded these riskier assets (Griffin 2020). Since 2015, CA increased its Tier 3 assets portfolio by 50 percent to €15 billion while SocGen raised its holding by 14 percent to about €10 billion, according to Berenberg. As the economic crisis worsens, investors will be watching Tier 3 assets, which are the coal-mine canaries of the French banking sector.

Another source of weakness for French banks is the sprawling retail networks they have built throughout the European market. The French banking sector faces significant contagion risk in Italy, for instance, which is its second-largest market outside of France. Six French banks do business in Italy. The biggest,

BNP and CA, operate more than 100 retail branches in the country. Data from the European Banking Authority (EBA) reveals French banks have €285.5 billion in credit exposure in Italy, more than double that of Luxembourg's banks which are the next most exposed (Salzano et al. 2019). A sell-off in Italy, where sovereign debt volatility is a major concern, would be problematic for French banks.

However, a review of the fundamental strengths of the French banks, in terms of asset quality and funding structure, reveals they are well-prepared to handle the economic downturn. For instance, capital buffers are at or near their mandated regulatory levels and data from the fourth quarter of 2019 shows French banks are well-capitalized to withstand the liquidity shock. The ratio of non-performing loans (NPLs) for the French banking sector is 2.5 percent, below its peak of 4.7 percent reached in 2013. European Central Bank (ECB) figures show the ratio of Tier 1 capital to risk-weighted assets was 15.9 percent in the fourth quarter of 2019, double the 8.0 percent minimum required under Basel III regulations. The loan-to-deposit (LTD) ratio currently at 113 percent (as of Q419) is at a more sustainable level than its peak of 140 percent in 2008 (Fitch Solutions 2020). Though the LTD may not be the best indicator of French banking health, considering loan deposits account for just 20 percent of all liabilities, ECB data indicates the banks have enough liquid assets to cover their short-term obligations. Since 2010, the net-stable funding ratio for French banks has hovered around the regulatory 60 percent, which means French banks receive the majority of their funding from sources other than deposits (Fitch Solutions 2020).

A loan guarantee program enacted by the French government in its 2020 Finance Act helped to build confidence in the banking sector and allow NFCs to access credit as they ride out the crisis. In March, the European Commission accepted France's exemption request for a package of state-aid schemes, clearing the way for the government to underwrite up to €300 billion worth of loans in cooperation with the state-run Bpifrance bank (European Commission 2020e). The scheme will allow businesses of any size to request a government-backed loan to bolster their cashflow for payroll and other immediate expenses. It covers guarantees on loans with a limited maturity and size and restricts the risk taken by the state to a maximum of 90 percent in order to adhere to the Commission's Temporary Framework rules.

The speed with which the scheme was conceived, approved, and launched, is a testament to the institutional strength inherent in the French financial system. In fact, the loan guarantee scheme is comparable to a loan scheme launched during the 2008 crisis, which allowed the state to mutualize financial assistance without having to take an equity stake in specific banks (Massoc and Jabko 2012). The institutional idiosyncrasies of the French banking system that enabled the successful program are discussed in the next section.

At the European level, the European Union (EU) regulators and the European Central Bank (ECB) have worked to loosen credit conditions in Europe. In Brussels, EU regulators announced on April 28 they would relax some of the macroprudential regulations of the Capital Requirements Regulation (CRR), including the leverage ratio (a measure of bank indebtedness) to keep credit flowing through the European economy (European Commission 2020f). Commission officials said the proposed amendment, which still requires approval in the European Parliament, could increase lending up to €450 billion in 2020. Meanwhile, the ECB has unlocked further liquidity with the enhanced 'pandemic emergency longer-term refinancing operations' (PELTROs) (European Central Bank 2020a) and increased its asset-purchasing through the €1.35 trillion Pandemic Emergency Purchase Program (PEPP), which aims to close bond spreads between countries (European Central Bank 2020c). Barring disruption caused by the German legal challenge to PEPP, these and other monetary tools the ECB has mobilized in recent months will serve as temporary relief for euro area economies and banks. However, they will not solve the immediate solvency issues or the slowdown in economic activity at the core of the crisis.

Looking beyond the pandemic, France has the benefit of being the next best choice as a European financial and regulatory hub in the long run now that the UK has left the EU. Three of the largest U.S. banks, Bank of America, Citigroup, and BlackRock, have announced plans to grow their Paris operations since the Brexit countdown began. The regulatory certainty Paris offers is no doubt a driving force behind the announcements.

France's reputation as a financial hub is also bolstered by its playing host to the corporate headquarters of the pan-European stock market, Euronext. Paris is the leading investment destination of the alliance, accounting for 62 percent of public company listings at the close of 2019 (Economist Intelligence Unit 2020). And in June 2019, the European Banking Authority moved its headquarters from London to Paris, which already hosts the European Securities and Markets Authority. Though London banking will likely retain its competitive advantage as an investment destination for legal and linguistic reasons, the momentum towards Paris could one day make it a center of EU finance.

Lessons from the 2008 crisis

The French banking sector avoided most of the financial carnage that swept up other European banks beginning in 2008. In fact, the largest French banks (BNP, CA, SocGen) all netted profits from 2008 to 2009 and no major government bailout was needed (Howarth 2013). Only two smaller entities required direct support from the government. The first was Natixis, the investment branch jointly owned by Banque Populaire and Caisse d'Epargne, which was exposed to U.S. subprime mortgages. In 2008, the banks were merged into one entity, BCPE, and the state (in a deal directly arranged by President Sarkozy) invested €3 billion for a 20 percent stake to help recapitalize Natixis (Creel et al. 2014). The second entity, the Franco-Belgian joint venture, Dexia, was dissolved into the state-run Caisse des Dépôts and La Banque Postale in a €5.5 billion deal shared by the French and Belgian governments. Taken together, the French government's direct bailout spending at the height of the crisis totaled just €5.75 billion (excluding the second bailout of Dexia in 2011).

Then President Nicolas Sarkozy was deeply involved in spearheading the government's policies to address the weaknesses in French financial markets. These included a €20.75 billion (later increased to €40 billion) recapitalization program for banks (known as SPPE) and a €320 billion government loan guarantee program (known as SFEF) for the wider economy, a model for the program initiated in March 2020 (Creel et al. 2014). Almost all banks that accessed SPPE finances repaid within the first year of its five-year term. Unlike the experience of other European countries, where healthy banks fearing a downgrade in their perceived solvency refused to accept bailout money, the French government did not have to coerce the banks to accept the rescue plan *en masse*. Instead, healthy and distressed banks alike used the facility in a moment of solidarity that restored confidence in the financial sector. The amicable process around the 'Plan de Soutien' can be attributed to close relations between the French bureaucratic and banking elites (and even among competing banks), which facilitated cooperation without requiring the state to take punitive measures (Massoc and Jabko 2012). The cozy relationship between the state and the banks, of course, also creates the potential for moral hazard, by allowing bankers to take greater risks knowing the state will offer near unconditional support. But in French experience, it also has facilitated efficient responses in times of crisis that have helped to shore up confidence in financial markets. Given the generally low-risk tolerance of the French banking sector (Howarth 2013), the tradeoff is arguably a net benefit for France, and could be an asset as it plots its pandemic recovery.

Of the €320 billion in borrowing allowed by the SFEF scheme, only €93 billion was ever raised in capital markets. It can be inferred from the low demand for credit that liquidity was not as acute an issue in 2008. Considering the French economy contracted by just 2.8 percent at the height of the crisis between 2008 and 2009 (and reached pre-crisis levels of growth by 2011), this is unsurprising (World Bank 2018). Credit supply also remained strong due to limited securitization in the French banking sector. Collateral in asset-backed commercial paper held by French banks at the end of 2008 was only 1.4 percent of GDP – far lower than most Western European countries at the time (Howarth 2013).

On the asset side, however, French banks were heavily exposed to euro area countries with a higher risk of default, such as Greece, Italy, and Spain (Blundell-Wignall 2012). The geographic spread of French banking activities in those countries led to large portfolios of international loans and government sovereign debt. As the financial crisis spiraled into the debt crisis, the stakes for French banks increased drastically. If it were not for then ECB president Mario Draghi's 'whatever it takes' declaration in 2012 and subsequent monetary policy action, French banks may have struggled to remain solvent. Since the last crisis, sovereign exposures of French banks have increased according to IMF data. Today, 70 percent of PNB Paribas' credit exposure falls outside of France (14 percent in Italy), and across the board, 50 percent of sovereign bond holdings of French banks are held in foreign government debt (International Monetary Fund 2019).

In response to the euro area financial crisis and the following sovereign debt crisis, France updated its domestic financial regulatory framework in 2010, and again in 2013 under President François Hollande. The first reform in 2010 involved the creation of a new unified regulator for the financial and insurance sectors, known now as the Prudential Control and Resolution Authority (ACPR). The second, in 2013, involved handing the new entity bank-resolution responsibilities. It also required banks to contribute €10 billion to a national resolution fund, an increase over the original requirement of €2 billion (Economist Intelligence Unit 2020).

Though the new regulations are meant to shore up the domestic deposit insurance scheme, the €8 billion increase represents a fraction of most French banks' balance sheets. Should a systemically important French bank fail, the state would have to rely on borrowing or the EU's Single Resolution Mechanism (SRM) which does not yet have a large enough fund from which to draw the capital needed, especially in the event of a wider financial collapse (Gros and De Groen 2020).

Paradoxically, EU regulators have now eased the Basel III capital controls designed to prevent another financial crisis in the aftermath of the 2008 crash. As intended, loosening capital controls should give the French banks, which have built large buffers since the last crisis, increased margins to inject liquidity into the economy. But given France's higher debt-to-GDP ratio today than in 2008 and further demands for fiscal stimulus, it is possible the government could exhaust its fiscal firepower as the crisis endures, taking the option of a banking bailout off the table. Though this may not be necessary now, in the long-term, conditions across the eurozone could deteriorate if there is a pandemic 'relapse'. If countries reopen for business before the virus has run its course, it may lead to another round of crippling lockdowns. The threat of fiscal shortfalls and the inadequacy of national resolution schemes under such a scenario brings fresh urgency to debates at the EU and euro area level about how to pool the bloc's resources more effectively.

France and the EU's financial markets agenda

Since his election, President Macron has advocated for sweeping structural reforms to the EU and the euro area, starting with the creation of stalled macro-prudential institutions. With the recent history of Europe's sovereign debt crisis and the near collapse of the eurozone in the early 2010s fresh in their minds, Macron and his predecessors have pursued policies in the EU that would boost confidence in Europe's financial markets and give the EU greater fiscal powers to avert future crises. In his signature policy speech to the Sorbonne in 2017, Macron called on policymakers in Brussels to create a fiscal union with a separate euro area budget to provide a fiscal backstop (Macron 2017). Since then, his administration has endorsed other institutions such as the Europe-wide deposit insurance scheme (the final pillar of the Banking Union), and the creation of a European safe asset. Similar to his plea for unity this year, Macron has argued ensuring the success of the Economic and Monetary Union will require deeper political integration. To achieve such integration, France has positioned itself as a deal-broker, toggling between the negotiating priorities of the periphery and the North. Paris hopes to use the pandemic as an impetus for political compromise to usher in permanent changes to the EU's fiscal and financial infrastructure.

France has positioned itself as the interlocutor between the two camps because its fiscal situation is not as urgent as that of the Southern countries. Although its public debt is high, France can still borrow at better rates than its Southern neighbors, Italy, and Spain. Spreads between the German 10-year benchmark and Spanish and Italian bonds remain elevated over their levels at the beginning of the year despite the ECB's massive asset purchasing program. And while neither Italy nor Spain have had trouble raising debt in their latest bond issuances, a large share of that government debt is held domestically (more than 50 percent in Spain) which raises risks of a sovereign-bank doom loop if the spreads become untenable (European Council 2020b).

The French banking system is also still robust enough to help finance its recovery, whereas Fitch Ratings and the ECB have found Spanish and Italian banks are the most exposed to the crisis due to slim capital reserves and weak asset portfolios (Long 2020). Nevertheless, Paris has consistently sided with the Southern countries during the crisis. This is partially out of self-interest (French banks are large holders of their sovereign debt) but it is also because of genuine belief among French leaders that greater economic unity can solidify the political alliance underpinning the EU. And yet, some of the latest French proposals in the EU have failed to gain serious support, even among the Southern countries that would be natural allies.

Earlier in 2020, France, in coordination with the ECB and eight other countries, including Belgium, Greece, Italy, and Spain, proposed 'coronabonds' as a mechanism for governments to share risk as they issue debt to pay for fiscal stimulus policies (see chapter by Lawrie). The proposal, which was a repackaging of the familiar eurobonds idea introduced during the sovereign debt crisis, was dead on arrival. Northern countries with cheap borrowing costs, such as Germany and the Netherlands, argue mutualizing debt without strict conditions encourages moral hazard, which is anathema to their economic philosophies. Deeply indebted Southern countries, whose economies cannot sustain themselves indefinitely without a new funding instrument, counter that the current crisis is not a result of fiscal profligacy.

The same debate nearly derailed talks on overhauling the European Stability Mechanism (ESM), which will now offer member states a pandemic-focused credit line of up to 2 percent of their GDP. Questions about conditionality (i.e., requiring austerity or using funds to service old debts) and length of maturity threatened to spoil ESM negotiations until a final hour compromise between Italy and the Netherlands resolved the impasse. Despite the compromise, few observers believe countries will use the ESM's new lending facility out of concern for a domestic political backlash (Fleming and Khan 2020a).

Convening in Brussels on July 17–21 for a special summit of the Council, EU leaders finalized a deal on a more than €1 trillion budget for 2021–2027 (known as the Multiannual Financial Framework) within which the Next Generation EU fund will sit. The largest and most important instrument in the fund, the Recovery and Resilience Facility, will allow those European economies that have borne the brunt of the pandemic to access €312.5 billion in no-strings-attached grants as well as €360 billion in loans. In total, €390 billion will be made available to struggling countries (Darvas 2020a) in the form of grants funneled through various programs.

To placate the so-called "frugal" countries (Austria, Denmark, The Netherlands and Sweden), Macron and his allies pared back the grants figure from the European Commission's original proposal, which called for €500 billion in grants and a further €250 billion in loans. He and other EU members also agreed to concessions in the form of budget rebates, which would allow net-contributor countries to recoup some of their initial payments. These rebates are controversial (Darvas 2019) and will no doubt become a sticking point in the future.

Despite the smaller sum for grants, the deal sets a major precedent for the EU, which will issue mutualized debt as part of its budget process for the first time and require member states to transfer up to 0.6 percent of GNI to the EU budget per year until 2058, when the last bonds would be repaid. The introduction of a new tax facility for the Commission, tasked with raising offsetting funds, furthers the momentum towards greater EU fiscal consolidation. Though it remains to be ratified by national parliaments, and the funds may not be mobilized until 2023 (Darvas 2020b), the deal is a badly needed confidence boost for European markets experiencing tightening credit conditions (Arnold 2020).

Conclusion

The source of today's economic crisis is entirely unrelated to what triggered the 2008 financial crisis, but the underlying risks to the French banking sector are familiar. Weak points in the French banking sector include the alarming levels of Tier 3 assets on French bank balance sheets since 2017 as well as risk from exposure to international loans and sovereign bonds. There are also novel challenges. A crash in the market for dividend futures has tanked the share price of French banks compared to their European competitors. This was not a problem in 2008, when most corporations and banks continued paying dividends.

Yet, there are built-in safeguards today that are stronger than they were in the last crisis. French banks are well capitalized. Tier 1 capital ratios of the major banks range from 13–16 percent and NPLs are at their lowest rates in more than a decade. The state has also responded well. Using the blueprint from 2008, French policymakers have moved swiftly this year to ensure the banking sector can withstand the onslaught of bad loans and maintain easy credit conditions for the economy. In the immediate term, no bailout or recapitalization funds have been needed, but it may be too soon to call.

Macron has pursued reforms in the EU and euro area that would satisfy two objectives. First, stronger macroprudential EU institutions would tame the cross-border distortions that have weakened the European financial system. Self-interest is a prime motivator for these reforms. French banks, with their large holdings of international loans and sovereign debt, would benefit from greater risk-sharing. Enhanced confidence-building measures would also be a win for banking sectors across Europe, reducing the need for costly bailouts. Second, Macron and the French financial elite earnestly believe deeper fiscal integration would augment the political and monetary union. A more integrated Europe, Macron says, would strengthen the bloc's liberal order. France has signaled it is prepared to make sacrifices. Whether that will be enough is unclear.

4

SETTING THE STAGE: THE ECB BEFORE CORONAVIRUS

Rebecca Neri

The European Central Bank (ECB) is one of the pillars of the European Union (EU). Its foundations lie in the Maastricht Treaty of February 1992. This was an ambitious project through which national governments decided to give up part of their sovereignty, creating a community held by solidarity and reciprocity.

The creation of the EU started a new era for the European continent: however, the Treaty of Maastricht was the first step of many. The foundations were solid, but Europe is still too heterogeneous and needs to be more integrated. The outbreak of the COVID-19 pandemic demonstrated that we need solidarity if we want to recover economically. Is the European Central Bank ready to play a role in the pandemic and in the post-pandemic EU? Its role is going to be challenged by the next moves it takes.

In order to develop an accurate analysis of the decisions made by the ECB's Governing Council, it is necessary to focus on the decisions it took during the months before the onset of the crisis. The following paragraphs will provide a timeline of events from the last important press conference of Mario Draghi on 12 September to the days before the speech of Lagarde on 12 March. This is the period during which the Governing Council took the first steps to counter the risks associated with the coronavirus and the lockdowns in Europe. The chapter will focus on the initial impact that the European Central Bank has had, and the consolidation of its monetary policy towards the crisis. As Mario Draghi (2012) said at the Global Investment Conference in London in July 2012: 'The ECB is ready to do whatever it takes to preserve the euro. And believe me, it will be enough.' The question at the start of this pandemic was whether that commitment still applies.

Every institution has a primary goal, and every decision taken should reflect that goal. The European Central Bank was created in order to maintain the price stability: every action the Governing Council takes is done to preserve the value of the euro currency. Therefore, the European Central Bank should reflect the integrity of the common market, should avoid the sovereign debt crisis, and maintain the stability of the European financial system. However, this almost perfect mechanism, created some decades ago, has defects that arise when a shock hits the region.

The coronavirus crisis is a unique event. The measures that governments undertook to halt the spread of the virus stopped much of the world's economy and so generated a near-collapse of the economic system as a whole. The role of the European Union and all the member states is to design the optimal solution in order to contain the consequences. The European Central Bank should work with the member states and the other institutions: its objective is not to solve a crisis, but rather to prevent it from getting worse. That is no easy task. The crisis adds to an already long list of problems that the member state had, including the lack of consensus among them and a lack of solidarity. The measures considered by the Governing Council need to be reinforced by fiscal actions that lie in the hands of the member states. The role that the ECB has in this crisis is only one piece of the enormous puzzle represented by the European Union.

This chapter will start by analyzing the problems that existed before the outbreak of the coronavirus pandemic in order to provide a context for understanding current events and decisions. The basic message is that the eurozone was already in trouble, even before the 'collapse' of the system.

Mario Draghi's last attempts as president of the European Central Bank

On the 12 September 2019, Mario Draghi decided to make his last big policy move as president of the European Central Bank. The economic outlook in Europe was negative: the eurozone risked facing a serious recession in two of its largest countries, Germany and Italy, and a possible sovereign debt crisis. The forecasts for economic performance in the coming winter suggested that matters were getting worse rather than better: downside risks included Brexit, the probable slowdown of the Chinese economy, and the unstable political situation. The rate of inflation had been decreasing since June 2019. The Governing Council was one of the few policy actors able to respond in a coordinated fashion. The ECB decided to apply the remedies it used in the past: a new round of unconventional monetary decisions was about to start in order to stop the slowdown of the euro area economy.

Such actions fell within the ECB's mandate to ensure price stability. As mentioned in Article 282, paragraph 2, of the Treaty on the Functioning of the European Union (2007):

> The primary objective of the [European System of Central Banks] shall be to maintain price stability. Without prejudice to that objective, it shall support the general economic policies in the Union in order to contribute to the achievement of the latter's objectives.

The Governing Council defines 'price stability' as an expected rate of inflation that is close to, but below, the 2 percent per annum over the medium term. However, the inflation had been below the Bank's target since 2013. Moreover, the growth of gross domestic product (GDP) in the euro area was expected to decrease: in fact, it was already decelerating from 1.4 percent during the first quarter of 2019 and to 1.2 percent during the second quarter (Statistical Data Warehouse 2020). The ECB's macroeconomic projections showed that the real GDP would increase by just 1.1 percent over 2019 as a whole (European Central Bank 2019a). As a result, the Governing Council tried to use both conventional and nonconventional monetary policy instruments to stimulate economic activity.

The Governing Council decided to decrease the interest rate on deposit facility by 10 basis points to negative 0.50 percent, while the rate on the marginal lending facility and the interest rate on the main refinancing operations would continue unchanged at 0.25 percent and 0.00 percent respectively. This decision was taken in order to push inflation to reach the ECB's desired level: the Governing Council made it clear that the decision would be maintained until expected rates of inflation converged on the ECB's definition of price stability. Only at that point, the Governing Council would begin to unwind these policies (Draghi 2019a).

The Governing Council decided to restart the Asset Purchase Program (APP) for an extended period of time. This included €20 billion per month starting from November 2019. At the same time, the ECB would continue to reinvest maturing securities (under the program) until necessary in order to ensure adequate liquidity in the financial system. The APP consists of four separate programs:

- corporate sector purchase program (CSPP);
- public sector purchase program (PSPP);
- asset-backed securities purchase program (ABSPP);
- third covered bond purchase program (CBPP3).

These asset purchase programs started in 2014 and the volume of assets they have accumulated is huge. The public sector purchase program corresponds to the largest percentage of reinvestment from maturing securities performed by the ECB. They improved the possibility of purchasing the assets of the third covered bond purchase program (CBPP3), the asset-backed securities purchase program (ABSPP) and the corporate sector purchase program (CSPP).

The CBPP aims to improve the liquidity in covered-bond markets. In addition, it is important because it encourages banks to lend by easing lending conditions for non-financial corporations and banks (European Central Bank 2020d). Although not officially a goal of the program, the commitment of the Governing Council should help the member states to borrow currency in order to inject it into the national economy, promoting new projects and investments.

Mario Draghi ensured that the new policies would continue as long as necessary (Draghi 2020a). This was consistent with the promise he made in 2012. Nevertheless, the decision was not completely welcomed inside the Governing Council. Indeed, it widened the divisions among participating countries. Germany's newspaper *Bild* accused the ECB President – 'Count Draghila' – of 'sucking dry' the accounts of German savers. Some German politicians referred to Draghi as 'the gravedigger of German savers' (Arnold 2019b). Many of these claims were directed at the decision to maintain negative interest rates. This policy caused increasing frustration among German citizens, and especially, among politicians. Even the President of the Bundesbank, Jens Weidmann, suggested that Draghi was 'overshooting the mark' (Financial Times 2019). Moreover, the restart of the APP caused criticism in other countries, not only in Germany: the Central Banks in Austria and the Netherlands were opposed to the changes, because they worried that the savings of the North were, and are, used to help Southern European countries (Arnold 2019b).

The stimulus program that Draghi announced played an important role in the following months, changing also the approach of the upcoming President of the ECB, Christine Lagarde. The benefits of that program have outweighed the criticism. As Draghi (2019b) pointed out during his monetary dialogue with the European Parliament in Brussels on 23 September, the APP accelerated the reduction of unemployment, one of the main sources of income inequality: in 2015 the unemployment rate (considering the active working population) was 10.9 in the euro area; by 2019 it had declined to 7.6 (AMECO 2020).

In order to implement an expansive monetary policy, the ECB needs to inject money (liquidity) in the system, and since Europe is a bank-based economy, monetary policy only works when the process of lending-transmission to the banks is activated. There are other policy options that could enhance this process: most of these entail allocations of fiscal measures which are beyond the scope of the ECB (Draghi 2019b). If national governments would work in partnership with the ECB, they could provide a more suitable policy mix. Short of that, however, the Governing Council has no choice but to set its instruments in unconventional ways.

During his last speech as President of the ECB on 24 October 2019, Mario Draghi underscored the influence that political pressures had, and still have, on the Central Bank (Draghi 2019c): last year there were plenty of events which compromised the political independence of the institution, and added to the political divisions within the Union. Brexit was still ongoing, although it should have been a positive and transparent goodbye from the EU. Populism became more and more prominent in European politics, and this has been reflected in the deliberations of the Governing Council, especially since the financial crisis in 2008. Frictions between North and South have risen again as well. Such factors added to the downside risks weighing on the economic performance of the euro area. Only a robust policy response can hold them at bay.

By the end of October 2019, Draghi was leaving, and the end of his mandate left a sense of uncertainty about the future. Should the ECB do less, or should it do more? Should the institution have a sort of partner in difficult times? Should the policy be uniform or adjusted to every situation? Unfortunately, there is no easy answer to these questions.

From Mario Draghi to Christine Lagarde

'Where you stand depends on where you sit' is a famous quotation from *The Essence of Decision: Explaining the Cuban Missile Crisis* by Graham Allison (1971). The point is that your preferences (therefore where you stand) depend on and reflect your position (where you sit). Every decision made is a reflection of the role you have to play. When on the first of November 2019 Christine Lagarde became the new President of the European Central Bank, her predecessor had already left important measures which were ongoing.

The position she took reflected her preferences: the continuity of the steps taken in September 2019 by the Governing Council. During an interview prior to her appointment, Lagarde also expressed where she stood on the policy decisions that governments in Germany and the Netherlands should take. Her recommendation was that those governments should use active fiscal measures to invest more domestically, even if that meant spending down their budget surpluses. The main reason was to rebalance their macro-economies (Arnold 2019a).

These recommendations added to the tensions inside the Governing Council: the Netherlands, as well as Germany and Austria, had persistent account surpluses; on the other side, countries such as France and Spain ran current account deficits. The main problem is to decide which countries should adjust. There are different points of view among economists: some suggested that countries with current account surpluses should invest more; others argued that countries running deficits should raise their competitiveness. Therefore, all the countries would have to adjust and rebalance. However, this is not a perfect approach, considering the euro area as a whole, and as part of a globalized world (Dombret

2013). The solution to succeed should be to make Europe more productive and integrated (Dombret 2013). In this context, Lagarde argued for that more integrated approach.

Lagarde's take on this issue is subtly different from Draghi's: their backgrounds are not similar, as well as the developments of their modus operandi. As mentioned before, Draghi was, and still is, the economist who saved the European currency from bankruptcy and collapse, innovating the monetary measures. His interventions saved the euro area, but also raised skepticism among Members of the Governing Council. By contrast, Lagarde was the former Managing Director of the International Monetary Fund, and she represented the future of the eurozone. Her leadership competences from her past job experiences could be what the ECB needs (Wolff and Christie 2019).

Lagarde had been known for her diplomatic and political skills, so the European Union should expect to see the Governing Council work more closely with the rest of EU institutions and with national governments. She will have to manage the criticism inside the euro area due to the expansionist monetary policy: by following the steps of her predecessor, her role will be defined by her capacities as a politician, promoting consensus among different opinions and within a more fragmented Governing Council.

Lagarde expressed her intent to involve the national governments more and to encourage them add as much fiscal stimulus as necessary to jump start the economy of the euro area (Jones 2019a). At the same time, she committed to review the strategy of the ECB. This was a delicate balancing act. Lagarde could not go too far during the first phase of her mandate, otherwise, she might compromise the political independence of the ECB as an institution. In turn, a loss of independence could lead to a loss of credibility – which is crucial in how monetary policies influence economic performance.

In her speech to the European Parliament, Lagarde stressed how important it is that Europeans have faith in the European Union (Lagarde 2019a), especially in the common currency and in the ECB as an institution: therefore, the ECB must be ready to respond with all the measures which might be necessary to ensure confidence. She was not eager to change course quickly.

On 12 December, the Governing Council decided to maintain the interest rates unchanged: it followed the decision to keep those rates until the inflation level would converge to the target (close to, but below 2 percent) (Lagarde 2019b). The Governing Council also expressed its intention to continue buying and investing from maturing securities (APP) in order to guarantee liquidity, and to support the growth in the euro area. However, the macroeconomic projections for GDP (done by the ECB) reflected the risks of the euro area growth. The downside risks remained the same and so did the justification for holding onto the existing policy (Lagarde 2019b).

Importantly, that policy showed signs of working. Real GDP growth continued to decelerate during the last quarter of 2019, and the ECB forecast that growth would remain down around 1.1 percent in 2020. But they foresaw that growth would increase to 1.4 percent in 2021 and 2022 (European Central Bank 2019b). Meanwhile, the unemployment rate was expected to continue falling gradually to 7.1 percent in 2022 (European Central Bank 2019b). Downside risks remained due to uncertainties in the market and in global trade. Nevertheless, the ECB had laid solid foundations for improvement.

The beginning of the 'Roaring Twenties'

The year 2020 started with a fragmented financial system: the United Kingdom was ready to begin its transition process that would end with the departure of the country from the European Union. Brexit had consequences in every aspect for the European Union, and it was a shock to the financial system in particular. The City of London had played an important role: many European firms relied on UK banks and financial infrastructures. Whether and how those financial relationships and activities would relocate to other financial hubs in the euro area, including the Netherlands, France and Germany, remained unclear. This movement affected all parts of the financial system – meaning not just banks, but also insurance companies and trading platforms. As a consequence, the reorganization of European financial markets increased the challenges that the European Union needs to solve (De Guindos 2020).

ECB Vice President Luis De Guindos (2020) set out these challenges at the SUERF/De Nederlandsche Bank Conference 'Forging a new future between the UK and the EU' on 8 January 2020. He made it clear that the European Union's banking union needs to be completed: more integration is required in order to advance the multiple resolution frameworks. In addition, the EU should provide uniform protection to depositors, without considering the bank's location. In this sense, the new decade focused initially on how to make the EU's markets more attractive in order to incentivize trade within the euro area. At the beginning of the year, the President Christine Lagarde said the Europe should turn 'challenges into opportunities in our natural, digital and economic environment' (Lagarde 2020): this was the motto in order to implement the system and go beyond the uncertainties of the past months, because a strong economic and financial environment affects all the European population, protecting banks, firms and the individuals.

The ECB monetary press conference on 23 January underscored how monetary policy had continued to rely on the decisions taken in 2019. It also underscored the influences operating on Europe from the outside world. The slow growth rate of GDP of the euro area was due to global weakness, as reflected in international trade, causing a slowdown of the European manufacturing sector. International trade had suffered because of the trade war between US and China, and, as a consequence, it had impacted also other regions of the world (Pope 2020). Moreover, inequality in the EU is a strong indicator of the need to reform the system. Consequently, Lagarde confirmed that the ECB was ready to start the first strategy review since 2003 (Lagarde 2020).

This strategy review focused on the changes that had taken place in monetary policy everywhere and similar reviews were underway in the United States and Canada as well. Lagarde sought to include the opinions of the Europeans in order to consider ideas and perspectives from academics, citizens and officials in other EU institutions (European Central Bank 2020e). The strategy review began in a divided Governing Council: one of the first debates concerned the Inflation target (close to, but below 2 percent per annum). The target had been questioned in the past because of its ambiguity and lack of efficacy. There have been different proposals about an 'appropriate band width': some argued that the target should provide flexibility in order to accept periods of low or high inflation (Randow 2020).

These debates are highly technical, but Lagarde believed they could not be reserved for technocrats. Public involvement in the conversation is important in order to create a deeper connection with the citizens, encouraging them to give advice on how to improve the functioning of the ECB. Moreover, the strategy review has to touch on issues that matter to the public and not just to monetary policymakers. In that sense, the strategy review included the mitigation of climate change as one of the objectives of the Central Bank. This expansion of objectives fit within the language of the treaties and yet nevertheless provoked controversy: the ECB's asset purchase program requires 'market neutrality'. As a consequence, the exclusion of polluting companies from the bond-buying programs could undermine the independence of the bank (Giugliano 2020a). Moreover, even if the goals proposed could be achieved, first and foremost the institution must fulfil its mandate, providing economic stability.

The outbreak of the novel coronavirus in China threatened everything. Leaving aside the political side of the problem, markets suffered from the lockdown of the world's second largest economy (China). It became clear that an economic crisis would follow the outbreak as the lockdown in China started and then proceeded to the EU. Nevertheless, as the virus began to spread, European financial markets EU were not exactly ready for another shock. Neither, it seems, as the ECB's Governing Council.

By the end of February, the response of the ECB had not arrived. As Europe started its lockdown in early March, and the economic outlook became more uncertain. The Governing Council's patience, turned out to be terrible for the markets: the silence of the institution gave the impression of a lack of consensus among the member states, and as a consequence, the markets speculated more and more that the institution would fail to respond decisively. Market participants also began to wonder whether the slowness of response of the ECB should be considered as a warning to the national governments to ensure that they come up with comprehensive fiscal policies (Giugliano 2020b).

Conclusion

Lagarde's honeymoon ended abruptly at the press conference she gave on 12 March. The content and outcomes of that press conference are the subject of the next chapter. For this chapter, the conclusion is about the context.

The main problem that remained at the European level was the lack of integration: there was the hope that consensus would bring a consolidation of the institutions and, first of all, of the banking system. But were Europeans ready to avoid another crisis? The divisions between North and South were still present, and politicians were fueling them. It seemed that the countries were not ready to give up the part of sovereignty which is necessary in order to make the system more robust. The creation of the common currency was the first step, and now they should be ready to adopt a common risk-free asset to consolidate the financial system. As Lagarde said during her first months of mandate, 'small rivers make very large oceans eventually when they are protected (Lagarde 2020).' The time had come to protect the small rivers, which include the weaker countries, that are entering in the crisis with already fragile foundations.

The analysis of the months before the crisis has been useful to understand the precarious position of the ECB and its permanent fragmentation. Looking back, it is clear that an integrated approach was required. Before that could be achieved, however, Lagarde had to change her position, and accept that the ECB would have to play a more active role in stabilizing the eurozone economy. That was a difficult evolution for her to make. Time was running out, and it seemed to many that the ECB did not have much room left to maneuver, after a large part of its arsenal had been deployed in September. Lagarde needed to set her priorities and to reveal her capacity to reassure the markets with the same level of confidence that her predecessor used during the previous crisis. The press conference she gave on 12 March was her first major test. She almost failed; but she found her feet quickly and soon moved to the forefront of European efforts.

5

THE EUROPEAN CENTRAL BANK: WHATEVER IT TAKES

Moritz Osterhuber

> This particular crisis might be different .... It could well be that what we have gone through collectively has transformed the way in which we look at what we value .... And my real hope is that by virtue of that change ... we pay more attention to women, we pay more attention to the environment, we pay more attention to those who are likely to be more affected than others.
>
> Christine Lagarde, European Central Bank President (European Business Leaders' Convention, 2020)

Making monetary policy for a fairly heterogenous group of 19 countries is a different beast than what central banks have been doing for much of modern financial history. While Europe's Economic and Monetary Union (EMU) brought about significant convergence of key monetary indicators, in the absence of a fiscal union it failed to deliver the stability and coherence typically associated with national jurisdictions. The global financial crisis (GFC) and the ensuing sovereign debt crisis have demonstrated that increasing market stress can easily turn intra-European disparities into vulnerabilities and impair the transmission mechanism of monetary policy. This is the financial backdrop against which the COVID-19 pandemic forced European governments to impose restrictions of unprecedented scale (in peacetime) on individual rights and economic liberties. The resulting paralysis of European economies created exceptional uncertainty that subsequently encumbered economic forecasting and complicated monetary policymaking. In fact, economic projections by the European Central Bank (ECB) carry a large error term and have become highly sensitive to changes in underlying economic variables. Forecasts locate negative GDP growth for 2020 between 5 and 12 percent conditional upon global containment measures, the pace of economic recovery, and a potential second wave of infections (Lane 2020).

Without a revenue-generating taxation system and limited competences in health care, social protection, and labor market policy, the hands of supranational EU institutions were tied beyond repurposing cohesion funds and what little remained in the multiannual financial framework. Decision-making in the more intergovernmental EU institutions had been characterized by gridlock until the Eurogroup endorsed a €540 billion fiscal stimulus package on 9 April that was adopted by the Council on 23 April and operational on 1 June. At the time of writing, the Commission's proposal for a €750 billion recovery plan supported by France and Germany is still in the negotiating phase and is facing major headwinds from Northern European states. Without such an ambitious plan however, Europe's fiscal response appears somewhat underpowered in a €15 trillion economy – particularly compared to the $2.2 trillion program in the United States. The political inertia and tepid fiscal response by European institutions have ascribed a paramount role to the ECB in finding a European response to the COVID-19 crisis. Yet, the success of monetary policy continues to be predicated on an 'ambitious and coordinated fiscal stance' (Lagarde and de Guindos 2020b).

This paper investigates the monetary policy response of the ECB to the 'sharpest and deepest [recession] ever recorded in non-war time' (European Business Leaders' Convention 2020). It addresses the two-pronged question of why the ECB devised the monetary policy program that it did and how the measures impacted markets. Through the course of the analysis, it interlaces the reasons that underpin the ECB's decisions with the early discernible effects that its policy had on key indicators in the eurozone. The central argument is that a dramatically changed risk environment and a contraction of bank funding conditions exacerbated Europe's problem of financial fragmentation that is reflected in diverging sovereign refinancing conditions and an intra-European flight to safety. The ECB recognized the negative implications for the monetary transmission mechanism and the substantial risk posed to the integrity of the common currency area. The Governing Council subsequently put forward an ambitious package of measures but remains subject to significant constraints like the capital key. In its current form, accommodative monetary policy addresses the symptoms but not the origin of distressed markets that lie in the absence of a banking union and a common fiscal policy. Understanding the ECB's unprecedented monetary policy and its short-term effects on markets is not only critical in devising and adjusting policy as the crisis unfolds but yields important insights into the vulnerabilities of the Eurosystem and the health of the single market.

The analysis starts by outlining the ECB's strategic response and recapitulating the intentions behind key policies. It classifies monetary policy decisions since 12 March into the three separate strands of non-standard instruments, collateral management, and banking supervision. The second section draws upon financial market data to explain why it was imperative for the ECB to intervene. Specifically, it discusses the risk environment, the funding conditions for financial corporations, intra-eurozone capital flows, and sovereign debt markets to shed light on the drivers behind different ECB programs. Moreover, it analyses the impact of ECB communications on sovereign yield spreads of Spanish and Italian debt securities over the German Bund. The third part examines potential vulnerabilities in the Eurosystem in a forward-looking analysis of disparities across different countries in the euro area. Moreover, it looks at the negative side-effects of unprecedented accommodative monetary policy and the consequences of the ECB's role as European crisis manager.

The ECB's strategic approach

According to the ECB staff projections of June 2020, the eurozone faces a fall in GDP of 16 percent over the first two quarters of 2020 (European Business Leaders' Convention 2020). The ECB's response since March 2020 has been characterized by three complementary lines of action. First, the Governing Council acted to safeguard the monetary transmission mechanism through open market operations, including non-standard monetary policy measures that raise available liquidity in the markets. Second, the ECB eased collateral requirements to ensure financial corporations have continued access to central bank liquidity. Third, the ECB Banking Supervision temporarily loosened the regulatory framework which affords financial corporations flexibility in servicing the economy.

Non-standard monetary policy measures

The ECB eased its monetary policy stance primarily through non-standard monetary policy measures whose purview goes beyond that of Keynesian tools of monetary stimulus. Non-standard instruments are geared toward safeguarding the central bank's monetary transmission mechanism by limiting the divergence of funding conditions across a heterogeneous system of 19 jurisdictions (Cour-Thimann and Winkler 2013). On the one hand, the pandemic impelled the ECB to set up novel programs like the pandemic emergency purchase program (PEPP) and the pandemic emergency longer-term refinancing operations (PELTROs). On the other hand, the ECB also moved to lower the refinancing rates of existing liquidity-providing programs like the longer-term refinancing operations (LTROs) and targeted longer-term refinancing operations (TLTROs). In the aftermath of the last financial crisis in 2008, non-standard instruments had become the principal determinant of liquidity conditions in the eurozone and therefore represent a powerful lever for the ECB during the present crisis (Carrión Álvarez 2020). The significance of benchmark interest rates on the other hand dwindled as fixed rates, full allotment tenders since 2009 and open market operations since 2015 provided cheap finance to banks and created excess liquidity in the Eurosystem.

The ECB formulated the first significant response to the financial consequences of containment on 12 March. The Governing Council provided a liquidity stimulus by extending the asset purchase program (APP) by an envelope of €120 billion, announcing additional LTROs, and adjusting conditions for TLTROs. The larger envelope for the APP is reflected in a marked upturn in net purchases to €20 billion per month which fall predominantly under the public sector purchase programme (PSPP). The larger APP envelope also inflated asset holdings on the ECB's balance sheet between February and June 2020. The uptake in purchases likely upends the ECB's efforts to reduce deviations from the capital key. Maturing principal from the APP had been used since early 2019 to decrease relative holdings of Spanish and Italian assets in order to return to the capital key distribution (Cœuré 2020).

By scheduling additional LTROs, the Governing Council sought to prevent a tightening of liquidity conditions in between the quarterly TLTRO tenders. These TLTROs will offer more favorable conditions for financial corporations in the Eurosystem: The ECB raised the upper funding limit from 30 percent to 50 percent of eligible loans. Additionally, the ECB lowered TLTRO borrowing costs by cutting interest rates to 25 basis points below the main refinancing rate (0.25 percent) and to 25 basis points below the average rate on the deposit facility (-0.75 percent) for counterparties that maintain their credit exposure (Lagarde and de Guindos 2020a). Making favorable refinancing terms conditional on providing credit created a strong incentive for financial corporations to maintain high lending levels to the real economy. This mild conditionality went beyond the already existing benchmark lending rules according to which banks can borrow more from the ECB at a lower cost if they exceed a bank-specific net lending target (European Central Bank 2019c). Additional full-allotment tenders (LTROs, PELTROs, and TLTROs) increased the volume of open-market operations on the ECB's balance sheet particularly between mid-March and mid-April.

As yields on sovereign debt particularly between Italy and Germany continued to diverge through mid-March, it became clear that the increased APP envelope would not be sufficient to keep spreads under control (Bouvet and Schroeder 2020). On 18 March, the ECB therefore embarked on a more aggressive policy and announced the pandemic emergency purchase program (PEPP), a temporary asset purchasing program for public and private debt in the eurozone (European Central Bank 2020c). Asset purchase programs in general are intended to shield against a self-fulfilling prophecy as investors start to reprice redenomination risk despite recurring commitments to the euro's irreversibility. Financial markets have indeed reacted positively and the spreads between Spanish and Italian 10-year sovereign bonds over the German Bund narrowed significantly since March.

The ECB further loosened its monetary policy stance during its meeting on 30 April as downside risks on the pervasiveness of COVID-19 containment measures materialized and the pessimistic macroeconomic outlook projected a GDP shrinkage of 15 percentage points for the euro area in 2020. The ECB slashed TLTRO rates by a further 25 basis points relative to its decision in March, positioning them 50 basis points below the main refinancing rate (-0.5 percent) and 50 basis points below the deposit facility (-1.0 percent) for financial corporations maintaining their credit exposure (Lagarde and de Guindos 2020b). Moreover, the ECB announced seven rounds of fixed-rate PELTROs with full allotment whose interest rates will be 25 basis points below the average rate on main refinancing operations (MROs) measured until the PLTROs' maturity in mid-2021. This move is significant because TLTROs are effective tools that increase interest rate pass-through and promote favorable lending conditions in the real economy (European Central Bank 2017a).

When the ECB held its Governing Council meeting on 4 June, the euro area economy showed the first signs of 'bottoming out' amid careful optimism that the worst could be over. At the same time, ECB President Christine Lagarde noted that the unprecedented economic contraction would bear a legacy of 'exceptionally elevated uncertainty' which would translate to a continuously high-risk investment environment in 2020 and beyond. Similarly, medium-term projections of the real economy hinted at a recovery that would be 'incomplete', 'sequential', and 'restrained' (European Business Leaders' Convention 2020, Lagarde and de Guindos 2020c). ECB modelling shows that while the economy will likely see lasting transformational change with a decisive bias toward the digital and the local, international trade, productivity, consumption, and investment will remain depressed for the foreseeable future.

The most significant news on 4 June concerned the PEPP which since March 2020 represented the bedrock of the ECB's response to COVID-19. In the context of a higher-than-expected purchasing pace and the looming specter of early depletion in October 2020, the Governing Council decided to extend the program until June 2021 and to enlarge its envelope by €600 billion to reach a total of €1.35 trillion. The size of the envelope is based on the depressed inflation outlook and thereby diverts from its initial purpose of containing escalating spreads and sovereign refinancing costs (European Central Bank 2020l). The program's extension was a prudent move that bought the ECB time to produce more dependable projections in the hope that uncertainty and volatility gradually recede from markets. Yet, if the current pace of asset purchases were to continue, the envelope would reach depletion by February 2021, well before the program's end date. This hints at the ECB's bet that spreads will stabilize and stay low in the second half of 2020.

A second significant decision taken on 4 June was to reinvest any maturing principal of the PEPP and APP until at least the end of 2022. This move signals the Governing Council's commitment to maintaining an accommodative monetary policy stance in the medium-term. It represents a powerful forward guidance intended to buttress market confidence. Yet, it also means that the ECB's balance sheet will remain larger and riskier for longer. The decisions taken on 4 June reaffirmed the ECB's strategy since March and dispelled concerns that the Governing Council could succumb to pre-emptive self-regulation after the German Court decision on 5 May drew into doubt the proportionality of the ECB's asset purchases. The impact of the judgement was nevertheless noticeable in the ramped-up efforts to communicate and explain why and how the PEPP adheres to principles of proportionality.

Requirements for collateral

The second line of action was a loosening of the minimum standards for eligible collateral by accepting a wider range of credit claims, increasing risk tolerance, and lowering regulatory thresholds (European Central Bank 2020h). This ensured that banks' access to central bank liquidity remained intact even as deteriorating asset quality and risk-averse markets rendered equity-financing increasingly onerous. By extension, continued access to central bank finance supported banks' capacity and willingness to offer loans and engage in uncollateralized lending on the interbank market, which is critical for financial corporations to meet short-term liquidity needs (de Guindos and Schnabel 2020).

On 7 April, the ECB announced a package of far-reaching collateral easing measures. The most significant adjustment is perhaps the widening of the eligibility of credit claims for collateral. This has a dual effect on the credit channel and bolsters money creation since issued loans can be pledged as collateral to participate in further refinancing operations. Additionally, the ECB uniformly reduced haircuts by 20 percent, which decreases the cost of central bank liquidity particularly for holders of distressed government debt. Lastly, regulatory adjustments include the temporary recognition of bank-internal credit assessments, a lowering of reporting requirements to unburden smaller banks, acceptance of small loans from SMEs as collateral (the previous minimum threshold was €25,000), and authorization to hold larger amounts of debt instruments issued by other financial corporations. This last measure promoted transactions of promissory notes and financial paper, which effectively constitutes uncollateralized lending with maturities of up to 270 days. The underlying objective was to reinstate investor confidence in the private and financial sectors and bring down yields for commercial and financial paper that had previously experienced an upward shock in March 2018.

On 22 April, the ECB reinforced the measures taken on 7 April and decided to make marketable assets like sovereign bonds retroactively immune to downgrades occurring after April 7 that would have otherwise pushed them below the minimum credit quality requirements for eligibility as collateral (European Central Bank 2020j). This process termed 'grandfathering' ensured that financial corporations can continue to access central bank liquidity by providing sovereign bonds of distressed eurozone countries as collateral. Notably, Hellenic bonds had already been expressly exempted from eligibility requirements in a move that reflected a strong commitment to the integrity of the euro area. Grandfathering already proved to be crucial in maintaining ample liquidity conditions in the eurozone's periphery after on 29 April Fitch relegated Italy's creditworthiness to BBB-, one grade above sub-prime status (Stubbington and Johnson 2020).

Banking supervision

Banking supervision in the Eurosystem has applied significantly more flexibility since the inception of the crisis to avoid a scenario in which the higher operational burden on banks turns liquidity challenges into solvency issues (McCaul 2020). Supervisory flexibility was thus critical to counteract incentives to deleverage and reduce loan provision. To guarantee that the capital released is directed toward the stabilization of the banking sector and the real economy, the ECB Banking Supervision has asked commercial banks to suspend dividend disbursements at least through October 2020.

On 12 March, the ECB Supervisory Board allowed financial corporations to temporarily operate at a lower capital adequacy ratio under the Pillar 2 Guidance (P2G), which means that banks can deviate from the minimum liquidity coverage worth 30 days of capital outflows and the capital conservation buffer of 2.5 percent of total exposures (European Central Bank 2020f). Moreover, the ECB relaxed regulation that normally requires banks to satisfy more than 50 percent of the Pillar 2 requirements with the highest-quality capital (Common Equity Tier 1, CET1), allowing increased reliance on private equity and liabilities.

On 20 March, regulators addressed concerns pertaining to a potential flood of non-performing loans (NPLs) and allowed for some flexibility in the application of the IFRS 9 accounting standard. In 2018, the IFRS 9 marked a shift from measuring objective impairment to estimating credit quality, obliging banks to calculate expected losses over a 12-months period even for performing assets. Under this framework, the lockdowns would have forced banks to write-down or increase impairment allowances for any loans that showed 'significant increase in credit risk' (Baudino et al. 2018: 8). Facing a large number of potentially impaired loans, banks can avoid classifying debtors as 'unlikely to pay' if loans have been put under a public guarantee or are subject to a moratorium (European Central Bank 2020g). In this context, moratoria in Spain (see chapter by Nesplyak) and in Italy under the 'CuraItalia' decree (see chapter by Hintermayer) continue to be critical to avoid spikes in banks' short-term capital requirements due to losses from NPLs on income statements (Ministero dell'Economia e delle Finanze 2020). Moratoria constitute a valuable contribution to managing liquidity risk (European Banking Authority 2020) and financial stability (Magyar Nemzeti Bank 2020) since banks can presently compensate foregone interest rate revenue with cheap central bank liquidity in the short-term.

In its decision on 16 April, the Supervisory Board further defrayed banks by reducing the qualitative market risk multiplier, an instrument designed to catch the elements of market risk not accounted for by banks' internal modelling. This was intended to compensate the rising capital requirements for financial corporations demanded by the quantitative multiplier which soared in March due to uncertainty, risk-aversion, and market volatility. Therefore, the decision granted financial corporations the necessary room for maneuver to continuously perform their 'market-making activities' (European Central Bank 2020i). The decision also reinforced the downward adjustments of countercyclical capital buffers and systemic risk buffers undertaken by national regulators and underpin an overall strategy of reducing the regulatory burden to enable a countercyclical rise in credit supply.

What the ECB did not do

The ECB deemed non-standard measures to be the more effective tools and did not lower benchmark interest rates. Already before the inception of the crisis, key interest rates that signal and govern the conduct of monetary policy have reached unprecedentedly low levels. Particularly the deposit facility which allows banks to deposit liquidity overnight has been in negative territory since June 2014. Low refinancing rates in recent years have increased banks' exposure to both credit and risk and therefore passed on accommodative liquidity conditions to the real economy (Demiralp et al. 2019). This relationship is robust even in negative territory as banks are able to pass on negative rates to corporate clients that subsequently have been shown to increase investment activity (Altavilla et al. 2019). This correlation suggests that interest rate pass-through is intact and that the ECB is not currently operating at or close to the reversal rate. Notwithstanding the evidence for pass-through of negative rates, the Governing Council considered headline rates sufficiently accommodative and left rates for the deposit facility (-0.50 percent), the marginal lending facility (0.25 percent, and main refinancing operations (MRO, 0.00 percent) unchanged at very low levels.

In contrast to the Federal Reserve and the Bank of England, the ECB refrained from actively intervening on repo markets (International Capital Market Association 2020a). Moreover, taking a different approach than the Japanese and Australian central banks, the ECB did not commit to a yield curve control (YCC) that would provide a ceiling to bond yields (and spreads) in the eurozone. This would have required an open-ceiling asset purchasing program with no temporary limit. Instead, in what likely reflects a compromise between hawkish and more dovish central bankers in the Governing Council, the ECB combined the roll-out of an ambitious €750 billion purchasing program (which now stands at €1.35 trillion) with the reassurance to do more if necessary. The downside risk to this approach is that a high burn rate of the PEPP would unsettle investors and resuscitate the pricing of redenomination risk. While the program's extension on 4 June has reassured markets of the ECB's commitment to control spreads, a further enlargement may be needed if peripheral bond markets lose traction in the latter half of 2020.

Why the ECB acted – indicators underlying monetary policy

In the first half of 2020, the ECB reacted to the unfolding of the COVID-19 crisis with unprecedented action in both type and magnitude. The decisiveness of monetary policy instruments distinguished the Governing Council markedly from the inertia in the European Council and the arduous negotiations of the €540 billion stimulus package. In the emerging vacuum, the ECB's asset purchases and liquidity injections became the public face and mainstay of the European crisis response. By implication, monetary policy had to serve the dual purpose of responding to global risk factors and mending the emerging imbalances between euro area countries. Not unlike the financial crisis, the COVID-19 pandemic accentuated the heterogeneity of conditions within the common currency area, prompted a fragmentation of financial markets, and threatened to undermine the monetary transmission mechanism. As such, the ECB Governing Council had to grapple not only with a rapidly deteriorating risk environment and threats to bank funding but also with diverging sovereign refinancing costs and flight-to-safety dynamics from the periphery toward the center.

The risk environment

Already before far-reaching containment measures gave a real economic dimension to the pandemic, markets had begun re-pricing uncertainty and elevated risk. On the one hand, the VIX, a measure of implied volatility based on index options, signaled high levels of expected market turmoil and more than quadrupled between 19 February and mid-March. On the other hand, market participants reappraised credit and default risk which set off a period of rising capital costs. In fact, the spread between the London Interbank Offered Rate (LIBOR) and the rate on Overnight Indexed Swaps (OIS), a measure of credit risk and indicator of financial sector health, had started to widen in late February. Coming from a multiweek low that coincided with a sprint of the S&P 500 on 19 February, the LIBOR-OIS spread rose 126 basis points until late March 2020, indicating increasing reservations on the part of financial corporations concerning the creditworthiness of their counterparties. Elevated market risk and volatility were reflected in equity selloffs in early March that burdened the private sector which had already been strained by major supply chain disruptions and collapsing expenditure levels. On 12 March, the Governing Council therefore reasoned that liquidity injections would be appropriate to buttress investor confidence and safeguard the flow of credit to the real economy (European Central Bank 2020k).

Bank funding: equity, interbank, and repo markets

Rising LIBOR rates not only heralded a reassessment of risk but also hinted at tightening funding conditions for financial corporations. In the eurozone, bank funding conditions had become a particularly sensitive issue after the last crisis left scarring memories of credit crunches, bank bailouts and fiscal austerity. The dominance of bank finance in Europe also makes it an economically momentous issue as uncertainty about funding conditions depresses credit provision and imperils interest rate pass-through (Ritz and Walther 2015). With the fundamental role that distressed banks play in propagating crises, the ECB decided to expand collateral eligibility and loosen regulatory requirements in order to lower banks' operational burden. This has been crucial to mitigate the deteriorating funding conditions on the equity, interbank, and repo markets and to instill confidence that markets were sufficiently liquid to absorb selloffs.

The spread of the pandemic caused the cost of both short- and longer-term bank funding to increase. Equity valuations of financial corporations reacted as early as mid-February and fell by more than 40 percent. This is significant because equity financing 'plays an important role in banks portfolio allocation decisions, including lending activity' (European Central Bank 2016: 27). Equity values have stabilized since March and individual banks registered moderate gains, which dissipated fears of a downright banking crisis. Nevertheless, bank losses in early 2020 have been ubiquitous in the Eurosystem. In fact, none of the large financial corporations in Germany, France, Italy, Spain, and the Netherlands avoided equity losses of well above 20 percent and in some cases more than 40 percent.

The Euro Interbank Offered Rates (EURIBOR) for maturities exceeding one month surged in mid-March and indicated a tightening of funding for uncollateralized short-term borrowing. They also signaled interbank market fragmentation, which during the GFC was more pronounced in the eurozone's periphery (Mayordomo et al. 2015). Shorter maturities, on the other hand, remained stable around the mark of –0.5 percent. Overall, funding conditions on the interbank market remained favorable as all maturities continued to demand a premium for holding cash. Nevertheless, rising rates were a sign of distress and elevated uncertainty about creditworthiness in a market that had to absorb unprecedented new debt issuance by sovereigns. This was important since rising interbank rates significantly depress credit provision (Cingano et al. 2013). Additional refinancing operations by the ECB managed to dissipate concerns about counterparties' liquidity and anchored interbank rates close to the deposit facility rate as banks accumulated excess liquidity and ceased to rely on MROs (Purps 2017).

Signs of funding stress extended also to short-term, collateralized lending in the repo market. Declining rates since March indicated that certain debt securities were becoming scarcer on account of the ECB's asset purchases and a general flight to safety (Arrata et al. 2018, International Capital Market Association 2020b). Safe debt securities increasingly traded under conditions of specialness, meaning that they commanded higher cash premiums than general collateral. This happened even as bonds targeted by purchase programs became less liquid, suggesting that the repo market presents an anomaly of the price liquidity trade-off associated with purchase programs (Corradin and Maddaloni 2017, Ferdinandusse 2020). Sinking rates had their origin in the scarcity of eligible collateral and implied that repo markets became increasingly asset-driven (Encío 2018). Low repo rates also emerged as a symptom of a broader flight to safety and suggested that collateral management was becoming more arduous for banks. Against this backdrop, the ECB's collateral easing measures on 7 April and 22 April in connection with the collateral lending program bolstered access to open market operations especially for undercapitalized banks and safeguarded the monetary transmission mechanism.

Cross-border payment balances

Investors' flight to safety at the onset of the crisis manifested itself in the TARGET2 balances, the cross-border payment balances in the Eurosystem.

Risk-aversion incited investors to shift capital from debtor systems to more liquid creditor systems, thereby accentuating existing net positions. The roll-out of the APP and PEPP amplified this trend since purchases are associated with excessive liquidity positions and are often implemented via non-domestic counterparties concentrated in liquid creditor systems (European Central Bank 2017b).

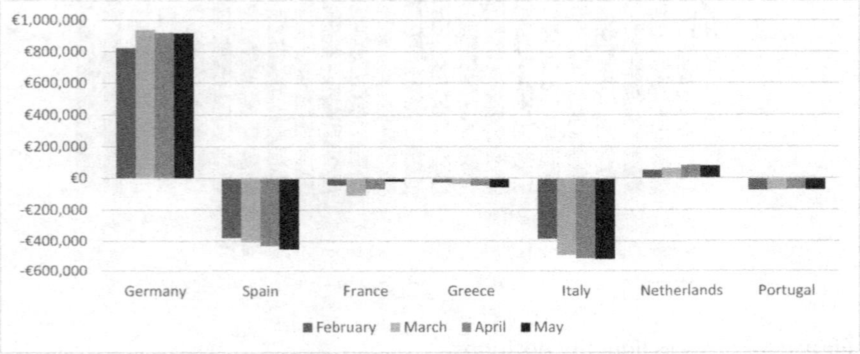

Figure 5.1 TARGET2 balances (selected eurozone countries)

Source: European Central Bank.

Importantly, TARGET2 positions do not in themselves reflect financial risk since credit risk in the Eurosystem is accounted for through collateralization, haircuts, and burden-sharing in the event of default. However, an increase in net balances indicates a segmentation of bank funding along national lines (European Central Bank 2013). On the one hand, sizeable negative changes in Italy and Spain implied a withdrawal of funds and tightening liquidity conditions. The ECB's liquidity injections via favorable LTROs, TLTROs, and PLTROs subsequently publicized private liabilities between banks and absorbed capital outflows from these countries. On the other hand, cross-border claims created excess liquidity positions in the central bank system, which was most conspicuous in Germany between March and April 2020. Generally, liquidity holdings that exceeded the reserve requirement became more prevalent during the COVID-19 crisis with overall net changes being predominantly positive throughout 2020. Rising excess liquidity positions are a sign that holding cash is very costly even when inflation is low (Darvas and Pichler 2018). Moreover, excess liquidity indicates strong risk aversion as emerging market (EM) and high-yielding assets are deemed too risky even as returns on safe haven investments become prohibitively low and, in many cases, negative (Baldo et al. 2017). Therefore, rising TARGET2 net balances point toward a depressed market environment and signal the need for a more accommodative monetary policy stance.

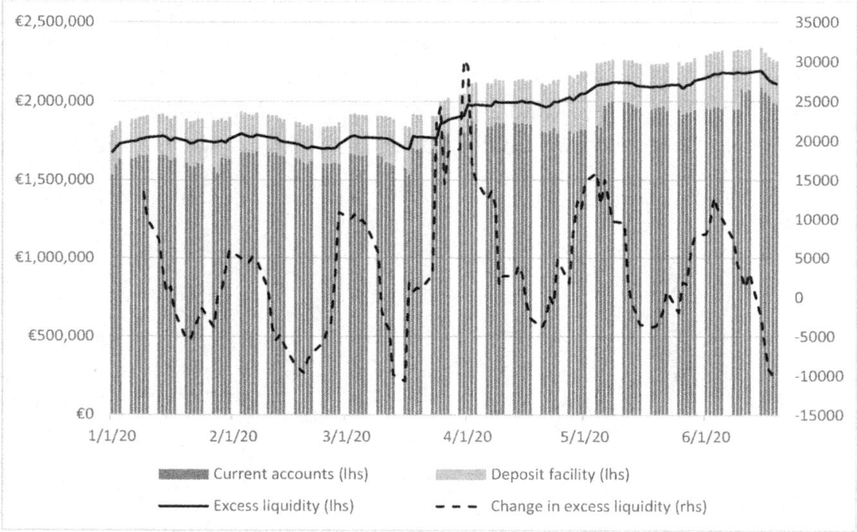

Figure 5.2 Excess liquidity positions

Source: European Central Bank.

Sovereign debt markets

Arguably the most pertinent development for monetary policy in the early days of the crisis has been the divergence of sovereign refinancing conditions across the eurozone. Similar to the last crisis, the COVID-19 pandemic conjured doubts about the euro's resilience and the steadfastness of political commitment to the integrity of the common currency area. As investors reappraised redenomination risk and calculated the odds of a euro country failing, European financial markets showed tendencies of fragmentation along national lines. Market participants were particularly skeptical of whether Greek, Spanish, and Italian bonds carried a comparable risk profile to German bonds and subsequently took refuge in 'safer' assets. In the eurozone periphery, the withdrawal of funds expressed itself in a decline of bid-ask spreads, an indicator of liquidity and measure of demand overhang, and a surge in sovereign refinancing costs. Crucially, in a moment of unprecedented need for fiscal stimulus, swelling yields not only imperiled the capacity to make the necessary investment for economic recovery but decisively skewed the playing field in the single market. Moreover, in the absence of monetary autonomy, the road of market fragmentation could ultimately lead to sovereign bankruptcy. Widening yield spreads have therefore been the main motivator behind the ambitious PEPP passed by the Governing Council on 18 March.

The evolution of sovereign yields since the start of Europe's economic and monetary union suggests that doubts about the euro's irreversibility are neither novel nor a unique feature of the COVID-19 crisis. Rather, redenomination risk appears to lay dormant in periods of growth only to resurface periodically when financial or economic outlooks darken. This is ultimately a symptom of Europe's unfinished transfer union where investors cannot be certain that the commitment to repay sovereign debt is the same in all eurozone countries. Therefore, idiosyncratic fiscal and debt characteristics that determine a country's individual default risk continue to play an important role in sovereign debt pricing even during episodes of minimal spreads (Codogno et al. 2003). In fact, yield decompositions show that increases in sovereign debt levels are associated with higher yields and refinancing costs (Schuknecht et al. 2009, Grande et al. 2013). While political, spillover, and contagion effects are non-negligible, this hints at the relatively high levels of public debt in the eurozone's periphery as explanation for the divergence of spreads in March and April 2020.

Sovereign refinancing costs not only have fiscal implications for crisis management and recovery programs but have an important impact on the real economy. The banking sector by way of its role as intermediator acts as transposing mechanism between the sovereign and private markets. Because it is hard for private enterprises to convince lenders that their creditworthiness is superior to that of their sovereign, yields paid on government debt instruments effectively provide a floor for capital costs in the private sector. Data for Italy demonstrates that rising yields increase the funding costs for financial corporations and in turn disincentivize the provision of cheap credit (Albertazzi et al. 2014). In fact, banks tend to pass on tighter funding conditions in a non-linear fashion by raising interest rates and reducing loan provision particularly for small and medium-sized enterprises (Al-Eyd and Berkmen 2013).

Rising bank funding costs also reduce the profitability of banks which represents an additional layer of risk for financial stability. More importantly still, disparate lending conditions run counter to the idea of common monetary policy and uniform interest rate pass-through and may help entrench economic inequalities in the single market (Horvath 2018). The divergence of retail rates in some peripheral euro area countries from the ECB's policy rates suggests that the sensitivity of peripheral banking sectors to monetary policy is reduced. By extension, this impinges on the ECB's capacity to pursue its mandate of price stability laid out in Article 127(1) of the Treaty on the Functioning of the European Union (TFEU). Therefore, sovereign bond yields are significant not only because they represent redenomination risk but because they have tangible consequences for the real economy, the integrity of the single market, and the ECB's mandate in common monetary policy.

Besides fiscal fundamentals, salient political events have significant impacts on bond spreads in the eurozone's periphery (António and Strauch 2007, Büchel

2013). Political communication, too, can have a quantifiable, short-term impact on spreads (Gade et al. 2013). Against this backdrop, it seems difficult to account for the precipitous movements in eurozone spreads since February 2020 purely based on country fundamentals, contagion, and international risk factors. In the weeks before 18 March, Italian spreads over the German Bund have more than doubled, a rise only partially and temporarily reversed by the €25 billion fiscal stimulus package by the Italian government announced on 10 March.

Just how much of an impact the ECB's communication isolated from the pass-through of its monetary policy has on spreads became clear on 12 March, when Christine Lagarde, pressed by a journalist on potential refinancing problems of individual eurozone countries, said that closing spreads would not be part of the ECB's mandate (Lagarde and de Guindos 2020a). Yields vis-à-vis the German bund rose after the press conference and increased the borrowing costs for the Italian and Spanish governments within the next trading day by 51 and 24 basis points respectively. Christine Lagarde personally tried to limit the damage by stating in a CNBC interview that large spreads imperil the monetary transmission mechanism and that she is 'committed to avoid any fragmentation ... of the euro area' (Lagarde and de Guindos 2020a: 6). Institutionally, the ECB achieved a soothing of market sentiments by the ambitious PEPP that was reinforced by a commitment to do more if necessary (Segreti 2020).

Spreads widened again in April and almost returned to pre-PEPP levels for Italy (2.57) and Spain (1.57) as the ECB's cues were overpowered by political signals coming from the Eurogroup and the European Council. The emerging fault line between Northern and Southern European states over instruments to mutualize debt and finance the recovery brought back uncertainties about peripheral states' fiscal space and liquidity. The political disagreement surfaced most clearly during the European Council meeting on 26 March, which stopped and reversed the sizeable downward trend of the Italian spread after the PEPP had been announced (European Council 2020c, De Miguel et al. 2020, Rankin 2020).

The rise of spreads since 9 April is less clearly attributable to any single event. Instead it reflects continuous bickering over debt mutualization and the politicization of the European Stability Mechanism (ESM). During the Eurogroup summit on 9 April, finance ministers could not agree on community-backed bonds and floated a low-conditionality credit line by the ESM as a viable alternative. This underwhelming outcome was amplified by the contentious nature of the ESM in many peripheral countries. In Italy, the country most severely affected by COVID-19 at the time, opposition leaders Giorgia Meloni of *Fratelli d'Italia* and Matteo Salvini of the *Lega* likened the ESM credit line to a sell-out of the Italian economy and vigorously opposed any conditionality. Eventually, cracks opened within the governing coalition of the center left *Partito Democratico* and the *Movimento Cinque Stelle*, forcing the independent Italian Prime Minister to rebuff the EMS emergency credit line even under reduced conditionality (Perrone and Trovato 2020). Giuseppe Conte has since walked back on his categorical refusal and put a decision on the ESM in the hands of parliament, where Silvio Berlusconi suggested that his *Forza Italia* would support the government in accepting ESM loans.

The hesitant fiscal response on a European level burdens national paths to recovery. At the time of writing, Italy's decision-makers are still negotiating the country's recovery plan, a process that is complicated by the country's meagre fiscal space and the unclear prospects of EU emergency assistance. The political environment in Italy reveals the toxicity of the ESM as a sovereign bailout mechanism as countries continue to associate the safety framework with conditionality and austerity. Despite the political and fiscal difficulties, financial markets give reason for careful optimism as bond spreads narrowed significantly since March and kept refinancing costs bearable. Low yields in the eurozone's periphery were achieved at the expense of large asset purchases and were sustained by positive economic signals and the PEPP extension on 4 June. However, the pending issues of a European recovery plan and debt mutualization mean that spreads are not sustainably anchored and may therefore rise again if the economic or financial outlook in the eurozone's periphery darkens.

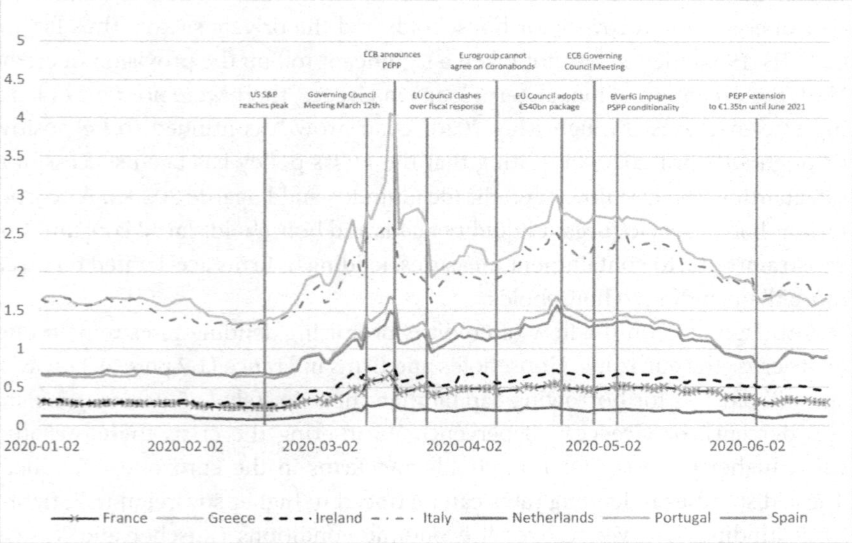

Figure 5.3 Sovereign bond spreads over German bunds (10Y maturities)

Source: IHS Markit.

A look ahead: disparities and vulnerabilities

The future trajectory of the COVID-19 crisis is mired in uncertainty with risks firmly tilted to the downside. On the one hand, structural disparities and weaknesses in the banking sector pose a threat to financial stability and the recovery process in the eurozone's periphery. On the other hand, the ECB's crisis response precipitated a politicization of central banking and may encourage excessive risk-taking on the part of undercapitalized banks. Getting a grasp of these issues is significant as it may yield an indication of how the crisis will impact economies and livelihoods across the eurozone.

As banks assume an increasingly central role in absorbing the pandemic-related losses, the risk to financial stability is two-pronged: tightening funding conditions on the liabilities side and the still-developing deterioration of asset quality on the asset side will likely compress bank liquidity and capital reserves for the foreseeable future. While Eurosystem banks have suffered comparable equity losses, their balance sheet compositions and exposures differ widely across countries. In fact, pre-crisis lending rates, exposures to domestic assets and bonds, and incidences of non-performing loans (NPLs) are disparate across the eurozone. As a consequence, risks to the banking sector are unlikely to manifest themselves homogeneously across the 19 jurisdictions of the eurozone.

The first significant variable to watch are lending rates as they determine the cost of economic recovery for households and the private sector. Thus far, the COVID-19 pandemic has not taken a significant toll on the provision of credit. With the exception of longer-term loans in Greece, there were no signs of lending rate increases through May 2020. Loan growth continued to be positive throughout April 2020, indicating that the ECB's policy has been successful in safeguarding the free flow of credit (de Guindos and Lagarde 2020c). As corporations had to service urgent liquidity needs and households faced consumption constraints due to containment measures, lending to firms accelerated relatively more than lending to households.

Although data on the flow of credit is promising, lending rates remain unequal across the eurozone. Households and firms in France (1.2 percent) on average still pay less for borrowing capital than those in Italy (1.5 percent), Ireland (3.0 percent), or Greece (5.3 percent). Weathering the crisis therefore often has a higher price tag for households and firms in the eurozone's periphery. These disparities in lending rates can be traced to higher sovereign risk, tighter bank funding, and worse overall economic conditions (Ruscher and Vašíček 2016). The long-term risk is that the COVID-19 crisis affects lending and helps increase and entrench economic inequalities in the eurozone.

Another important risk factor on banks' balance sheets is exposure to high-yielding domestic assets. Advancing market fragmentation during the GFC had already increased domestic-foreign asset ratios and reversed a previous trend of rising financial interconnectedness in the eurozone. The onset of the COVID-19 crisis has further promoted fragmentation and home biases as documented by the increase in TARGET2 net balances. Particularly banks with pre-existing 'solvency-critical exposures' to risky sovereign debt had an incentive to double down on their bet and buy more of the same (Acharya et al. 2018: 2862). For banks whose solvency had already been linked to the non-default of a sovereign, rising yields in March lost their risk-signalling function and turned into a potentially lucrative investment opportunity. The incentive to shift risks was reinforced by better information in the home country which promoted the retreat into domestic assets (Andrade and Chhaochharia 2010). Moreover, exposure to deposits and assets in the same jurisdiction held the additional benefit of neutralising redenomination risk, which effectively affords domestic banks a competitive edge as soon as the possibility of conversion is priced into assets (Battistini et al. 2014).

Yet, rising home biases at a time when government bond valuations are falling bear the risk of curtailing banks' access to funding. Marked-to-market losses on sovereign debt are associated with a contraction of short-term funding from US Money Market Mutual Funds and a reduction in more longer-term equity funding (De Marco 2019). During the GFC, impaired bond valuations inflicted average equity losses of 10.8 percent on banks in the eurozone's periphery (Acharya et al. 2018). Banks with risky debt holdings therefore were forced to deleverage and disproportionately scaled down credit provision and raised borrowing costs. The corporate clients of these banks subsequently boasted lower growth rates of investment, employment, and sales than clients of less exposed banks, showing the negative real sector implications of home biases and reduced bank funding (Acharya et al. 2018). In the present crisis therefore, the accentuation of home biases bears the dual risk of causing financial instability and transmitting funding distress to the real economy via a credit crunch.

Despite the ECB's success in stabilising spreads and alleviating bank funding constraints, systemic and bank-level risks remain significant beyond 2020. As the magnitude of fiscal deficits and the damage to the economy and debt sustainability will become clearer, rating agencies may further downgrade the creditworthiness of states in the eurozone's periphery. Given the contagious qualities of credit events, redenomination risk could quickly spread to other countries with better fundamentals (Constâncio 2012). Institutional investors bound by internal or legal minimum rating requirements may subsequently be forced to retreat from debt markets and would thereby contribute to reigniting a divergence of yields. Systemically, this may trigger a self-reinforcing dynamic toward sovereign bankruptcy for individual euro area countries. On a bank-level, impaired bond valuations would simultaneously increase the reliance on central bank finance and decrease the collateral that home biased corporations have at their disposal. The ECB may therefore have to reinforce its collateral easing measures that currently still enforce market discipline on the basis of a BB minimum rating requirement and regressive haircuts.

Non-performing assets (NPAs) are another potential balance sheet weakness and have long been a concern for regulators because of their effects of propagating crises and contracting credit supply (Fredriksson and Frykström 2019). Data on NPLs, a subset of NPAs, show that exposures have decreased since the GFC but remain disparate across the eurozone. The incidence of NPLs as a share of total loans is particularly elevated in Italy (5.9 percent), Portugal (7.4 percent), and Greece (33.4 percent). This points toward a pre-existing burden on the banking sectors in these countries and reduced capacity to shoulder bad loans arising in the wake of future insolvencies. This is particularly relevant in light of the lasting downward effect on consumption that the COVID-19 pandemic is likely to have. Moratoria and state guarantees have been instrumental in avoiding a flood of NPLs in the first half of 2020, but state programs will only provide a real solution if they are sufficient to help businesses to weather the crisis (Carrión Álvarez 2020). Again, the lasting economic effects of the pandemic suggest that some measure of structural adjustment will be unavoidable, which may disproportionately reduce interest revenue and increase write-offs for commercial and retail banks in the eurozone's periphery.

Aside from structural weaknesses in the eurozone, the ECB's unprecedented accommodative monetary policy is not without caveats. Yet, the most significant ones today only partially reflect the popular criticisms that the ECB's rates approach the reversal rate and that its asset purchases distort markets. Loose monetary policy matters not because it unhinges market-pricing mechanisms but because it may incite excessive risk-taking and because it bears distributional consequences.

In the absence of outright recapitalization, the ECB's liquidity injections may lead to an accumulation of risk on banks' balance sheets. With cheap crisis finance available, risky assets tend to shift from solvent banks to undercapitalized banks (Drechsler et al. 2016). This is because undercapitalized banks have a particularly strong incentive to invest in risky, high-yielding assets to increase revenue and avoid default (Acharya and Steffen 2015). In what is akin to a carry trade, banks attempt to exploit the duration mismatch between the ECB's short-term crisis finance and longer-term, high-yielding assets to generate net interest margin. Key risks of carry-trades include glitches in cash management as the duration mismatch may cause liquidity shortfalls and, crucially, a significant solvency risk in case of impaired valuations or asset defaults. If crisis finance is reinvested domestically in distressed government bonds, carry trade behavior also compounds the disadvantages associated with excessive home biases. In the context of risk-taking, the ECB's accommodative monetary policy therefore carries a clear element of moral hazard since systemically relevant banks may come to expect the publicization of the downside risk on their portfolios.

Alongside its financial effects, loose monetary policy creates distributional consequences that imply a politicization of the ECB (Jones 2019b). Non-standard measures create economic winners and losers in the short-term, a side-effect of monetary policy that goes beyond the ECB's mandate to manage long-term inflation expectations. Distributional consequences are therefore imperfectly justified by technocratic necessity and threaten to undermine the European consensus for central bank independence (Jones 2019b). The most recent expression of the ECB's politicization are the legal quarrels around some of its non-standard instruments. While the European Court of Justice (ECJ) in a case brought by leading anti-EU politicians in 2018 confirmed the PSPP's compatibility with EU law, on 5 May 2020 the German Federal Constitutional Court (BVerfG) came to a different verdict regarding the program's conditionality. In the wake of the judgement, the Commission publicly considered initiating an infringement procedure against Germany to defend the primacy of EU law and make a statement about the ECB's independence (Khan and Fleming 2020). Overall, the ECB's involvement in what is essentially a political debate is a preoccupying sign that its crisis response is not only under increasing scrutiny by judges and politicians, but that the doctrine of central banks independence is increasingly up for interpretation and debate.

Conclusion

The COVID-19 pandemic quickly matured from a health emergency to an economic crisis. In the eurozone, markets became volatile and risk averse as they began to reprice credit, default, and redenomination risks. Preying on existing vulnerabilities, the COVID-19 crisis subsequently resuscitated fears of sovereign defaults and a financial crisis in the eurozone. European institutions struggled to coordinate a political response in the early period of the crisis. While the fiscal package of €540 billion adopted on 23 April constituted a good start, debt mutualization remains politically toxic and a more ambitious €750 billion recovery plan is still the subject of fierce disagreement at the time of writing. Against this backdrop of political vacuum, the ECB assumed a preeminent role in addressing the COVID-19 crisis on a European level. This paper's aim was to shed light on the ECB's unprecedented monetary policymaking, asking why the ECB devised the monetary policy program that it did and how the measures impacted markets. On the one hand, understanding the drivers behind monetary policy can teach us valuable lessons about the persisting vulnerabilities in the Eurosystem. Based on the analysis, these vulnerabilities lie in the absence of a transfer union and banking union and find expression in an intra-European flight to safety and diverging sovereign refinancing conditions. On the other hand, gauging the short-term effect of monetary policy on markets can provide crucial insights in how monetary policy could be adjusted and optimized as the crisis unfolds.

In February 2020, market indicators began showing signs that the Eurosystem would come into troubled waters. First, the sudden deterioration of the global risk environment exemplified by the soaring LIBOR-OIS spread demonstrated heightened credit risk and lacking investor confidence. Second, equity selloffs and rising rates on the interbank market signaled a tightening of funding conditions for financial corporations. This was compounded by low rates on the repo market that indicated increasing scarcity of certain 'safe' assets. Tight bank funding was problematic as it raised the risk of a banking crisis and threatened to propagate financial distress to the real economy by way of reduced credit provision and higher lending rates. Third, a capital flight from the eurozone's periphery accentuated net TARGET2 balances between countries, indicating a financial market segmentation along national borders. The differences were quickly absorbed on the ECB's balance sheet but represent a risk if banks in debtor countries experience liquidity shortfalls. Fourth, rapidly rising refinancing costs for sovereigns in the eurozone's periphery threatened the monetary transmission mechanism and the common currency area. Significantly, rising spreads also skewed the single market and demonstrated that disparities in key economic indicators like debt levels can turn into sources of instability as individual countries may be heading for default without monetary policy intervention.

Particularly the phenomena of diverging spreads and intra-European capital flight are symptoms of incomplete financial integration. The ECB addressed these symptoms by capitalizing on three complementary lines of action that go beyond a Keynesian-type monetary stimulus. First, the ECB provided additional liquidity for banks through non-standard measures like the PLTROs and TLTROs and through an ambitious asset purchase program. Second, collateral easing measures ensured that banks retain access to central bank liquidity through refinancing operations. Third, regulatory flexibility decreased the operational burden on banks and liberated capital reserves that can contribute to servicing the economy. Overall, the policy package is designed to safeguard financial stability, prevent the transmission of financial distress, and create financial conditions conducive to recovery.

Tentative evidence suggests that the ECB succeeded in mitigating the impact of the crisis. Bank funding conditions have stabilized on both the equity and interbank markets since March 2020 and the PEPP significantly narrowed the yield differentials across the eurozone. Moreover, the high burn rate suggests that the program played a key role in preventing a further escalation of sovereign funding costs after the German Court impugned the conditionality of asset purchases. Against the preliminary stabilization on markets, the eurozone faces a myriad of risks as it enters the second half of 2020. Balance sheets in the eurozone's periphery are likely to develop a stronger home bias, while the cost of capital and the incidence of non-performing loans remain unequal across the eurozone. With unavoidable structural adjustments, these disparities are prone to be accentuated and entrench economic differences in the single market. Finally, the ECB's intervention itself does not come without caveats. While its accommodative stance may incite excessive risk-taking on the part of undercapitalized banks, it has already precipitated a politicization of the ECB that threatens to undermine the long-standing consensus for central bank independence.

6

THE GREAT LOCKDOWN: NATIONAL FISCAL POLICIES IN THE EURO AREA

Zoë Katharina Strauss

The effectiveness of national fiscal policies to respond to the coronavirus recession differs across euro area countries. This is due to existing country-specific vulnerabilities, the size of the expansionary fiscal stimulus packages, and disparate borrowing constraints to raise additional debt. This chapter will look at Germany, Italy, the Netherlands, and Spain to illustrate that these three factors are leading to an uneven recession in the eurozone, distorting already existing disparities.

First, Italy and Spain are more vulnerable than Germany and the Netherlands because their macroeconomic conditions prior to the crisis and the structure of their economies expose them more heavily to the lockdown crisis. On top of that, Spain and Italy have been hit harder by the virus than most other countries in Europe. Second, Italy and Spain are likely to experience a longer and more profound economic downturn because they are spending relatively fewer fiscal resources than what is needed to prevent lasting economic harm. Third, increases in direct fiscal support of Italy and Spain are constrained by the uncertainty of rising yield spreads. This uncertainty further limits the possibilities for the Italian and Spanish governments to navigate the crisis successfully. Although the coronavirus has also pushed Germany and the Netherlands into a recession, their circumstances are significantly more stable. The impediments to adequate national fiscal responses from Spain and Italy are, therefore, exacerbating economic and financial imbalances in the eurozone.

The importance of fiscal policies

National fiscal policies are playing a prominent role during the coronacrisis, due to the weakness of a coordinated European action, the nature of the crisis, and the severity of the shock. The difference in national fiscal measures is so apparent because national political dynamics have prevented agreement on an ambitious pan-European recovery plan. The European Union (EU) has settled on a €540 billion initial stimulus package (Michel 2020). This package is to a large extent symbolic rather than an actual attempt to provide a strong fiscal response to ensure that all countries of the EU can recover to the same extent and at the same pace. The package involves different EU institutions and provides various ways for national governments to borrow, but the amount is far too small to provide any significant aid or macroeconomic impact.

The European Commission's recovery plan, 'Next Generation EU', starts to look like the scale that is needed. However, even such amounts might not suffice given the dire economic outlook in Europe (Darvas 2020c). Moreover, just like the so-called coronabonds did not win support, the Commission's plan is unlikely to succeed in the way initially envisioned: national politics of eurozone countries have rather opposing views on any kind of mutualization. Although member states seem to be willing to find some compromise and help harder-hit countries in the South in the form of loans and some light form of conditionality, they have been more reluctant to support any form of structural transfers or lasting debt mutualization. [This chapter was written before the European Council adopted the Commission's proposal in modified form. That agreement is important and yet does not alter the argument made here substantially, especially since the ratification, implementation and actual pay-outs will take time.]

Besides the missing European response, the nature of the coronacrisis implies that fiscal policies are an important way to mitigate the economic repercussions of the virus. The coronacrisis is a pandemic which has direct effects on the real economy. Containment measures have halted most global economic production, disrupted supply chains, and reduced domestic and foreign demand to a minimum. In addition, heightened uncertainty is impacting expectations negatively and putting downward pressure on future expenditures and their financing (Lagarde and de Guindos 2020a). The economic crisis, therefore, stems from a supply shock that quickly turned into a demand shock.

This is a different story compared to the global financial crisis of 2007, which in Europe turned into a sovereign debt crisis in 2011 and 2012, because that crisis had its origin in the financial system. Many determinants created a toxic mix: financial innovation, global imbalances in trade and financial flows, extraordinary levels of leverage and mismanagement of risk led together to the real estate bubble (Obstfeld and Rogoff 2009). Restoring financial stability was a priority while fiscal stimulus was less central. The nature of the coronacrisis, on the other hand, implies that policies of governments are at the forefront in tackling the recession as they can provide targeted assistance such as minimizing the health impact and ensuring households and businesses survive the economic downturn. Especially in the initial phase fiscal policies made the difference in terms of counterbalancing the slowdown in economic activity, ensuring that productive capacity survived, and stabilizing rising unemployment rates.

Furthermore, the scale of the economic crisis is why fiscal policies are a crucial instrument during this recession: government decisions determine to a large extent how bad the state of the economy will look in the aftermath of the crisis and how difficult the recovery phase will be. In the World Economic Outlook Report of April, the IMF announced that the pandemic will cause the worst recession experienced since the Great Depression (International Monetary Fund 2020b). The eurozone is no exception as output is expected to contract by 7.7 percent (European Commission 2020a). This implies that the coronacrisis will impact our lives economically, but also socially, for a long time to come.

Stimulus packages of unprecedented size are necessary to have a positive impact on the economy. Even current fiscal policies might not be enough to prevent 'lasting damage to the productive capacity of the economy' according to the chair of the Federal Reserve, Jerome Powell (Powell 2020). He mentioned that the initial US fiscal stimulus of $3 trillion, amounting to more than 14 percent of GDP support (of which 9.1 percent in direct fiscal stimulus) might need to be increased. Already this first stimulus package was more aggressive compared to what the majority of European countries have employed. However, it seems that this large fiscal support in the US might have a too limited duration due to political divisions in the House of Representatives and the Senate.

In Europe, Christine Lagarde, president of the European Central Bank (ECB), has made remarks on fiscal policy similar to Powell's. She has even specifically called upon the governments of the EU to come up with a joint fiscal stimulus as monetary tools are necessary but not sufficient (Hall and Arnold 2020). The ECB and its monetary policies, in particular the Pandemic Emergency Purchasing Program (PEPP), have so far played an essential role in this crisis by stabilizing European financial markets. However, they must be complemented by fiscal measures: overreliance on the ECB increases its balance sheet which brings it into political controversies that an independent institution should not face. The coronacrisis is perhaps an extreme example of the relevance of fiscal policies due to its devastating effects on the real economy, but already before the crisis, central bankers and economists called for more fiscal intervention as a stabilization during recessions as well as in normal times given the global macroeconomic climate (Blanchard and Summers 2017).

While most governments have acknowledged the importance of fiscal stimulus packages, those so far implemented differ between countries within the EU. Moreover, the virus has caused more deaths and more pressure on the health system in some countries implying stricter containment measures, more economic damage, and consequently a more pressing need for fiscal stimulus. In addition, the different economic situations prior to the crisis also determine how equipped countries are to fight the coronacrisis. Germany, Italy, the Netherlands, and Spain provide excellent examples of how these trends are playing out in the eurozone. Depending on how the virus and the economic crisis will evolve in the coming months and years, the disparities in the euro area could, combined with a lack of political will, pose a serious threat to the future of the eurozone. To understand why, the following sections will cover the pre-existing vulnerabilities, the similarities and difference of the national fiscal policies, and the borrowing constraints of these four countries.

The vulnerabilities of Germany, Italy, the Netherlands, and Spain

The coronacrisis is a symmetric shock to the entire world: no country in the EU and the rest of the world is shielded from the economic repercussions of the pandemic. There are, however, clear differences in terms of the vulnerability of countries. Germany, Italy, the Netherlands, and Spain have not experienced the same public health crisis, they did not enter this crisis under the same economic conditions, and they do not have the same economic exposure to the lockdowns and social distancing measures (Redeker and Hainbach 2020).

First, the extent to which a country and its health system have been hit by the virus, influences how long and how strict the lockdown measures had to be. In Europe, Italy and Spain have been two of the worst-hit areas by the virus in terms of deaths. This has led to more extreme and longer lockdowns, including more aggressive restrictions on movement of people and business activities compared to Germany and the Netherlands (Hirsch 2020). In other words, the greater the health crisis, the longer more restrictive measures had to persist, which means less production and consumption. As businesses cannot operate at all or only at a limited capacity, they do not generate (enough) revenues but certain fixed costs continued to accrue. This, in turn, implies liquidity or solvency issues.

Second, the vulnerability of Italy and Spain becomes even more evident when one looks at their macroeconomic data before the crisis started. Although none of the European countries has performed outstandingly well over the last decade, economic stagnation has been particularly visible in Italy. It has had persistent low real growth rates in gross domestic product (GDP) throughout the last decade (almost all below 1 percent) (Eurostat 2020a). The forecast from the European Commission projects the Italian economy to shrink by 9.5 percent in 2020. Given the uncertainty about the evolution of the virus and its economic consequences, this number could turn out to be larger (European Commission 2020a).

Spain was one of Europe's fastest-growing economy since 2015, but it has had a different problem to tackle. While unemployment peaked over 25 percent in the previous crisis, Spain still faced an unemployment rate of 14.1 percent in 2019 (AMECO 2020). Unemployment rates were also not particularly great in Italy in the aftermath of the eurozone crisis (fluctuating between 8.4–12.7 percent). Germany and the Netherlands, on the other side, managed to decrease their unemployment levels considerably after the financial crisis (3.2 percent and 3.4 percent at the end of 2019, respectively). In addition to growth rates and unemployment, the divergence in pre-corona economic conditions is also reflected in the debt levels. These have been much larger in Italy (and Spain to some extent) compared to Germany and the Netherlands.

Third, the economies of Germany, Italy, Spain, and the Netherlands are exposed in different ways to the coronacrisis. The relative importance of certain industries, enterprise sizes, job transferability, and global value chain dependence are some of the most meaningful determinants for the exposure. Economies that depend on service sectors that including retail trade, accommodation, transport, and food service activities are particularly vulnerable (Battistini and Stoevsky 2020). Both in Spain and Italy, these are the economic activities with the largest share of gross value added to GDP with 23.80 percent and 21.63 percent, respectively (OECD 2019b). For the Netherlands and Germany, these are not the largest industries but still have a sizable impact with 20.63 percent and 16.23 percent, respectively.

Another important difference is the role of tourism in domestic spending in the cases of Spain and Italy. A depressed tourism industry means an even larger economic drop for those two countries (Ewing 2020). An OECD report on tourism calculated that for Italy it represents 13 percent of its national GDP and 14.7 percent of total national employment, while in Spain tourism accounts for 11.8 percent of GDP and 13.5 percent of employment (OECD 2020b). In the Netherlands and Germany, tourism makes up less than a third of that (around 4 percent for both countries) and employs less than half the amount in Spain and Italy.

Industry, manufacturing, and construction are the other three sectors that will experience relatively more losses as a consequence of this crisis. Especially Germany, and to a lesser extent Italy, relies on industry and manufacturing. Construction is a rather small part of value-added for all four economies (OECD 2019b).

The size of businesses and types of jobs also matter for the exposure of the economy: a large number of small companies can be problematic as liquidity issues can quickly turn into solvency issues. Smaller enterprises often do not have the possibility to create buffers and they rely on a continuing revenue stream to operate. In all four economies, small companies make up around 18 percent (10 to 49 employees) of all firms. But in Italy micro-companies (less than 10 workers) account for almost 45 percent of the total enterprises (OECD

2019c). Spain finds itself in a similar situation with around 40 percent of micro firms. This means that all four countries run the risk of losing many private small firms during this crisis, but the micro-firms in Italy and Spain are a particular cause of concern.

In addition, jobs that can be more easily transferred to remote work, determine to what extent the economy can operate in the coming months. The Netherlands has a significant advantage in that perspective since about 45 percent of the jobs can be performed through working remotely. On the other hand, Spain only has around 30 percent of transferable jobs.

Finally, economies whose predominant industries rely on global value chains will find the coming times particularly troublesome. An example is the German manufacturing industry, especially its car and machinery makers, that have links to businesses all over the world. This the result of the 'supply chain contagion' (Baldwin and Freeman 2020). The entire EU is more susceptible to supply chain disruptions than other parts of the world due to the integrated nature of the European economies, especially those in western Europe. Supply chains present therefore a problem for all four countries.

The indicators described in this section show that Spain and Italy went through a greater health crisis, found themselves in more fragile economic situations, and are relatively more exposed to the lockdown crisis. Overall, this puts these two countries in a relatively weaker position. A vulnerability measure constructed by the Hertie School indicates the same conclusion: Spain and Italy will endure a bigger economic strain (Redeker and Hainbach 2020). While one would think that consequently they would need a relatively larger fiscal support, this is not happening as explained in the next part.

The similarities and differences of national fiscal policies

To smooth the fall in output caused by the coronavirus the fiscal stimulus has to be (1) timely, (2) targeted to those who need it most, (3) of a temporary nature but long enough to provide sufficient support to boost the economy (4) and large enough to have an impact on the economy (International Monetary Fund 2020a). These criteria will be followed to assess the details of the fiscal policies of the countries analyzed in this chapter. This will reveal that the first three points are remarkably similar across the countries, whereas the size of the responses varies a lot.

The announcement of policies took place around the same time. Germany, Italy, the Netherlands, and Spain all announced their plans starting from the beginning or mid of March and continued to take additional measures in throughout the following months (Anderson et. al. 2020). One can argue that governments across Europe should have started taking precautionary measures at the time China was still the epicenter, but that does not make a difference for the analysis comparing four European countries. The point is that as governments started to announce lockdown measures, they also immediately acted in terms of extra spending. The timeliness is, therefore, not a determinant that makes the fiscal measures of one country more effective than those of others.

The target of the fiscal stimulus does not show big discrepancies between the four countries either. In the first place, they all aim to reduce the pressure on the health system to ensure that hospitals can provide the necessary treatments. Another focus is the private sector including the self-employed. Governments are providing liquidity support through credit guarantee schemes for micro firms and SMEs as well as different degrees deferrals or even reliefs of taxes and other payments. This should ensure that businesses have enough liquidity and can easily attain further loans. In this way, governments hope to reduce the damage to the private sector and prevent bankruptcies.

Further employment schemes, wage subsidies and transfers to firms and self-employed are being used such that employees do not lose their income and stay employed. Some governments also established emergency cash funds to inject extra liquidity into the markets through small grants to businesses that have experienced the largest hit. Overall, the main goal of these fiscal policies is that households as well as businesses survive this crisis and that consumption, production and investments will pick up as fast as possible as lockdowns are gradually lifted.

The fiscal intervention of all four countries is temporary, not permanent. The policies are aimed to minimize the economic fallout in the short run and assist households and companies for the duration of the crisis – which may turn out to be a long time. A decade ago, the common belief among economists was that only temporary expansionary fiscal policies are effective and sustainable (Spilimbergo et al. 2008). However, this view has changed over the years to favoring permanent increases in government spending as a consequence of low interest rates, low growth, and strong international economic and financial connections (Krugman 2020, Furman 2016). Regardless of these changing trends in monetary literature, it is not a point of difference between Germany, Spain, Italy, and the Netherlands.

The size of the fiscal stimulus does vary. The severity of the crisis makes this size arguably the crucial point causing the fiscal policies of Germany, Italy, the Netherlands, and Spain to differ in terms of the duration and amount of support they can provide. Data from Bruegel illustrates this by listing the government intervention relative to the size of the economies and dividing the fiscal measures into three categories: immediate fiscal impulse, deferrals, and other liquidities provisions and guarantees (Anderson et. al 2020).

Table 6.1 National fiscal measures implemented as of 19 June 2020 (% of 2019 GDP)

Country	*Immediate fiscal impulse*	*Deferral*	*Other liquidity/ guarantee*
Italy	3.4	13.2	32.1
Germany	13.3	7.3	27.2
Netherlands	3.7	7.9	3.4
Spain	3.7	0.8	9.2

Source: Anderson *et al.* 2020

The immediate fiscal impulse includes expenditure and revenue measures since they deteriorate the budget balance of 2020. Such government expenditures include efforts that support the health system, subsidize firms, and keep people employed. Examples of foregone revenues are cancellation of certain taxes and social security contributions. Many sectors have been disrupted, economic production has practically come to a complete halt in March and April 2020, and the European economy has only slowly started to pick up in May, June and July. Immediate support is therefore key to ensure that productive capacity, both capital and labor, do not get lost. Without such support, a country risks facing a larger number of bankruptcies of businesses in the private sector and even larger increases in unemployment. In other words, direct stimulus is highly effective but very costly.

Tax deferrals are a second kind of stimulus. The main aim of the deferrals is to improve the liquidity situation of households and firms by postponing some of the tax payments, social security contributions, bills, and loan servicing payments. Deferrals, therefore, help reduce the immediate expenses, but such measures might not always be enough for firms and self-employed to bridge the lockdown period and survive the recovery phase facing reduced demand. These deferrals also worsen the budget balance of 2020 but should improve it later.

Guarantees and other liquidity assistance, the third category, are an additional way to provide liquidity and access to credit through loans. The main advantage is that guarantees do not have an impact on the budget balance this year and are less costly than direct support. However, they might not be as effective if the damage to incomes of households and profits of firms is long-lasting (Caracciolo et. al. 2020).

The data from Bruegel shows that all countries acknowledge the severity of the economic fallout by providing an unprecedented amount of support. Since these numbers can still change as the coronacrisis continues, they should be interpreted as a first reference point of what a country can provide to its citizens rather than a final decision. Besides, depending on how the response at the European level will develop, the need for national programs might decrease. However, one does notice some differences at this point in time. For Germany, the size of the fiscal stimulus is not an issue and the country is spending as if the 'schwarze null' (or 'black zero', representing a balanced budget) has never existed. Germany has even stated that there is no limit to the support it is willing to provide to businesses (Posanar 2020). The direct support of 13.3 percent of GDP is even larger than the expected decline in output of 6.5 percent in 2020 (European Commission 2020a).

The Netherlands seemingly limited fiscal measures given that GDP is assumed to drop around 6.5 percent in 2020 is because they are intended to cover only the first months of the crisis (Nederlandse Omroep Stichting 2020). In addition, households, firms, and the government went into this crisis in a relatively good position (Nauta and Vrieselaar 2020). This implies that as the economic situation worsens, fiscal support could still easily increase because the government still has room to maneuver and can easily borrow additional money (Misérus 2020).

According to their vulnerable situations, Spain and Italy would need larger fiscal support to avoid coming out of this crisis significantly weaker than these Northern countries. However, Spain and Italy are not spending enough in direct support. This puts increasing pressure on the survival of firms and exacerbates income losses for households. A prolonged duration of the crisis in Spain and Italy becomes likely as these countries are facing larger declines in GDP and higher unemployment rates with relatively fewer fiscal measures.

A positive development is Italy's liquidity and guarantees section, which has significantly increased in April 2020 as it started off at a size similar to that of Spain. Italy's preference for this kind of support for the economy can be explained by the fact that in this way the government expenses do not grow too quickly. But as mentioned earlier, guarantees can be a less effective form of economic aid and will put further pressure on the finances of the Italian government in the near future. Data on Spain for deferrals and guarantees indicate that these figures are not even close to what is needed for the economic slump that is to come. If more vulnerable countries continue to allocate fewer fiscal resources to mitigate the one of the largest recessions ever, Germany and the Netherlands might very well come much stronger out of the crisis compared Spain and Italy.

Borrowing constraints

Instead of an unwillingness to spend more, the size of the discretionary fiscal stimulus reflects borrowing constraints that Spain and Italy face. Every country needs to finance the large increase in expenses by raising additional debt. The extent to which a country has cheap access to capital to finance their government expenditures is therefore important. The European sovereign debt market is not anywhere close to the extreme differences in yield spreads that have been experienced in the past. The massive interventions of the ECB through its Pandemic Emergency Purchasing Programme (PEPP) of €1.35 trillion are to thank for that. There have been some spikes in the yield spread between Italian and German 10-year government bonds since the outbreak of the pandemic as it has reached several times over 250 bps – the first time when Christine Lagarde said that it was not the ECB's job to 'close spreads' (Lagarde and de Guindos 2020a).

It remains to be seen for how long the ECB will continue its aggressive monetary policies. Uncertainties about the ECB's instruments, the economic recovery phase and the spread of the coronavirus make it impossible to predict if, whether, and when market participants could turn against Italy and Spain and make yield spreads explode.

Italy and Spain have to face less favorable conditions in the bond market due to their macroeconomic outlooks, their existing and future government debt, and expectations of market participants of the broader political and economic spectrum. There is no doubt that the coronacrisis will be a painful recession for Germany and the Netherlands, but none of their macroeconomic estimates and financing possibilities are as worrisome as those of Spain and Italy – as already reflected in the different economic forecasts for 2020. This shows that the coronacrisis is an unequal recession in which Italy and Spain suffer a lot more. These dire economic expectations are reflected in the ways the market prices government bonds which makes Italian and Spanish government bonds less attractive.

The expected debt-to-GDP ratios of 2020 are of course an evolution of pre-existing government debt. Italy has had higher debt rates than any of the other countries. This is, however, not a result of running primary budget deficits every year. On the contrary, Italy has run only primary surpluses since joining the Euro apart from two years, namely 2009 and 2010. The problem for Italy has been the persistent low growth in combination with the inherited large pile of public debt. Spain had rather low debt-to-GDP ratios at the beginning of the financial crisis and even after Spain survived its period of sovereign debt turmoil between 2011 and 2013, it managed to start bringing down its debt ratios. Economic growth is what allowed this to happen since Spain has run lower and fewer primary surpluses than Italy over the same period.

The Netherlands and Germany were impacted a lot by the financial crisis starting from 2007 but managed to shield themselves – to some extent at the cost of other European countries. More important, they were not part of the countries involved in the second stage of the Euro crisis that took place on the sovereign debt market. As a consequence, they committed themselves to further reducing their debt levels during those years.

The initial lower debt ratios at the start of the coronacrisis make a difference because all countries will come out of this crisis holding more public debt. The lower 'starting point' and buffers of Germany and the Netherlands created over the years through their surpluses, make it easier to borrow at cheap market rates. In addition to initial higher debt ratios and expected larger debt increases, the sizeable debt that matures this year in Spain and Italy do not help the situation either. Italy's maturing debt in 2020 will be 19.93 percent of GDP and for Spain it will be 13.53 percent, whereas for the Netherlands and Germany it will not even be half of that (6.14 percent and 5.5 percent, respectively) (International Monetary Fund 2020b).

However, it is not debt per se that constitutes a constraint on borrowing. It is the interpretation of it by market participants in terms of their expectations. As perceived riskiness of a country increases, it then translates into higher yields of government bonds. The ECB can push back against this (see chapter by Osterhuber). In the end, however, confidence of investors is what determines which way the markets decide to turn. Debt sustainability is, in fact, a relative concept without a defined threshold. But if no growth is in sight, unemployment is on the rise, parts of the productive capacity are destroyed due to the crisis, and already high debt levels are rising, it could take only a small event for Italy and Spain to find themselves in a difficult position in the markets.

Expectations of market actors do not only take into consideration macroeconomic data. National political dynamics are just as important. In Spain Pedro Sánchez's weak minority coalition is having difficulties dealing with the People's party, the far-right Vox, and the administration of Catalonia (Dombey 2020b). In Italy, the potential use of the European Stability Mechanisms (ESM) has resulted in deep divisions across parties in parliament as well as an internal crisis for Italy's Five Star Movement (Fonte and Amante 2020). Compared to such developments the political situations in Germany and the Netherlands are much more stable at the moment. The popularity of Merkel and Rutte have experienced a significant boost as a consequence of how they have handled the crisis so far (Erlanger 2020a). Higher yields that incorporate all these economic and political facts and expectations, explain partly why more vulnerable countries have to spend fewer fiscal resources than would be desirable.

Conclusion: Uncertainty

The duration of the recession and the persistence of the economic damage is still unknown. The evolution of the coronavirus and the effectiveness of the containment measures remain uncertain. How the private sector, especially the financial sector, will survive the coming months and how robust the European financial system will be under these stressful conditions is also hard to predict. Initially, a V-shaped recovery, where the economy would snap right back, was considered a feasible scenario. Now U-, L-, W-and 'Nike-swoosh'-shaped developments seem more likely (Kennedy and Jamrisko 2020). They follow different trajectories, but they all involve a slower recovery and long-term economic implications.

The nature of the coronacrisis makes it unlikely that consumption and investment will simply pick up again as lockdown measures are lifted. Households are questioning whether their future income could be anything like the past and will therefore hold off or limit certain consumptions and increase savings to face this uncertain period. At the same time firms have to cope with lower revenues, increased loan servicing costs if they borrow money to keep the business afloat, and fewer investors willing to finance new projects. A pandemic also has psychological and behavioral impacts that affect consumption and investment decisions negatively. It will take time and effort for citizens and entrepreneurs to believe that a return to normalcy and previous habits is possible. Perhaps life might be different so long as there is no drug or vaccine available nor certainty about immunity after being infected.

However, even in this moment of uncertainty, some points should be clear to all member states of the EU. The coronacrisis will depress the economy for a long time to come and the next generations will have to deal with extremely high levels of debt and politically sensitive issues such as the normalization of the ECB's monetary policies. The future of the EU economy is predicated on surviving this crisis as a bloc – not as individual countries. If solidarity does not convince member states to act together, the integrated nature of European economies should do so. The entire EU benefits from every member state to recover as best and as fast as possible. Different national fiscal capacities likely lead to more permanent distortions in the Economic and Monetary Union and the broader single market. In turn, these economic and financial divergencies between countries could pose a serious threat to the future of the European project.

7

UNUSUAL ISSUES: DEBATING DEBT MUTUALIZATION

Charles Lawrie

The coronavirus pandemic has prompted fresh proposals for the issuance of mutualized debt instruments in Europe. Such debt, it is argued, would provide a risk-free alternative to instruments such as the European Stability Mechanism (ESM) used during the euro crisis. This arrangement would be of particular benefit to member states such as Italy and Spain, which are expected to see their economies contract by 9.1 percent and 8 percent respectively but lack the fiscal capacity of the wealthier Northern states to counteract this drastic reduction in GDP (International Monetary Fund 2020b).

In the European context, discussions around shared debt instruments, known as 'eurobonds' or 'coronabonds', are hardly new (Jones 2019c). During the euro crisis that followed the Greek sovereign debt crisis, prominent European policymakers raised the possibility of issuing mutualized debt instruments, collectively underwritten by the EU member states, with the purpose of raising funds in international money markets. As in the previous crisis, however, the debates concerning mutualized debt have run aground. The reluctance of Northern countries to underwrite has proved impossible to overcome. On both occasions, constituencies in Germany, the Netherlands, Austria, and Finland have been unwilling to provide their savings for the benefit of what they see as their fiscally incompetent neighbors in the Southern periphery states of Spain, Italy, and Greece.

In the previous crisis, the Southern states were ultimately bailed out not by European Central Bank (ECB) liquidity but by the European Stability Mechanism (ESM), which provided credit facilities in return for significant fiscal restructuring. In the current crisis, the ESM has also pledged significant financial firepower in the form of a Pandemic Crisis Support mechanism, accessible to all member states for spending on their healthcare systems (Janse 2020a). In turn, the European Investment Bank (EIB) has also been called upon to provide support to small- and medium-sized enterprises (SMEs) that have found themselves in financially dire straits as a result of the global economic recession.

The central argument of this chapter is that the coronavirus pandemic has driven Europe to perform a magic trick: to a large measure, it has conducted forms of debt mutualization *without issuing mutualized debt*. On the one hand, the crisis has demonstrated the continued inability of member states to collectively agree to a mutualized debt issuance. On the other hand, member states have been able to rapidly agree to a series of mutually funded macroeconomic interventions on a significant scale. While discussions about the precise nature of the interventions remain ongoing at the time of writing, the European institutions have demonstrated their willingness to undertake a program of significant proportions. Of course, this significance can be debated. In macroeconomic or fiscal terms, there is still more Europe could do (see chapter by Strauss). But in historical terms, it is hard to deny that the European effort is unprecedented.

The chapter begins by exploring the historic debate over debt mutualization in Europe before continuing with an examination of the institutional response of two important European financial institutions – the ESM and the EIB – in the previous and present crises.

Debates over debt in the previous crisis

At the outset, it is worth briefly considering what debt mutualization actually entails. Debts are formalized by debt instruments – in this case, sovereign bonds – which are *contracts* between two counterparties. Under the terms of such contracts, one party undertakes to pay the other party sums of money at some later date. As with any contract, a degree of risk is represented by the likelihood of the debtor party being unable to meet its contractual obligations. In this form of contract, the debtor is solely liable for meeting its obligations.

When debt is mutualized, however, the debtor ceases to become solely liable for her obligations. Instead, the parties that undertake to mutualize the debt agree to accept 'joint and several' liability; that is, they become collectively required to meet the debt obligation. The creditworthiness of the individual borrower is significantly improved, and the cost of borrowing falls as a result. In the case of Europe, debt mutualization would involve a shared debt instrument being underwritten by the German central bank, the Bundesbank, whose significant creditworthiness would drastically reduce the cost of borrowing for other member states. This would have the effect of creating a common 'risk-free' asset. In turn, debt mutualization can either be applied to debt that has already been issued or debt that will be issued in future.

In the previous crisis, shared debt instruments were mooted as one way to address inefficiencies in European sovereign debt markets (Jones 2019c). These inefficiencies principally related to the inability of markets to distinguish between 'responsible' and 'irresponsible' government borrowing, since all government borrowing looked the same regardless of the proportion of GDP that it represented. The issuance of shared debt instruments, it was argued, would allow markets to make this distinction, since limits could be set on the amount of mutualized debt that individual countries could borrow before they were required to issue their own, non-mutualized debt (Jones 2010). The price differential that would emerge as a result of this distinction would discourage excessive borrowing by member states and prevent moral hazard (ibid.).

Although the Lisbon Treaty, which came into effect in 2009, made debt mutualization illegal in the European context, the Greek crisis prompted fresh discussions concerning the collective underwriting of member state sovereign debt (Tooze 2018). Following the spike in Greek sovereign bonds in October 2009, the European Central Bank (ECB), then led by Jean-Claude Trichet, was presented with the opportunity to calm the markets by intervening to buy Greek debt. The ECB failed to do so, however, and opted not to renew its Longer-Term Refinancing Operations (LTRO) program, which it had begun in May 2009 to provide liquidity to the banking system. Nonetheless, the ECB did introduce a second asset-purchasing program, the Securities Market Programme (SMP), in May 2010, and relaxed its collateral requirements in order to take on Greek sovereign debt (Gabor 2012). Yet the LTRO would only recommence in December 2011, following Mario Draghi's appointment as ECB President. At that point, however, the LTROs extended out to three years.

The ECB's reluctance to intervene in the Greek bond markets has been attributed to Trichet's desire to prompt the Greeks to get their fiscal house in order by subjecting them to market discipline (Tooze 2018). This also allowed the ECB to curry favor with the Bundesbank, the German central bank, which was suspicious of any interventions that seemed to be a Trojan Horse for debt mutualization. The reluctance of northern EU member states to provide credit to Southern countries proved a difficult obstacle to overcome. This stemmed from the perception held by interest groups in Germany, the Netherlands and Belgium, *inter alia*, that intervening to support other countries was tantamount to throwing good money after bad.

Despite the objections of the northern states, the European Council and the European Commission had both launched proposals for debt mutualization by the winter of 2012. These differed in certain important aspects, however. José Manuel Barroso, President of the European Commission, called for deeper fiscal integration including – in the long term – the creation of a eurozone-wide budget and the common issuance of public debt (Barroso 2012). The President of the European Council, Hermann Van Rompuy, called for the creation of a greater fiscal capacity which would allow for the issuance of collective debt 'without resorting to the mutualization of sovereign debt' (Van Rompuy 2012). By entering into 'contractual arrangements' with the EU institutions, the EU member states would be able to agree to comply with a reform agenda in return for access to a 'shock absorption function' – that is, to support during times of economic crisis (Van Rompuy 2012). Despite its explicit aversion to eurobonds, however, even this argument was not enough to persuade Angela Merkel and her fiscally conservative coalition partners, the Free Democratic Party (FDP) (Tooze 2018).

In this sense, the debate over debt mutualization in the previous crisis became a question of domestic politics, notably in Germany and France (Jabko 2015). During the Greek sovereign debt crisis, then-German Finance Minister Wolfgang Schäuble advocated the creation of a European Monetary Fund (EMF), modelled after the International Monetary Fund (IMF), with the objective of conducting sovereign debt restructuring at the European level. The proposal was ultimately derailed by Merkel herself, who was deeply reluctant to see increased European federalism. This was partly due to a June 2009 ruling on the Lisbon Treaty by the German constitutional court, which had rejected further EU integration (Tooze 2018). Merkel's argument for resorting to the IMF ultimately won out at an EU summit on 25 March 2010, and Greece would receive loans from the so-called 'troika' – the EU, the ECB and the IMF – while entering an austerity program without a trace of debt restructuring, let alone mutualization. This was no less true of France, where Nicholas Sarkozy used the 'golden rule' to frame Hollande as fiscally irresponsible in the 2012 presidential elections (Jabko 2015).

Debt mutualization in the current crisis

Debates over the issuance of common debt resurfaced during March 2020. A flurry of letters and op-eds in the *Financial Times* called on the European Council to agree to create eurobonds (Regan et al. 2020). A group of nine eurozone countries – France, Italy, Spain, Greece, Portugal, Slovenia, Luxembourg and Belgium – wrote a letter to the President of the European Council, Charles Michel, calling for the creation of a common bond (Dombey et al. 2020).

Remarkably, a group of German academics also took up the cause, arguing for euro zone countries to issue €1 trillion in the form of 'community bonds' (Hüther et al. 2020). These community bonds were to be jointly underwritten by the EU member states and made available to members who were at risk of being unable to borrow on capital markets, with interest and repayment obligations based on the respective shares, known as the capital key, held by member states in the ECB (ibid.). What was more, the German economists dismissed the idea of the ESM as the appropriate financial institution, suggesting that it was an 'institution from a different time' (ibid.).

Statements issued by the European Council on 26 March and the Eurogroup on 9 April, however, contained no mention of debt mutualization, suggesting that Germany and the Netherlands had won the argument once again (European Council 2020d, European Council 2020e). This came as no surprise, given the fragility of the German and Dutch ruling coalitions and the deep suspicion with which domestic constituencies viewed mutual bonds. In Germany, the Alternative for Germany (AfD) pledged not to allow German taxpayers to be 'bled' for the debts of other EU countries (AfD Kompakt 2020). In the Netherlands, the Dutch Finance Minister, Wopke Hoekstra, emerged as a principal critic of the coronabond proposal (Dutch House of Representatives 2020). While Hoekstra may have been motivated by his own personal political ambitions, his skepticism of mutualized debt reflects a broader Dutch cultural aversion to debt (The Economist 2020a).

For both Berlin and Amsterdam, the preferred mechanism for extending support to the crisis-afflicted South was credit lines offered through the European Stability Mechanism (ESM). Strongly associated as it was with the memory of Greece's sovereign debt crisis, the ESM emerged as a controversial candidate for support during the first two months of the pandemic in Europe.

The ESM and pandemic crisis response: a sheep in wolf's clothing?

The ESM was established in September 2012 during the middle of the previous euro crisis. It would emerge as the primary institutional response to the sovereign debt crises of the periphery states, offering credit lines to Cyprus, Greece, Ireland, Portugal and Spain. The ESM's establishment was Berlin's sole concession during the 2012 discussions on financial integration (Tooze 2018). Initially agreed to by the European Council on 17 December 2010, signed on 2 February 2012 and effective from 27 September 2012, the ESM replaced the European Financial Stability Facility (EFSF) and the European Financial Stabilization Mechanism (EFSM). As with the EFSF, all euro members would be shareholders in the ESM, and would have the power to raise funds in secondary bond markets up to a maximum of €500 billion, with Berlin insisting on this upper limit (ibid.).

For reasons that are by now well known, the ESM credit lines met with controversy. On the one hand, the stringent conditionalities that accompanied them would require Greece and other states to impose dramatic austerity measures, which would reduce economic growth (Blyth 2013). For Germany, on the other hand, the EFSF and the ESM threatened to become a permanent 'transfer' mechanism (Jabko 2015). Despite these concerns, the overall effect of the ESM was to reduce the cost of lending: wealthy countries such as Germany and France could lend to Greece at below-market rates but above the rate at which they could borrow themselves (Picketty 2020).

In the current crisis, the ESM has emerged as one of the principal pillars of the European institutional response. The ESM, which had €410 billion unused lending capacity at the start of the crisis, proposed to extend two credit lines for member states that found themselves in financial distress. On 9 April, the Eurogroup agreed that the ESM could provide a Pandemic Crisis Support Credit Line (PCSCL) aimed at providing up to 2 percent of the country's GDP at the end of 2019, with the sole condition that countries purpose it 'to support domestic financing of direct and indirect healthcare, cure and prevention related costs due to the COVID 19 crisis' (European Stability Mechanism 2020a).

The first of these, the Pandemic Crisis Support Credit Line, was based on a pre-existing ESM credit line, the Enhanced Conditions Credit Line (ECCL). This was what gave the PCSCL its advantage: it was based on a pre-existing facility, and so would not require the ESM to raise additional funds in secondary markets. The total value of this fund is €240 billion, although the Managing Director of the ESM, Klaus Regling, suggested in a 19 April 2020 interview that further funds could be made available were the economic crisis to continue unabated (Fubini 2020). In turn, a second credit line was proposed, the so-called Rapid Financing Instrument (RFI); this would have been a smaller credit line with even fewer conditionalities. The RFI, however, was ultimately rejected by the Eurogroup.

The European Council endorsed the Eurogroup proposal to create a Pandemic Crisis Support Credit Line on 23 April and the PCSCL became available for immediate disbursal on the 1st of June 2020. Mindful of the stigma associated with the earlier Greek program, the ESM sought to play down the comparison with Greece's ECCL by highlighting the lack of conditionalities associated with the Pandemic Crisis Support Credit Line (European Stability Mechanism 2020b). Unlike the ECCL, whose programs require significant and regular surveillance missions from Brussels and Luxembourg, the PCSCL only requires that the funds be spent on healthcare related costs. In spite of this, the PCSCL has been the subject of heated debate within Italy, where the political parties are split on whether to request a credit line form the ESM. Not only have splits emerged within the Five Star Movement, currently in government with the center-left PD, but La Lega has expressed significant opposition to the deal. On 25 April 2020, the Italian Foreign Minister, Luigi Di Maio, appeared to signal that the ruling coalition might be open to accepting ESM support, although later rescinded his comments, claiming that he had meant EU support instead (Za et al. 2020).

Notwithstanding ESM attempts to reduce the stigma, countries debating whether to request ESM assistance were faced with a dilemma. To take the example of Italy, the €36 billion that it would able to apply for would not only fail to cover many heath costs–which in Italy's case are expected to amount to some €120 billion in 2020 – it would likely require countries to renew their commitment to Europe's fiscal rules as enshrined in the Stability and Growth Pact (Italian Ministry of Government and Finance 2020). Accepting ESM assistance would be a confidence-boosting measure, sending a positive signal to markets and reducing the cost of government borrowing on sovereign debt markets – but would entail increased surveillance in the form of quarterly reports (European Stability Mechanism 2020b). Thus the political costs appeared to outweigh the economic benefits, which, in the case of Italy, have been estimated at around €150 million in direct interest savings (Corsetti and Erce 2020). No country appeared eager to turn to the ESM for support.

Against this backdrop, the ESM declared full-throated fiscal solidarity with the member states by reducing the cost of borrowing under the Pandemic Crisis scheme to nil, if not less. In the event that countries were to apply for seven-year loans, they would pay an effective interest rate of *minus* 0.07 percent – that is, they would be required to pay back less than their initial loan (Janse 2020b). In the event that countries borrowed over a ten-year period, the rate would increase to 0.08 percent. As with the ECCL, countries that requested access to the PCSCL would gain access to the ECB's Outright Monetary Transactions (OMT) instrument. In an interview given on 19 April 2020, the incumbent Managing Director of the ESM, Klaus Regling, indicated that countries would need to request access to the PCSCL in order to be eligible for the ECB's sizeable intervention mechanism.

While clearly not debt mutualization in the technical sense, the ESM initiative could represent a form of wealth transfer from the wealthier states in the European core to the more economically disadvantaged states at its periphery. This is because the negative rates on PCSCL credit – at least, in the seven-year scenario – effectively represent a subsidy on borrowers and a tax on lenders. At present, precisely which member states have expressed an interest in accessing PCSCL credit remains unknown. The ESM, however, has suggested that the ESM fund could be cheaper than capital market borrowing for eleven EU member states for both seven- and ten-year loans (Janse 2020b): that is, Greece, Cyprus, Italy, Spain, Portugal, Malta, Slovenia, Slovakia, Latvia, Lithuania, and Ireland. Of course, the ESM has also imposed its own charges over the cost of the credit line, meaning that the PCSCL interest rate will remain higher than the cost of borrowing. At the same time, the wealth transfer is not a simple question of capital flowing from wealthier states to poorer states, but from bond buyers, in the form of private investors and central banks, to the governments of these countries – who will inevitably have to make repayments on these loans, a percentage of which will accrue to the ESM.

The European Investment Bank then and now

The European Investment Bank is a development bank whose shareholders are the EU member states. The Bank was initially established by Articles 3(j) and 129 of the Treaty of Rome with the objective of 'balanced and steady development of the common market in the interest of the Community', and later by Articles 308 and 309 of the Treaty on the Functioning of the European Union. The Bank's principal role has been to promote European integration through the provision of loans for public and private development projects, often in economically underdeveloped regions of Europe (Treaty of Rome 1957). The EIB's capital was subscribed by all of the founding members of the EEC. This stock was gradually increased to account for new members, the expansion of the Bank's operations and inflation.

Following the appointment of Jean-Claude Juncker as European Commission President in November 2014, the EIB began to play an increasingly prominent role in Europe's response to the previous crisis (Mertens and Thiemann 2019). Juncker's proposals for an Investment Plan for Europe, which included a European Fund for Strategic Investment (EFSI), aimed to promote growth in the bloc by mobilizing public funds for private investment projects (European Commission 2015, Paternoster and Rakić 2019). Through a combination of €16 billion from the EU and €5 billion of its own capital, the EIB established a funding pool to invest €315 billion of loans in countries affected by the financial crisis. This was further extended to 'at least' €500 billion by 2020 to enable greater investment both in Europe and abroad (European Commission 2016). As of April 2020, all member states had accessed EFSI loans; of these, countries in the periphery had received the most funding in terms of EFSI-'triggered' investment per euro of GDP (European Investment Bank 2020a).

Despite its constitutional focus on promoting long-term investment in the bloc, the EIB saw its role rapidly repurposed during the first months of the coronavirus pandemic. Of the economic measures proposed by the Eurogroup on 9 April and endorsed by the European Council on 23 April, the European Investment Bank's pledge of €200 billion was almost as large as that offered by the ESM.

This €200 billion is enabled through a much smaller pledge of a €25 billion guarantee fund (European Investment Bank 2020b). Loans are to be provided through the EIB and the European Investment Fund, a subsidiary of the EIB that specializes in providing support to small and medium enterprises. This

€25 billion will in turn be lent to member states, which will then use the loans to make interest payments on up to €200 billion. As with the ESM's PCSCL, the fund will be based on a pre-existing fund, which in this case will be the EIB's Partnership for Funds (PFF). Capital for the EIB fund will be secured from individual member states and EU budget contributions (European Investment Bank 2020c).

The EIB had already announced €40 billion worth of guarantee loans for banks in March, aimed at providing emergency funding for urgent vaccine development and medical needs, as well as a fillip for banks threatened with the specter of non-performing loans (European Investment Bank 2020b). The loans were structured into three parts. The first tranche would support banks' existing liabilities, ensuring that customers could retain access to deposits. The second tranche aimed to provide 'working capital support' for small and medium enterprises as well as mid-cap firms faced with a liquidity crisis during the emerging economic downturn. Lastly, the EIB launched an asset-backed security purchasing program, which would allow the EIB to take non-performing loans off bank balance sheets and avert the risk of bankruptcy.

In the context of the debate over debt mutualization, the structure of the EIB debt suggests that a degree of risk pooling has already occurred (The Economist 2020b). Of course, recipients of EIB support are not governments, but banks and businesses; the EIB loan scheme is an attempt to guarantee the liquidity of the member states' banking systems and not to underwrite existing or future debt issuances. At the same time, however, the notion of mutualization was implicit in the creation of the European Investment Bank, which solved the 'collective action problem' of rebuilding Europe after the Second World War (Jones 2017). The collectivized structure of the EIB made it a leading candidate in calls for addressing the 2007–2009 financial crisis (Gros and Micossi 2008, De Grauwe and Moesen 2009) – and, in the context of the current crisis, its role as provider of risk-free capital has been deployed once again.

Conclusion: were coronabonds a red herring?

This chapter has argued that, in the heat of the debate over coronabonds, other forms of mutualization have taken place by stealth. In the technical sense, debt mutualization has yet to emerge: member states have not collectively undertaken joint and several liability for a debt issuance, whether for pre-existing sovereign debt or for the issuance of future debt. Yet, in what appears to be a collective pooling of risk, the EIB initiative to underwrite banks and support SMEs and mid-caps clearly involves guarantees provided by the member states.

At the same time, while the idea of coronabonds has remained unacceptable to Germany, Merkel has proved more amenable to borrowing through the European Commission. In a joint press conference on 18 May 2020, Germany and France announced proposals for a 'recovery fund' (Élysée Palace 2020). German impetus may have been provided by a German Constitutional Court ruling on 5 May 2020, which had deemed the European Central Bank's Public Sector Purchase Programme (PSPP) incompatible with German law (Hackenbroich 2020). In turn, the Franco-German proposals were followed by a European Commission announcement on 27 May proposing the establishment of the so-called Next Generation EU program, a €750 billion recovery instrument to be spent on economic recovery between the years 2021–2024 (European Commission 2020c). This would be provided alongside €1.1 trillion in an expanded Multiannual Financial Framework (discussed in greater detail in the next chapter by Rave).

Rather than tolerate individual states borrowing on capital markets, then, Germany has given permission to the European Commission to do so instead. The Next Generation EU mechanism would be funded through capital market bond issuances with varying maturities, with the earliest to be repaid in 2027 and the last to be repaid in 2058; these will be repaid through 'additional new own resources at a later stage of the financial period' (ibid.) – in other words, through unspecified future taxes and individual member state contributions. In the short-term, the European Commission has also committed to providing member states with unemployment support in the form of the Support to mitigate Unemployment Risks in an Emergency (SURE) (European Commission 2020g). At €25 billion, this comparatively smaller intervention will be used to cover interest payments on loans up to €100 billion for member states facing sudden increases in public expenditure. This fund has permitted the EU to assuage any fears that individual member states would spend money on their own businesses during the economic downturn (Motta and Peltz 2020).

As we have seen, the issue of debt mutualization in the EU is nothing new. Indeed, the animated debate that took place during March and April 2020 has demonstrated that the concept of shared risk remained unacceptable to northern member states, notably Germany and the Netherlands. Yet the European response to the coronavirus pandemic has shown that this does not matter, given that ESM and EIB support represents an alternative kind of debt sharing. When considered alongside the ECB's PEPP and the major European Commission fiscal proposal alluded to above, these measures suggest that the Europeans have demonstrated an ability to conduct coordinated fiscal and monetary interventions, which may ultimately pave the way to greater economic integration in the wake of the pandemic.

8

THE EUROPEAN COMMISSION, COVID-19 AND FISCAL FEDERALISM

Thomas Rave

History does not repeat itself, but it often rhymes. Until now the response to the economic and fiscal fallout of the coronavirus pandemic in the European Union (EU) has been dominated by the European Central Bank (ECB) – (see chapters by Osterhuber and Neri in this volume). This is similar to the approach we saw during the sovereign debt crisis in the euro area a few years ago. In contrast, the EU's main executive body, the European Commission, has struggled to take the lead in coordinating a common response with the member states. Then and now, the Commission is lacking the means and position to take on the European Council. Obviously, the ECB has organizational and structural advantages that make it easier to take swift and effective decisions. The Commission, however, has a much more limited scope for crisis action, especially in the realm of macroeconomic governance.

Nevertheless, President von der Leyen and her institution have tried to take a proactive role in the coordination of the public health and the ensuing economic crisis early on (see European Commission 2020i). Most importantly, there has been a substantial push for granting the Commission new temporary fiscal capacities in order to respond to the diverging economic fallout in the member states. This initiative rests on two pillars: the reinsurance for national short-time work schemes SURE ('support to mitigate unemployment risks in an emergency') and the expansion of the EU budget. The former covers €100 billion in loans to governments. The latter aspires to collect up to €750 billion on capital markets, which shall be distributed as grants and loans to member states. Both would represent an unprecedented expansion of the Commission's borrowing and spending activities.

Considering the political rifts among the member states during the sovereign debt crisis, those proposals for risk sharing are inherently controversial. The EU finds itself again in a power struggle not foreseen by the treaties. The decision about the Commission's proposals is being taken in the Economic and Financial

Affairs Council or in the European Council. In times of crisis intergovernmentalism trumps supranationalism. Therefore, this crisis reveals that it is not only about the appropriate policy responses. The overall architecture and power balance in the community are put into question. More precisely, the effectiveness of the macroeconomic governance model is being tested. Compared to the swift and powerful actions of the United States, the European Union looks like a laggard. And that is despite the party-political discord in America.

Hence, this chapter tries to make a case for fiscal federalism. While the monetary union has been in existence for two decades, and the banking union is in the making, a fiscal union is still lacking. The Commission proposals do point into the right direction, but they have lacunae which might undermine the effectiveness of these programs. However, the point of a fiscal union is that it allows for interregional smoothing of economic shocks through (automatic) stabilizers. Nevertheless, these initiatives might set precedents leading to even more fiscal integration in a subsequent crisis.

This chapter begins by examining the theoretical background. The EU's existing and potential dispositions for fiscal federalism and automatic stabilizers will be explained. The second part will describe the Commission's plans for a common European fiscal response. The SURE program and the negotiations of a coronavirus recovery fund within the Multiannual Financial Framework (MFF) will be at the heart of this. Throughout this analysis, it is important to keep in mind that even for EU standards, these measures appear to be of an unprecedented and idiosyncratic nature. Therefore, the presented argument will be a combination of description, some historical comparison, and theoretical references.

Fiscal federalism and automatic stabilization – theory and implications

Monetary policy is perhaps the single most powerful policy competence the EU's member states delegated to the supranational level. In contrast, fiscal policy remains a sovereign attribute of the national level. This creates a dichotomy in macroeconomic governance of the community. Therefore, there has been a lot of academic and public discussion about a fiscal union in recent years. Not least the French President Macron has been very vocal in that regard. Indeed, the current crisis reemphasizes this issue. Whereas fiscal federalism is not being discussed explicitly, it constitutes the underlying question. Hence, it is useful to review the academic literature on fiscal federalism and automatic stabilization in the EU.

The theory of fiscal federalism is a normative theory about the provision of public goods (Oates 1999: 1121). Therefore, macroeconomic policy is a task that should be conducted at the federal level (Inman and Rubinfeld 1997: 50). More specifically, 'fiscal union is defined by a budget at the federal level that has its own tax revenue and can thus act as a kind of overdraft facility on present and future taxpayers.' (Schelkle 2013: 107) In the context of the EU, own resources via a European tax appear to be politically unacceptable. But the current crisis points to some degree of an enhanced budget. A certain level of redistribution for example through intergovernmental grants, such as in Germany or Canada, is a second consideration. Such redistribution is important to level off interregional differences (Oates 1999: 1127 f). This kind of fiscal balancing helps to sustain the cohesiveness of the federation. A third issue with split fiscal capacity between the supranational and national level is moral hazard. This problem emerges from the possibility that the federal level bails out regional governments (Hallerberg 2013: 89). That is an argument frequently brought forward by the fiscally conservative countries in the current debate.

Fiscal federalism in European integration differs greatly from what theory teaches. While there is a certain common budget, fiscal union mainly takes other forms. The EU's fiscal power is first and foremost of regulatory nature deploying rules that are applied to national budgets (Hallerberg 2013: 93, Schelkle 2013: 106–108). That is why European macroeconomic coordination is a function of fiscal policy surveillance (Jones and Fuller 2015: 341–343). Even during the sovereign debt crisis, the member states refrained from installing a larger fiscal capacity, instead they set up the European Financial Stability Facility and the European Stability Mechanism, and elaborated new regulations complementing the Stability and Growth Pact (Hallerberg 2013: 95–98). In place of resorting to redistribution within the Union member states opted for an even more tight fiscal control mechanism combined with new intergovernmental institutions.

Counter-cyclical policy and the minor role of Commission spending have contributed to that problem (Dullien and Schwarzer 2011: 93). As fiscal policy was underperforming something else happened to promote fiscal integration. Schelkle states that the reluctance of national governments to shift proper fiscal capacity to the European level lead to the intervention of the European Central Bank. She calls this monetary action 'fiscal integration by default' (Schelkle 2013). Just as other scholars note national fiscal stabilization will not be efficient in the wake of large shocks, especially for those countries with already high sovereign debt stocks (Buti and Carnot 2018). Consequently, there is a gap between the assumptions of fiscal federalism and the fiscal structure of the EU.

This gap between what theory says is necessary and what European institutions provide has repercussions on the Union's ability to react to economic shocks. Fiscal policy can be the crucial tool for adjustment between nations in a monetary union with low wage flexibility and labor mobility (Dullien and Schwarzer 2011: 98). Some sort of fiscal capacity is necessary for automatic stabilization to function in a federal system. In a currency union, there is a collective action problem in terms of responding via fiscal stabilizers, hence the stabilization should take place at the aggregate level of the monetary union (Dullien and Schwarzer 2009: 161). Thereby, automatic stabilizers have the advantage that they react immediately to economic difficulties and do not suffer from any information or implementation lags (ibid.: 158). But at the national level in the EU, some argue that these instruments are restricted by the common deficit rules (Collignon 2004: 147). The aim of these tools is to smooth out shocks. The EU has already intertemporal smoothing in exceptional cases through loans by means of the European Stabilization Mechanism, but not interregional smoothing which could help prevent economic divergences from becoming greater in a crisis (see also Collignon 2004: 151).

Nevertheless, there is a lively academic discussion about a European unemployment reinsurance scheme as a supranational stabilizer (Doll 2019: 2). The Commission's SURE program does take up such academic proposals. This is relevant for this analysis, because an unemployment reinsurance scheme has a similar purpose and effect as a short-time work scheme. Both alleviate the impact of an economic downturn on the labor market. Some scholars explicitly emphasize that fiscal stabilization should be linked to changes in the unemployment rate (Buti and Carnot 2018). A European unemployment reinsurance could take the form of a fund with contributions from and payouts to member states (Brandolini et al. 2016: 1124). So-called 'experience rating' would circumvent outright redistribution, as those who receive funds will pay higher contributions (ibid.: 1126). Insofar, there is also a point for the fact that SURE only allows for intertemporal smoothing through its loans. In the end, the sustainability of the debt might be linked to the maturity – which as will be noted later depends on an agreement between the receiving country and the Council. Here politics comes back in.

A fiscal response to the pandemic

In order to explain the Commission's effort to assemble some kind of mutualized fiscal response, two different instruments have to be assessed. Though, they are linked by the overarching issue of fiscal federalism. In a communication from mid-March, the Commission put forward initiatives based on the EU budget. This includes a €1 billion guarantee to the European Investment Fund, a Coronavirus response investment initiative reallocating €37 billion from the cohesion fund, and the permission for member states to redirect resources of the structural fund (European Commission 2020i: 5–8). These funds do not represent any new loans or spending but are repurposed resources from the current multiannual financial framework. Due to this fact, it is plausible that the effect of it on tackling the crisis will be marginal. Thus, they will not feature in this analysis.

SURE – a first step towards a European unemployment reinsurance scheme

The Commission put forward the idea of a support scheme for alleviating the repercussions on the labor markets with a specific tool for short-time work schemes already in mid-March (European Commission 2020i). This is in line with the preexisting discussion for a permanent European unemployment reinsurance. The European Parliament has been interested in such a scheme (see Beblavy and Maselli 2014) and the von der Leyen Commission initially planned to put forward a proposal in 2020 according to its work program from January (European Commission 2020h). Such a European unemployment reinsurance could function as a stabilizer between countries in times of economic distress.

The creation of the SURE instrument seems to be more revealing about the functioning of the crisis response. First, it is important to mention the legal background to this scheme, because generally debt mutualization and state financing are prohibited by primary law. This builds on article 122, paragraph 2, of the Treaty on the Functioning of the European Union. This provision allows the Union to assist member states financially upon a decision by the Council of the EU, as a reaction to a natural disaster or other kinds of special situations. Whereas the treaty does not attach any conditionalities to this instrument, the Commission is well aware of the opposition of some member states with respect to fiscal transfers within the Union. Hence, it decided to propose assistance via loans instead of outright grants at this early stage of the crisis.

The scheme itself functions as follows. Only those countries that face an increase in public expenditure due to the implementation of short-time work schemes or similar instruments are eligible. The member states receiving such assistance will get them in the form of loans and are bound to use them for the mentioned purposes. The Commission will be able to make these loans by borrowing from the financial markets or financial institutions for a sum of up to €100 billion. Any member state requesting a credit will have to rely on an implementing act by the Council, which will determine the precise conditions, such as the maturity and the amount. Due to the limited amount of loans available the regulation proposal provides one rule for the allocation: the three largest loans shall not exceed €60 billion. If a member state fails to pay back its credit, the Commission will roll the debt over. This instrument will only be operational as soon as member states have contributed on a voluntary basis to the guarantees of €25 billion total according to their portion of the Union's Gross National Income (GNI) (European Commission 2020g).

This facility looks small, but it is well focused. Short-time work schemes appear to be an important instrument during this recession. As Landais and Giupponi (2020) emphasize, the usefulness of such schemes is due to the fact that they prevent even higher numbers of unemployment and help the private sector cope with the liquidity shock. Indeed, countries have extended short-time work programs, and some countries without such an instrument are working to implement similar measures that avoid outright layoffs (Müller 2020). The question is to what extent countries actually are in need of a supranational reinsurance scheme, backing up national programs. And if there is a substantial demand, which specific countries are interested in these loans. Generally, all member states are eligible as outlined in the Commission proposal, given that states can either apply with an existing scheme or a plan to set one up.

The assessment of which country has an effective need depends primarily on the unemployment rate and the refinancing conditions on the bond markets. That is to say, a country with an already high unemployment rate pre-crisis has a particular interest to prohibit further lay-offs. Also, those states expecting a very high increase in the unemployment rate (in relative terms) would likely want to expand their short-time work. Considering the evolution of unemployment rates since before the financial crisis no fewer than seven countries seem to have an interest to apply for SURE assistance.

The European Commission expects joblessness to at least double in Czechia, Estonia, Hungary, and Poland (AMECO 2020). Hence, short-time work might be a useful tool to alleviate this spike, although the rates are still comparatively low. Then there are three countries which have two-digit unemployment rates respectively since 2008, 2010, and 2012: Spain, Greece, and Italy (ibid.). This structural problem combined with the rise expected for 2020 makes them presumably candidates for the program. It is important to note that this group includes Eastern and Southern European countries. As opposed to the general perception, major contraction on the labor markets is not a problem exclusive to the Mediterranean countries. Due to the fact that Spain and Italy are populous member states with high GNI per capita and a high potential for short-time work, they will most likely be the biggest recipients of loans.

At the same time applying for SURE assistance only makes sense for those governments having less advantageous credit ratings than the European Commission has (Alcidi and Corti 2020). This is because the commission will borrow the funds from the markets with its top rating (European Commission 2020j: 11 f, Quatremer 2020). Thus, countries such as Germany with a big national short-time working scheme and with a negative yield on its government bond would have no incentive to apply to SURE.

Overall, it seems as though the European Commission has initiated a useful tool. It caters to the needs of some severely impacted member states. At the same time, its most vulnerable trait – giving out loans instead of grants – is perhaps also its most powerful. Because this loan-based configuration makes it more acceptable among national governments. Therefore, it is more likely to succeed and to set a precedent for more elaborate insurance schemes during a future economic crisis. Indeed, the instrument has been adopted in mid-May (Council of the European Union 2020). Although SURE is placed outside the MFF, limiting the Commission's sway over the instrument, it does give it more leverage in the future.

Expanding supranational budgetary capacity

While the temporary labor market reinsurance scheme has already entered into force, other fiscal initiatives on behalf of the Commission are still under negotiation. Notably, there are plans to expand the EU budget MFF, combined with a proposal for a coronavirus recovery fund. So far, the MFF for the period from 2021 until 2027 is not agreed, which makes it prone to being entangled in the current crisis action. Therefore, it could be leveraged for two things: fiscal transfers and Commission power.

The budget usually does not exceed 1.1 percent of Europe's GNI (European Commission 2019: 16, Wyplosz 2020). Thus, any substantial extension of the MFF would be a considerable success for proponents of a fiscal union – and an extension of the Commission's competences as well. Against that background, the Berlaymont published its pandemic-updated budget proposal at the end of May (see European Commission 2020c, European Commission 2020b). That was a bold proposal raising multiple issues.

There was the question of the institutional framework. The recovery program could be incorporated within the budget or detached in a separate entity in different ways (Vallée 2020). Overall, this new instrument is being referred to as a recovery fund. The European Council has given the Commission a mandate to explore such a scheme in April (Fleming and Khan 2020b). This reflects the political acceptability of fiscal expansion at EU level and shows that member states are aware of a need for common action. This awareness was actually spearheaded by the French and German governments. They proposed a temporary fund within the MFF to give out grants to member states, with an emphasis on expenditures related to COVID-19, as well as digital and green policies (Presse- und Informationsamt der Bundesregierung 2020: 2 f).

The Commission was clearly in favor of locating it inside the multiannual budget (European Commission 2020c, European Commission 2020b). Any increase in the budget would result in a precedent for the member states' commitments to the community finances (Wyplosz 2020). This is something that the Commission could use to expand the framework further in the future.

Moreover, the Commission also wanted to attach the grants and loans to specific programs and policy goals for a digital and green transition (European Commission 2020c, European Commission 2020b). Hence, targeting the money towards defined ends attaches a certain conditionality. Therefore, this might be more agreeable than outright grants to member states' budgets. Also, this allows the Commission to maintain a say over the spending of the funds.

In addition, both the Franco-German and the Commission proposal pointed towards new own resources for the EU in order to possibly finance the enhanced budget (Presse- und Informationsamt der Bundesregierung 2020: 3, European Commission 2020c: 3). Indeed, locating the fund within the MFF enabled Brussels to make a case for the necessity to allow the EU to raise its revenue stream. Ultimately, this might be an issue that is less related to the current crisis, than it is to the logic of European integration. The Commission as a supranational body favors a transfer of competences, whereas the governments generally favor intergovernmental decisions. Indeed, during the sovereign debt crisis, national governments managed the fiscal response among themselves (Vallée 2020). Perhaps this crisis is different. A shift towards more supranationalism with some form of recovery fund seems plausible.

There is also the question of the amount available to the tool. The Spanish government has promoted the idea of a recovery fund with a magnitude of €1.5 trillion, which would be financed by a perpetual bond issued by the Commission (Dombey 2020c). The Commission's own initiative was not quite as bold, but still an increase in resources of historic size: €500 billion shall be allocated as grants and €250 billion shall be handed out as loans under the new facility (European Commission 2020c: 14). Berlin and Paris have proposed €500 billion in grants (Presse- und Informationsamt der Bundesregierung 2020: 2), whereas the 'frugal four' coalition of the Netherlands, Austria, Denmark, and Sweden advocates for loans only (Grüll 2020).

The allocation via grants or loans is a crucial issue, as this determines the fund's impact on the economy. Loans will simply push back the payment obligation into the future. The affected countries which started already with difficult conditions into the crisis might end up in a similar situation as post-2008. An economic crisis could turn into a sovereign debt crisis yet again. In order to avoid such negative effects, Gros suggests transfers via the MFF. The member states most affected would be partially exempt from their payments to the EU budget (Gros 2020). With the Commission, France and Germany supporting a similar scheme in this vein, there will likely be substantial cross-country redistribution at a significant scale during the upcoming MFF.

Politically, such an allocation through grants is highly contentious. The already complex MFF negotiations have only gotten more complex due to the pandemic as clear-cut coalitions are fraying (Bayer 2020). As a consequence, there has been no agreement at the European Council on June 19 (Herszenhorn et al. 2020). But the heads of state and government reconvened in July for an in-person summit (Valero 2020). As so often in European integration the common action of France and Germany was crucial. Especially Berlin's realignment with the Élysée's push for more European spending was a decisive step (Karnitschnig 2020, Taylor 2020). Germany's shift also puts the frugal coalition in a weaker position (Taylor 2020). The crisis response seems to upend traditional patterns of fiscal policy coalitions, leading to more supranational spending power at least temporarily.

While European governments have already put together substantial fiscal packages (see chapter by Strauss), the EU is still developing a common approach. The agreement on the European recovery fund is only the start of the process and not the end. The Commission is pushing for an expansion of the MFF in order to deal with the economic fallout over the coming years. Some member states are also in favor of a significant increase in resources for the community. Enderlein and Guttenberg call this expansion of fiscal capacity in times of crisis a 'federalism by exception' (Enderlein and Guttenberg 2020: 400 f). Already during the sovereign debt crisis this logic was applied by implementing temporary and conditional instruments of fiscal and monetary policy – a pattern repeated now again (ibid.: 401 f). If such a fund will be implemented, it might have an impact on the overall performance of the Union during this pandemic. But more broadly, this is also a question about the finality of European integration. The issue here is to what extent does the EU need and want fiscal federalism.

Conclusion

The European Commission has tried to assemble a meaningful common fiscal response to the coronavirus crisis as a complement to the monetary policy reaction and the national fiscal policies. SURE is a new instrument that allows quick financial assistance to countries with distressed labor markets. Though, it remains to be seen whether the loans will be an effective instrument, or whether the debt burden will merely be pushed into the future. The MFF is surrounded with more uncertainty at this point. It seems most likely that there will be a recovery fund within the budget. The magnitude, the conditions, and the allocation key remain to be decided by the member states. These aspects will determine how impactful the fund will turn out to be. Clearly, both initiatives point towards more fiscal capacity at the European level. Thus, both indicate small steps toward fiscal federalism. SURE resembles the function of an automatic stabilization instrument. And an enhanced EU budget could lead to substantial spending capacity beyond the common agriculture policy and the cohesion funds.

The comparisons with the sovereign debt crisis have shown that the current actions go beyond what has been done at that time. The new crisis requires new instruments and therefore further integration. Also, this chapter pointed out that the European Commission will likely leverage any new fiscal competence in order to further increase the budget in the future. Hence, incremental steps could lead to fiscal federalism by default rather than by a grand design with treaty reform. But this must not underestimate the resistance on behalf of national governments. As SURE and the MFF negotiations show, there is sustained demand for conditionality of any assistance among countries. Fiscal redistribution seems to be almost unthinkable from a political perspective. There remains indeed a gap between what the theory of fiscal federalism and automatic stabilization teaches and what is politically feasible under the structural constraints of European integration. However, the question is how long the gap between European monetary policy and fiscal policy can persist. Ultimately, this crisis is a test for the macroeconomic governance capacity of the EU.

9

COVID-19 AND THE NETHERLANDS: TESTING EUROPEAN RESILIENCE

Isabeau Mensing

The COVID-19 crisis has exacerbated one of the issues at the core of the European project; the divide between the traditional creditor and debtor countries, in the North and South, respectively. Most European countries have suffered a significant economic blow as a result of diminished economic activity, increased medical expenditure, and the mobilization of state funding to support domestic enterprises. In addition to domestically mitigating consequences of the COVID-19 crisis, EU countries have tried to agree on adequate common measures to minimize an EU-wide recession. As part of this debate, a renewal of the demand for debt mutualization has come up in the form of so-called coronabonds (see chapter by Lawrie).

Different countries have responded antagonistically to this demand, proposed by the harder-hit countries of Southern Europe. The Netherlands has taken a particularly hard stance in opposing instruments of common debt, arguing that this would allow Southern countries to free-ride on more beneficial credit rates, in addition to pointing out how the insufficient financial security of the South is a result of their own economic and fiscal choices. This 'harsh' Dutch response to calls for solidarity has been openly scrutinized by the leaders of Italy, France, and Portugal, stating that turning away from European solidarity will decrease faith in the EU and might ultimately even cause the European project to fail.

This paper will analyze the Dutch response to the COVID-19 crisis, both domestically and within the European framework. Dutch economic performance, political identity, and its position within Europe will be examined, in order to clarify both the Dutch response and the Southern European reaction to that response in the debate on debt mutualization. This will be used to assess the possible future position of the Netherlands within the eurozone. In order to efficiently do so, this paper is divided into five sections.

The first two sections outline the pre-COVID-19 situation in the Netherlands, looking at the political and economic conditions in the country. These sections discuss political support for the European Union and its part in the rise of populism in the Netherlands. Then follows an analysis of the Dutch economy, specifically focusing on the role of the European Union. In doing so, Dutch economic dependence on and contribution to the European Union are at the center of analysis. Furthermore, it will review the influence of EU fiscal regulations.

The third section describes the actual economic response to the COVID-19 crisis on a domestic level. This includes an overview of the most significant policy measures that the Dutch government has implemented in order to minimize the economic backlash of the lockdown. Subsequently, the third section discusses the real consequences the crisis has had on the Dutch economy so far.

The fourth section analyzes the response to the COVID-19 crisis on a European level, focusing on the Dutch position within this response. It discusses the 'harsh' position the Dutch leadership has taken in opposing the idea of shared debt and how this debate has evolved.

The fifth and last section of this paper explains the Dutch response to the debate on debt mutualization, before analyzing the Southern European reaction. Information from the previous parts is integrated in order to clarify the current divide within European politics.

This paper concludes by assessing how this divide could alter the future Dutch position within Europe, and by making recommendations for how this divide can possibly be overcome.

Pre-COVID-19 political situation in the Netherlands

As one of the six founding members of both the European Coal and Steel Community (ECSC) in 1951 and the European Economic Community (EEC) in 1956, the Netherlands has been a part of the European project since its very start. Since the Netherlands is a relatively small country, cooperation on the level of the European Union (EU) enables it to exert more influence than it ever could independently (Janning 2019). As such, the Netherlands actively participates in almost all facets of the EU framework. However, the Dutch government mainly pushes for further integration of EU policies on themes such as migration, security, and climate change. On these issues, the country's main partners are Germany and, previously, the United Kingdom. With these countries, the Netherlands shares common liberal and capitalist values, causing them to agree on most issues (Janning 2019).

EU support

Initially, the European project could count on nationwide support in the Netherlands. This caused the Netherlands to be one of the most europhile countries in the Union until about two decades ago. At the beginning of the 21st century, however, EU criticism started to grow in the Netherlands. This was partially a result of the EU accession of Eastern European countries in 2004 and 2007 (De Waard 2012). Furthermore, the period was characterized by public scrutiny over EU contributions. As the Netherlands increased payments, many felt the country was not seeing sufficient, direct benefits in return. In June 2004, around 20 percent of the Dutch votes cast for the European Parliament, was cast on parties voicing concerns regarding the European Union, such as *Lijst Pim Fortuyn* (LPF) and the *Socialistische Partij* (SP) (Oomkes 2004). In 2005, the Netherlands was one of the two countries to vote against the establishment of a European Constitution; 61.5 percent of the Dutch population voted against it in a national referendum (Europa Nu 2005). All in all, Dutch support for further European integration decreased significantly over the years 2004–2007. EU support increased again during the financial crisis in 2008–2009 since the Euro turned out to be a form of protection. However, the eurozone crisis that followed again led to a decrease in Dutch support for further European integration (Burgerperspectieven 2020).

These fluctuations in European support over the last two decades are represented in Dutch politics by politicians who increasingly question the legitimacy of the European Union. This started at the beginning of the 21st century with the abovementioned LPF being skeptical of further European integration. However, two Eurosceptic parties remain influential in Dutch politics to this day that were established later. In 2006, Geert Wilders founded the *Party for Freedom* (PVV), followed by the foundation of *Forum for Democracy* (FvD) by Thierry Baudet in 2016. Both PVV and FvD party programs are centered around the idea of a distinct Dutch identity and culture, which causes them to criticize the effects EU membership has on national sovereignty. In the most recent Dutch elections, those for the Senate in 2019, the FvD came out as the second-biggest party, with 16 percent of the votes (Europa Nu 2020b).

Since then, Dutch attitudes toward the European Union have somewhat improved. This is partially due to increased economic prosperity. However, the lengthiness and complexity of the Brexit negotiations also seem to have scared off Dutch eurosceptics. In February 2020, the Dutch Social and Cultural Planning Office published their biannual report, estimating Dutch public opinion using the Eurobarometer and European Social Surveys. This report notes that support for the EU has increased over the last year; a clear majority of the Dutch population believes the EU to be beneficial for the Netherlands, and thus favors EU membership. The Eurobarometer even estimates that the Netherlands has the highest support for EU membership out of all EU countries. Nevertheless, almost half of those surveyed believe that the Netherlands has granted the European Union with too much power over domestic affairs, resulting in them being reluctant to support further deepening of the European project. The fraction of the Dutch population supporting an expansion of European power is also a lot lower than the European average; a net percentage of 9 percent in the Netherlands, compared to a 17 percent average across Europe. Moreover, a clear majority of 63 percent of the surveyed population believes the Netherlands should focus less on other countries in general, and instead concentrate on domestic issues (Sociaal Cultureel Planbureau 2020, Europa Nu 2020a).

Pre-COVID-19 economic situation in the Netherlands

With a population of 17.3 million in 2019, the Netherlands accounts for only 3.9 percent of the European population. However, it is one of the richest members of the European Union. In 2018, its GDP per capita was calculated at $53,024.06 or €45,082. This is more than four times larger than the world average, exemplifying the relative economic wealth the Netherlands enjoys (Worldbank 2018, Trading Economics 2018). In recent years, the Dutch economy has seen an increase in real growth of gross domestic product (GDP) after years of economic slowdown, due to the financial crisis and the eurozone sovereign debt crisis. For example, Dutch GDP per capita was €39,820 in 2014, making GDP growth for 2014–2018 equal to 16.7 percent in only four years. This increase in GDP per capita can partially be explained by lower levels of unemployment, and was accompanied by increased government taxes in recent years; from 2007 to 2017, the share of the Netherlands' GDP contributed by taxes increased from 35.4 percent to 39.2 percent (Centraal Bureau voor Statistiek 2019).

When comparing economic proxies from the Netherlands to European averages, the Netherlands surpasses the European average in almost every section. In 2017, Dutch GDP per capita, price level corrected, was €38,400, compared to an EU average of €30,000. In this year, the only EU countries with a higher GDP per capita in the eurozone than the Netherlands, were Luxemburg and Ireland (Centraal Bureau voor Statistiek 2019). Moreover, Dutch GDP per capita is well above that of the other big economies in the European Union, such as Germany, France, and Italy (Worldbank 2018).

Costs and benefits from EU membership

The contributions the European Union requires from its members are determined based on a GDP basis; those who earn the most, pay the most. Thus, as the sixth largest economy in the European Union, the Netherlands also is one of the largest contributors to its budget. In 2017, the Netherlands paid €3.4 billion to the European Union, equal to 1.3 percent of total government expenditure in that year (Frijters and van Uffelen 2019). In 2018, the Netherlands contributed a total of 5.15 percent of the total EU budget (Statista 2019). Despite opposition from the Netherlands, its contribution is expected to rise in coming years as a result of the budgetary gap left by Brexit (Algemeen Dagblad 2019).

In return, the Netherlands receives money from the European Union each year. The most important recipients of this money are in the agricultural sector together with research and development in universities and companies. In 2017, the Netherlands received a total of €2 billion from the European Union. Thus, in 2017 the Netherlands was a net contributor by €1 billion (Frijters and van Uffelen 2019). The fact that the Netherlands has been a net contributor for years, receives a lot of criticism from eurosceptic politicians in the Netherlands.

However, the Netherlands has also received indirect economic gains from being a part of the European Union. Within the economic sector, membership of the European Union has led to an increase in trade, competition, specialization, innovation, and an enlargement of the scale on which Dutch trade operates (De Waard 2012). It is difficult to measure exactly how dependent the Dutch economy is on the European Union, although estimates exist.

An analysis conducted by Statistics Netherlands estimated that over the last 65 years, 4–6 percent of Dutch GDP growth is a direct result of EU membership and participation in Europe's economic and monetary union. Annually, this adds up to one extra month worth of salary for the average Dutch citizen (Centraal Plan Bureau 2008). 71 percent of the goods the Netherlands exported in 2018 were transported to other EU countries, with Germany (23 percent) and Belgium (10 percent) receiving the largest shares. In that same year, imports also constituted the majority of the Netherlands' import; 53 percent of total goods imported came from other EU countries (Centraal Bureau voor Statistiek 2020a). It is thus safe to say that the EU's free movement, mobility of capital and goods, common market and agricultural subsidies have benefited the Dutch economy immensely.

What would happen to the economy if the Netherlands were to leave the European Union also remains speculative. Nevertheless, research conducted by the ING Bank in 2012 estimated that if this were to happen, the Dutch economy would shrink up to 10 percent in two years. This was mainly attributed to a decrease in exports of up to 25 percent, as a result of a more expensive monetary unit. In this scenario, the decrease in export is expected to lead to up to 300.000 people losing their jobs in the first year alone (ING 2012).

Compliance with EU fiscal policy

Most fiscal policy for the eurozone countries is still determined at a national level, which is one of the criticisms of those calling for further deepening of

European integration. However, some regulations with regard to fiscal policy are set by the European Union. These regulations, outlined in the Stability and Growth Pact (SGP), are mainly aimed at safeguarding the fiscal health of eurozone countries, by ensuring they have sufficient financial buffer in times of crisis. The main requirements for fiscal stability, taken up in the preventive arm of the SGP, are budgetary ceilings for public debt at 60 percent and government deficit at 3 percent of a country's GDP. Moreover, countries are supposed to comply with their country-specific medium-long term objectives, which are set every three years (European Commission n.d.-b).

The Netherlands' own Stability Program is supposed to comply with these EU fiscal policy regulations. Since 1994, the Netherlands operates with a trend-based fiscal policy, ensuring flexibility. Each government coalition sets its own national budgetary framework, which can be revised annually (Adema 2008). These frameworks include expenditure ceilings, that are translated into revenue ceilings by compensation through tax adjustments. Flexibility within the allocation of revenue and expenditure is allowed, but the ceilings are not supposed to be surpassed (Stability Program of the Netherlands 2019). In addition to reaching domestic fiscal stability, the Stability Program is supposed to keep the Dutch economy in compliance with EU fiscal policy regulations. Over the last years, the Netherlands has complied with the SGP requirements.

However, this was not always the case. As part of the Dutch government's efforts to minimize the effects of the financial crisis starting in 2008, the government increased its expenditure. This resulted in a government deficit of over 5 percent of GDP in 2009 and 2010. Likewise, government debt surpassed the threshold of 60 percent from 2011 to 2016. In these years, the Netherlands did not comply with European norms (Centraal Bureau voor Statistiek 2018). To make up for this increased expenditure, the Dutch government implemented strict austerity programs from 2011 to 2015. These programs consisted of tax increases (43 percent) and spending cuts (57 percent) (Centraal Bureau voor Statistiek 2015). Additionally, the government announced that it would gradually raise the retirement age from 65 to 67 years (Rijksoverheid 2012). In 2017, the austerity measures were effective in making the Netherlands comply with EU requirements again. However, the measures have proven a burden for the Dutch taxpayer. In 2012, the average household income for the Dutch population decreased by 3.2 percent, falling for the fifth year in a row (Centraal Bureau voor Statistiek 2013). Moreover, the impact of austerity measures affected lower income groups disproportionally (Oxfam International 2013).

Even though the EU requirement for government debt as a share of total GDP is 60 percent, many countries failed to meet this threshold. In 2018, the EU average was at 80 percent of government debt to GDP, equal to almost €13 trillion of government debt in the eurozone as a whole. That year, Dutch government debt was equal to 52.4 percent of GDP, thus staying well below the EU average (Centraal Bureau voor Statistiek 2019). In 2019, Dutch government debt decreased to 49.1 percent of GDP. Before the COVID-19 outbreak, government debt was expected to drop further to 47.1 percent of GDP (European Parliament 2020, Centraal Bureau voor Statistiek 2019).

In 2018, the general government balance of the Netherlands was equal to 1.5 percent GDP. This number decreased to 1.2 percent of GDP in 2019. Thus, the Netherlands has also stayed well below the 3 percent excessive deficit threshold set by the European Union in the SGP. Before the COVID-19 crisis, the excessive deficit was expected to further decrease in 2020, to reach 0.8 percent. In 2019, the Dutch structural government balance has decreased slightly but remained above its MTO of –0.5 percent (Stability Program of the Netherlands, April 2019).

Thus, as a result of the financial crisis and the Euro crisis, the Netherlands did not adhere to EU requirements from 2011 to 2016. Using strict austerity measures, the country was able to get its economy back in line with SGP's budgetary requirements in 2017. Since then, it has ensured to keep its economic indicators in line with EU regulations.

COVID-19 crisis: the Dutch response and consequences

After the first Dutch COVID-19 infection on 23 February, the Dutch government started enacting measures to counter the virus' spread. At first, this was done by urging people to work from home (12 March) and closing schools, cafes, and restaurants (16 March). When compliance with these measures proved insufficient, an 'intelligent lockdown' was announced on 23 March. This required the Dutch population to stay at home as much as possible and keep a 1.5 meter distance from others. Professions necessitating close contact, such as hairdressers, were forced to close and all large events were banned until 1 June. These measures were prolonged twice, to last until 20 May (Rottinghuis 2020).

Support mechanisms

When the inevitability of the COVID-19 crisis became evident at the beginning of March, the Dutch government acted quickly to try and limit the negative economic consequences of the lockdown. As such, the Dutch government put in effect policy measures and pledged to increase government spending to up to 60 percent of GDP, equal to around €90 billion for the Netherlands. By comparison, in 2019 the country's expenditure to GDP ratio was at 41.9 percent, the lowest it had been in the 2000s (Trading Economics 2020).

So far, the Dutch government has introduced two comprehensive emergency support mechanisms, the first on 17 March and the second on 20 May (Woudt 2020, Rijksoverheid 2020c, 2020d, 2002e, 2020f, 2020g). An overview of the most important measures that have been enforced, can be found in Table 9.1. The objectives of these measures were maintaining liquidity in the market by facilitating the easing of lending, preventing soaring unemployment and financially supporting affected sectors (Ballegeer and Kuppeveld 2020). At the start of May 2020, the Dutch coalition claimed that they had been able to support over 2 million Dutch citizens with the NOW and TOZO measures alone (Rijksoverheid 2020b).

The Dutch government has also attributed a significant amount of government funds to measures less directly related to the Netherlands' economic development, that are nevertheless important. This includes the implementation of support packages for lost education (up to €300 million), increased spending in the medical sector (by almost €900 million) and pledged state support to Air France-KLM (€2–4 billion), which has suffered immense losses as a result of the unprecedented lack of cross border mobility (Rijksoverheid 2020a). In total, an amount of €35 to €37 billion of government expenditure is expected to be allocated to the domestic mitigation of the effects of the COVID-19 crisis in 2020 alone (Rijksoverheid 2020e).

In addition to these measures taken by the Dutch government, De Nederlandsche Bank (DNB) lowered the reserve ratio required for the three biggest Dutch banks from 3 percent. This should make more credit available for companies suffering from the economic ramifications of the current crisis. Additionally, a relatively new DNB requirement obliging banks to maintain a buffer of €3 billion in case of a housing crisis, has been discontinued. As a result, an extra €8 billion has become directly available, resulting in an estimated €200 billion of credit available for lending (Rooijers and de Boer 2020). In this way, financial buffers built up in the Dutch economy are re-allocated to alleviate some of the economic repercussions of the COVID-19 crisis.

Economic effects

Despite these efforts, the Dutch economy has suffered severe consequences from the COVID-19 crisis. The most recent report by Statistics Netherlands (Centraal Bureau voor Statistiek, CBS), noted that the Netherlands' GDP had already shrunk by 1.7 percent in the first quarter of 2020 (Centraal Bureau voor Statistiek 2020a).

Since the Dutch lockdown only started halfway through March, these numbers do not represent the peak of the virus' impact on the Netherlands' economic performance (RIVM, 2020). Therefore, expectations for the second quarter of

Table 9.1 Economic measures implemented by the Dutch government as of 22 May

Measure	*Content*	*Desired effect*	*Expected Cost*
Expansion of *Borgstelling MKB-kredieten* (BMKB); BMKB-C	Offers an enhanced government guarantee for credit, from 50 percent to 75 percent. The premium has been lowered from 3.9 percent to 2 percent. SMEs of up to 250 employees are eligible. Increased guarantor budget to up to €1.5 billion. Measure is applicable to bridging loans and increasing overdrafts, lasting up to 2 years	Easing credit accessibility, maintaining liquidity	€203 mn
Tijdelijke Noodmaatregel Overbrugging voor Werkgelegenheid (NOW), NOW 2.0	Labor cost allowance Reimbursement of up to 90 percent of labor costs for three months, when expected to lose over 20 percent of turnover due to the current crisis. 80 percent of labor costs will be paid, provided that employees can keep their jobs and will receive 100 percent of their salaries. The measure was first implemented on the 17 March and announced to be prolonged on 20 May	Easing financial burden of labor costs, tempering expected unemployment	NOW 1: €10 bn NOW 2: €9.6 bn
Tijdelijke Overbruggingsregeling Zelfstandig Ondernemers (TOZO), TOZO 2.0	Independent entrepreneurs are viable for receiving up to three months of financial support to meet their basic living expenses and/or a loan for working capital. The measure was first implemented on the 17 March and announced to be prolonged on 20 May 20	Easing financial burden of independent entrepreneurs	TOZO 1.0: €3.8 bn TOZO 2.0: €1.1 bn

Table 9.1 Economic measures implemented by the Dutch government as of 22 May *(continued)*

Measure	*Content*	*Desired effect*	*Expected Cost*
Expansion of *Garantie Ondernemersfinancieringregeling* (GO)	Offers up to 50 percent of guarantee for banking loans. 80 percent for big companies, 90 percent for small companies. The GO ceiling was first raised from 400 million to €1.5 billion, and then to €10 billion on 20 May	Easing credit accessibility, maintaining liquidity	GO €80 mn (March) GO-C €1 bn (May)
Expansion of *Borgstellingskrediet voor de Landbouw* (LB)	Offers an enhanced government guarantee for credit in the agricultural sector	Easing credit accessibility, maintaining liquidity	€29 mn
Tegemoetkoming Ondernemers Getroffen Sectoren (TOGS)	Provides enterprises from affected sectors with an onetime €4,000 allowance	Easing affected sectors	€1.67 bn
Tegemoetkoming Vaste Lasten (TVL)	Offers a three-month-long allowance of 20,000 for fixed costs in case of a turnover loss of over 30 percent	Easing companies' financial burden	€1 bn

Source: Rijksoverheid 2020c, 2020d, 2020e, 2020f, 2020g.

2020 are grim (Centraal Bureau voor Statistiek 2020c). Assuming there will not be a second wave outbreak of the virus, the Dutch economy is expected to contract up to 5–7 percent this year (Barendregt et al. 2020, European Commission 2020a).

From March to April 2020, consumer confidence in the Dutch economy decreased from –2 to –22. This is the fastest monthly decrease ever reported for this proxy throughout CBS history. Moreover, the Dutch population has never been as negative about their economic prospects as they were in April 2020. As a result, their willingness to buy has plummeted; household consumption decreased an unprecedented 2.7 percent in the first quarter, and continued to decline (Centraal Bureau voor Statistiek 2020b).

Fixed investment fell by 1.1 percent in the first quarter of 2020. Likewise, producer confidence dropped significantly, reaching its lowest level ever measured. The level of goods produced in March 2020 decreased by 2.5 percent, compared to March 2019. In the coming months, this number is expected to decrease further, given the decreased consumption. Even though as of now there is no surge in the level of bankruptcies, this is most likely due to administrative delays. Bankruptcy numbers are expected to increase in the second half of 2020 (Conjunctuurklok 2020). The same phenomenon is occurring for unemployment; as of now, exact levels of its increase are difficult to detect. However, the first few weeks of lockdown showed a 13 percent decrease in working hours, as well as an unprecedented decrease in job vacancies (Prins and Barendregt 2020).

COVID-19 crisis: the European response and consequences

At the same time, efforts to mitigate the economic downturn following the pandemic have also been negotiated on an EU level. However, reaching a consensus on what the appropriate response is, has proven difficult. A fierce debate has gone on between and within the different eurozone countries and EU institutions.

Economic effects

As the European Commission notes in its economic forecast for the spring, all European countries suffer the impacts of the current economic crisis. Due to the EU's interconnectedness, this effect is exacerbated. However, the severity of this impact will be uneven (European Commission 2020a). When comparing the effects of the COVID-19 crisis on the Dutch economy to those on the European economy as a whole, the economic hardship in the Netherlands seems relatively limited.

Most of the detrimental trends that have occurred within the Dutch economy, can also be depicted in the rest of Europe. For example, decreasing consumer and producer confidence is a Europewide phenomenon (Centraal Bureau voor Statistiek 2020b, 2020d). According to economic forecasts by the European Commission, Dutch GDP will shrink by 6.8 percent in 2020. This decrease, although significant, is lower than the euro area's average of 7.7 percent. Especially when compared to Southern European countries, such as Italy with 9.5 percent and Spain with 9.4 percent decrease in GDP, the Dutch GDP decrease seems relatively moderate. Moreover, these numbers could worsen in case of a second outbreak of the virus or if EU economies prove to recover slower than expected (Stevis-Gridneff 2020). Other economic proxies, such as unemployment, also seem less affected in the Netherlands; the Netherlands' unemployment rate is expected to grow to 5.9 percent, compared to a eurozone average of 9.6 percent, and a soaring 11.8 percent and 18.9 percent in Italy and Spain, respectively (European Commission 2020a).

One of the reasons why the Netherlands seems to suffer less from the crisis is that the country has complied with EU regulations, guaranteeing fiscal stability in case of a crisis. As is discussed above, the Dutch government responded to the crisis with two comprehensive support packages. This makes the Dutch economy likely to suffer less and recover more quickly from the current economic recession. However, there are other, COVID-19 crisis specific, reasons why Southern European countries are affected more than the Netherlands.

For the first quarter, the Netherlands' most important trade partners, like Germany and the United Kingdom, did not yet suffer the real consequences of the crisis. On the other hand, countries in the European South saw high levels of COVID-19 infections early on. They had to implement lockdowns and quarantines before the rest of Europe, and thus for them, the negative effects of lockdown measures on their economic performance are already noted in data describing the first quarter of 2020 (Prins and Barendregt 2020).

Besides chronological differences, industries that are more hard hit by the current crisis, such as tourism and the car industry, are less important for the Dutch economy than they are for Southern European countries. In Spain and Italy, tourism accounted for 14.6 percent and 13.2 percent of GDP in 2018, respectively, while tourism contributed only 5 percent to the Netherlands' GDP in that same year (Knoema 2018). As a result, the Netherlands has suffered less of a blow due to the lockdown measures restricting tourism and certain industries than other eurozone countries.

Moreover, the Netherlands has the highest share of people working from home of the entire European Union – 14 percent, before the crisis. By comparison, the EU average is 5.3 percent (Eurostat 2020b). As a result, on average, Dutch people working from home are less likely to experience decreased efficiency as a result of a changing work environment, keeping Dutch productivity during lockdown more stable.

Last, the Netherlands never implemented a full quarantine, like the one in Italy. During the Dutch 'intelligent lockdown', more companies were able to stay open than during the Italian lockdown. As a result, the Dutch economy was hit less hard than the economies of countries enacting a full quarantine.

Support mechanisms

There are different possible ways in which the European Union can offer relief. While the European Central Bank (ECB) has already bought up large sums of Southern European bonds, the European Council debated fiscal measures, including the recovery plan (see chapters by Lawrie and Rave). Throughout this debate, the most divisive proposition seems to be the idea of mutualized debt instruments or 'coronabonds'. Since the start of the crisis, the most hard-hit Southern countries have asked for the issuance of common EU bonds, in essence mutualizing debt over the eurozone. Over the last few weeks, countries such as Belgium and France have voiced their support for this idea. Leaders of these countries, such as Emmanuel Macron, have urged the EU to act collectively and in solidarity with one another (Mallet and Khalaf 2020, Ballegeer and Hekking 2020).

However, the Netherlands, together with Austria, Sweden, Denmark, and previously Germany, strongly opposed the idea of coronabonds and providing other EU countries with unconditional grants. For these countries, that are traditional creditors, shared debt would mean higher borrowing costs and shared responsibility for EU wide debt. Moreover, issuance of shared debt would mean a step in the direction of further European fiscal integration, which is unpopular among Dutch voters.

On 20 March, Dutch Finance Minister Wopke Hoekstra expressed his concern over the current situation at a meeting of the eurozone Finance Ministers. In this meeting, he urged the European Commission to look into the inconsistent preparedness for economic setbacks, that had become apparent between different EU countries. This remark was not taken well by the Southern countries and caused outrage in international media. Hoekstra has since admitted he was too blunt and expressed that he did not have a specific country in mind when saying this (Walker and Schaart 2020).

To the dismay of the Dutch government, EU-wide pressure for shared debt did not fade. On 23 April, European leaders in the European Council agreed to cooperate on a recovery fund, which they urged the European Commission to outline as soon as possible. On 18 May, Emmanuel Macron and Angela Markel put forward a proposal for a €500 billion recovery fund, based on debt sharing (Erlanger 2020b).

With the leaders of the two strongest economies in Europe proposing debt mutualization, the Dutch position thus became even more precarious. As a response, the Dutch Prime Minister Mark Rutte announced that he would be working with Denmark, Sweden, and Austria to create a counterproposal to the plan. He repeated that the Netherlands would be willing to grant loans, provided that affected countries would commit to fiscal improvements (Den Hartog 2020). On May 23, the 'frugal four' presented their response to the Franco-German proposal. In this counterproposal, the group calls for a similar recovery fund, with one main difference; the financing should be provided through loans and not through the grants, financed by shared debts (Grüll 2020). Some of the 'frugal four' have softened their stance since then.

The European Commission presented its own proposal for an EU recovery fund 'Next Generation EU' on 27 May. The proposed fund consists of €750 billion, €500 billion of which would be in grant-form, and €250 billion in loan-form. In this proposal, financing of the fund is grounded in an adapted version of the Multiannual Financial Framework 2021–2027, which has been rebuilt around providing economic recovery in a sustainable matter (Europa Nu 2020c).

Hoekstra discussed the Dutch cabinet's position with regard to the Commission's proposal in a 9 June letter to the Dutch Parliament. In this letter, Hoekstra stressed that the Commission's proposal shares with the Dutch cabinet a profound belief in the necessity to support those EU countries most in need of financial aid, and the belief that this aid should be used to reach climate goals and improve digitalization. However, Hoekstra also reiterated the cabinet's opposition to providing aid in the form of grants, instead of loans. Additionally, he questioned the size and the specific distribution of different instruments within the recovery fund and restated that the cabinet believes money from the fund should only be directed towards COVID-19 related relief.

Furthermore, Hoekstra repeated that the cabinet believes 'more attention should be given to the way member states handle the implementation of structural reforms, necessary to strengthen economic fundaments, for example by lowering debts and reforming pension systems and improving administrative capacities' (Hoekstra and Blok 2020). Hoekstra also stressed that the Commission's proposal will result in a steep increase in Dutch contributions to the European Union; starting with an increase of €1.5 billion in 2021, and leading up to €2.3 billion by 2027 (Europa Nu 2020c).

On 19 June, the European Council convened to discuss differences in interpretation of the recovery fund, after which the plan moved into a negotiation period. European Commission President Ursula Von Der Leyen expressed hopes of reaching a final agreement in July (European Council June 2020). She was not disappointed on the timing, but the negotiations did reveal the strength of Dutch resistance. It also revealed the depths of the division between those who do and those who do not support the mutualization of debt.

Explaining the division

As a result of the COVID-19 crisis, a division between countries supporting debt mutualization and providing grants to mitigate the effects of an economic crisis, and countries opposing those measures has thus developed. Since Germany has recently broken its historic opposition to debt mutualization, the Netherlands now remains as the economically strongest opponent of sharing debt within the eurozone. In order to understand the responses of both the Netherlands and the Southern European countries to this debate, information from the previous chapters will be integrated below.

The Dutch position

Dutch opposition to eurobonds can be explained by looking at Dutch austerity measures, Southern lack of compliance with EU regulation, domestic support for eurobond opposition, domestic fear of populism, prejudices and stereotyping of Southern Europe, and the absence of Great Britain in the European Union.

As a result of the increased public debt and deficit the Netherlands encountered following the financial crisis, the Dutch government has implemented stark austerity measures. These austerity measures have been successful but have decreased the Dutch population's wealth. The majority of the Dutch population therefore has the idea that it has carried the financial burden of the previous crises.

According to the Dutch, Southern countries such as Italy and Spain have not implemented adequate austerity measures following the financial crisis and eurozone crisis, even though the public debt in these countries is higher than the Dutch public debt ever was. Additionally, the retirement age in Southern European countries is relatively low. The Dutch government has noted this and does not want to share the financial burden of countries that it does not believe tried to decrease their spending by implementing austerity measures like the Netherlands did. This perception, strongly present throughout Dutch politics, is likely part of the reason why Hoekstra has brought up the need to further research why Southern European countries were less equipped to deal with the current economic downturn than the Netherlands was.

This view is supported by the fact that Southern European countries did not meet their end targets for fiscal consolidation. Even though none of the Southern European countries was in an Excessive Deficits Procedure, they have been urged to improve multiple times. This can be seen throughout different 'Implementation of the Stability and Growth Pact' reports (European Commission n.d.-a). Italy, for example, has been urged to change its directory in order to comply with EU regulations multiple times. Therefore, the argument can be made that Southern countries were warned that they did not have their finances in order, and the Dutch government should not have to carry the burden for their inadequacy.

The Dutch population seems to support these views. A survey on the public's opinion of the Dutch government's handling of the crisis showed an overwhelming increase in support for both Rutte and Hoekstra (ANP 2020, Peilingwijzer 2020).

Moreover, the political debate on coronabonds within the Netherlands started off relatively homogenous. Initially, debates were mainly focused on how Hoekstra had given in too much, rather than too little. Only the parties D66, one of the current coalition partners, and ChristenUnie supported the issuance of shared debt. Other political parties were more hesitant about these measures. This creates a rare almost-unity across the political spectrum (BBC 2020). However, since the actual presentation of the European Commission's plan, it seems as though the Dutch tough position – at least within domestic Parliamentary discussion – has been somewhat softened. The question remains whether this is because Dutch politicians start to actually believe in EU solidarity, or simply realize they are not powerful enough to resist (Brouwers 2020).

An important reasoning often overlooked in the international depiction of the current issue, is the realistic threat of populism not just in the Southern European countries, but in the Netherlands as well. As has been seen in the past, an economic crisis tends to increase euroscepticism in the Netherlands. Therefore, it is not unthinkable that a sizeable contribution of the Dutch government to aiding Southern European countries will cause an enormous increase in domestic support for populist politicians such as Wilders and Baudet. This reasoning is supported by polling data: a recent increase in support for Rutte's *People's Party for Freedom and Democracy* (VVD), is facilitated by a large decrease in support for the 50+ Party, and smaller losses for FvD and PVV, the two populist parties, and D66, the party supporting the idea of debt mutualization (Peilingwijzer 2020).

With the departure of the United Kingdom from the European Union, the Netherlands has lost one of its most important allies. The UK and the Netherlands often had similar positions, cooperating on topics such as trade and fiscal policy (Janning 2019). Since the UK left the EU, the Netherlands thus has become more isolated in issues such as the current one. This has complicated the Netherlands' position within the EU, especially with its other ally, Germany, now speaking out in favor of debt mutualization as well.

With a populist party coming close to receiving the largest vote share in the last elections, if the Dutch government relaxed its opposition and supported the idea of shared debts against the wishes of the population it is supposed to represent, this could have disastrous consequences for the future of domestic politics in the Netherlands. This in itself thus poses a problem for the Dutch government; either they express solidarity on an EU level by supporting unlimited funding for suffering economies and they risk an increase of euroscepticism domestically, or they support the wishes of the Dutch population – those which they have ultimately been chosen to represent – and risk an increase of euroscepticism abroad, in addition to being called out for their selfishness.

Moreover, throughout the current crisis, the focus in Dutch media seems to lie on reinforcing existing stereotypes of Southern Europe. For example, one of the Netherlands' most-viewed political shows, *Zondag met Lubach*, devoted a 10-minute segment to ridiculing the idea of coronabonds. Throughout the show, with over 2 million views, the only aspect of the Italian economy that was discussed was its large public debt and its failure to resolve this (Zondag met Lubach 2020). This supports the stigmatization of the Italian and Spanish as inadequate and inferior. Moreover, by solely focusing on this aspect of the Italian economy, without analyzing how it gained its high debts or what this means, the Dutch population is misinformed *en masse*. This contributes to the already limited awareness of the origin of economic and financial differences in the eurozone.

The Southern European position

The Southern European position, on the other hand, can be explained by looking at the historical reasons for their high public debt and their precedence of decreased faith in Europe. With regard to the Netherlands specifically, their stance can be explained by analyzing previous Southern critique on the Dutch fiscal system, the Dutch precedent of speaking out against the South, and general prejudices and stereotyping of Northern Europe.

In line with this, public debt mismanagement of Southern European countries is stigmatized and twisted in Dutch media. For example, an important reason why Italy has such considerable debt stems from the 1980s. When comparing the last ten years of government debt between the Netherlands and Italy in real terms, Italy does not perform that much worse than the Netherlands (Peréz 2019, Dunford 1994).

Despite the fact that there is some truth in the Dutch criticism of Southern European fiscal policy, with deaths due to COVID-19 rising by the day, this did not seem like the right timing for such a concern. This insensitivity combined with declining the idea of coronabonds has fueled a strong feeling of lacking solidarity and even betrayal in most Southern European countries (Mercuri 2020).

Moreover, this unwillingness to help is often put in the context of earlier reluctance to provide aid in the eurozone crisis in 2012, as well as the more recent migration crisis. As a result, trust in the European project is expected to diminish in the Southern European countries. This growth in Euroscepticism forms a problem with regard to Italy, where already before the current crisis support for the European Union was very slim. A survey from the last months of 2019, showed that only 37 percent of Italians supported EU membership (Scazzieri 2020). This tendency has been reflected in recent Italian leadership. Therefore, politicians all over Europe have reiterated the need to cooperate on this issue, claiming that this could be a make or break for Europe.

Part of the reason why the Dutch response has been met with so much backlash is the historical precedence of Dutch politicians taking a stance. In March 2017, then Eurogroup chairman, as well as Dutch minister of Finance, Jeroen Dijsselbloem stated that he believed that support for countries encountering financial hardship should be paired with certain obligations. In an interview with the German *Frankfurter Allgemeine*, he went on to make the comparison that, similarly, he 'could not spend all his money on booze and women and then proceed to ask for help' (Verschuren 2017). Southern European countries were angered by this remark; the Portuguese government demanded Dijsselbloem's resignation and even the Italian leader of Dijsselbloem's own fraction in the European Parliament, Gianni Pittella, condemned his comments. The Dutch government, on the other hand, spoke out in support of Dijsselbloem, who expressed that he had not meant the words to come out like that, but did not apologize or take his words back (Beunderman 2017).

This is in line with more general criticism from the Southern European countries toward the Dutch for being arrogant. Just like in the Netherlands, the Southern European media also plays a role in enforcing stereotypes of the North as being 'cold and only after money'.

Part of the reason why the Netherlands is often viewed like this has to do with Dutch identity. In Dutch culture, honesty is one of the highest virtues. Therefore, a Dutch person abroad will often be perceived as being blunt or even rude. Although in recent years, the Netherlands seems to have become more 'politically correct', honesty, or bluntness, remains an integral part of Dutch culture. This probably explains part of Dijsselbloem and Hoekstra's insensitivity and reluctance to apologize for their words.

Another criticism the Netherlands often faces within the framework of the European Union, is its corporate taxation. Just like in Luxemburg and Ireland, a large part of why the Netherlands is such a wealthy country is due to their beneficial corporate taxation. The Netherlands creates special agreements with big multinationals and uses its subsidy system to decrease corporate taxation (De Hoon 2020).

In March 2018, the European Commission condemned seven European countries, including the Netherlands, for their tax policies. The EC claimed that the low corporate taxation in these countries leads to the undercutting of taxes, creating an unfair advantage within the internal market. The European

Commission stressed the need for countries like the Netherlands to resolve these issues, urging for harmonization of the EU tax system. Currently, in the eurozone annual revenues of up to €70 billion are estimated to be lost as a result of profit shifting (Casert and Pylas 2018). In a report published by Oxfam International in May 2020, the Netherlands came out as the top corporate tax haven in Europe, and third globally (Oxfam International 2020). Thus, Southern Europeans claim the Dutch are being hypocritical: even if Southern European governments have failed to live up to European fiscal norms, successive Dutch governments have failed to live up to European norms for taxation.

Conclusion

How the current crisis will shape the future of Europe is difficult to determine. As seen throughout the previous crises the European Union has faced, struggle can lead to further strengthening of the Union. Thus, the EU could come out of the COVID-19 crisis stronger than before, provided that it finds a way to come together. Given the multitude of divisive issues, overcoming them will take a long time and necessitates an EU-wide effort.

Throughout this chapter, the emphasis has been on Dutch reliance on the European Union. Therefore, specifically for the Netherlands, repairing the current situation is important. If this does not change, this could have long-term ramifications for the future trust other eurozone countries have in the Netherlands. In the short term, the eurozone should do whatever is in its power to overcome an economic recession. In this way, European trust can be rebuilt, both within and between countries. In the long term, the eurozone should work on the fiscal stability of its member states. In order to efficiently do so, certain European benefits could become conditional on reaching fiscal stability goals.

One of the ways in which that can be done, is by actively countering misinformation. For example, the international debate on coronabonds fails to address the likelihood that extensive financial support from the Netherlands to the rest of the eurozone will increase Euroscepticism in the Netherlands. Likewise, the international debate also fails to address the very real difficulties Southern European governments face when trying to improve fiscal stability, partially because they are a part of the eurozone. In order to improve European unity, these issues should be acknowledged and tackled on an EU level.

10

HOW COVID-19 IS CHANGING THE UNITED KINGDOM

Zixuan Feng

COVID-19, one of the most serious pandemics in recent years, has had an enormous impact on the world economy. No country could escape from this disaster, and most countries' economies and people's lifestyles have been negatively affected by this global pandemic. In a highly globalized world, the United Kingdom is no exception. By the time this paper was drafted (20 June 2020), according to the Johns Hopkins University's coronavirus map, 304,580 people are infected, 42,674 people dead, and the mortality rate is around 14.0 percent. The COVID-19 pandemic was slowing down in many areas of the world, such as Italy and China, but it was still suspending the work and affecting people's lives in many other areas.

Many questions remain about why the British Government failed to control the spread of the virus and how the virus entered the UK. At the moment, it is essential for the UK Government and Britain to find out how this virus has affected daily life, focusing on retail, transportation, restaurants, and housing. The COVID-19 pandemic has entirely changed people's lifestyles and disrupted normal life. Furthermore, the British are still in the process of Brexit and negotiations between the EU and the UK remain to be concluded. Hence, the UK Government needs to figure out how the COVID-19 pandemic will affect the final Brexit negotiations and with what results for the future of the United Kingdom.

This chapter discusses how the COVID-19 pandemic affects the United Kingdom in three different areas. The first section examines the similarities and differences between two major crises, the ongoing lockdown crisis and the financial crisis that took place in 2008, and how financial regulators reacted to stimulate British business and financial activities. The second section explores how the COVID-19 pandemic affected the UK's real economy, especially in the retail market, construction activities, car sales, and the education system. The third section discusses how the coronavirus will have an impact on the negotiations between the EU and the UK over their future trading relationship. The third section also considers how the combination of the COVID-19 pandemic and Brexit might affect the British economy.

Financial regulators during the 2020 lockdown crisis and the 2008 financial crisis

There are many differences between the current lockdown crisis and the 2008 financial crisis since the reasons behind these two crises are different. During the last crisis, banks were under significant pressure, some of them collapsed, such as the Northern Rock, and there was a public debt crisis in many parts of the world. This time it is a micro and macroeconomic crisis, which is caused by severe disruptions on both the supply and demand side. However, there are also some elements in common: both are fast, deep, long-term, persistent, and global. This part will discuss two questions: first, what are the differences in the approaches taken by financial regulators at the beginning of these two periods; second, what policy decisions did these regulators take during the two crises.

First, the financial regulatory authority was reformed after the 2008 financial crisis. This means two different groups of regulators face these two crises. There were some disadvantages to the regulatory system before 2008. Ahead of the outbreak of the 2008 financial crisis, the UK's financial regulatory framework was jointly supervised by the Bank of England, the Financial Services Authority (FSA), and the British Treasury (Daripa et al. 2013). The supervision of systemic risks was mainly the responsibility of the Bank of England. However, because the Financial Supervisory Authority was independent of the Bank of England, the Bank of England itself lacked practical tools or means to perform its duty to maintain financial stability, resulting in loopholes in systemic risk supervision. Even though the UK passed several reforms, they were not powerful enough to improve the whole financial system.

After learning the painful lessons from the 2008 financial crisis, the UK reformed its regulatory system. In June 2010, the British Chancellor of the Exchequer announced a proposal for a comprehensive reform of the UK's financial regulatory system, proposing reform of the UK's original model in which the Bank of England, the FSA and the British Treasury were jointly responsible for financial stability. In December 2012, the proposal was passed, the Financial Services Authority was formally abolished, and the Prudential Regulatory Authority (PRA) and the Financial Conduct Authority (FCA) were set up to undertake some of their functions, respectively.

The PRA is a branch of the Bank of England, which is mainly responsible for micro-prudential regulation, promoting the stability and prudent operation of the financial system. The FCA is directly responsible to the British Parliament and the British Treasury, and its primary responsibility is to regulate financial institutions to protect consumers and maintain the integrity of the financial markets. Moreover, in order to solve the problem of insufficient systemic risk supervision during the financial crisis, the British Government established a new financial policy committee within the Bank of England to prevent and respond to systemic risks with macroprudential tools. There are now two different groups of regulators to deal with crises and they have different functions.

It is also essential to analyze which policy decisions these regulators took throughout the crises, and how this impacted the crises. In the 2008 financial crisis, the UK regulators acted quickly: The United Kingdom passed the Banking (Special Provisions) Act on 21 February 2008, which provided temporary powers for the Government to deal with bank failures. This authority was used to resolve problems of Northern Rock, Bradford and Bingley, and two Icelandic banks that operated as British subsidiaries. This act provided regulators with significant power to deal with the crisis.

Furthermore, The Banking Act 2009 proposed the establishment of a complete set of bankruptcy procedures and a Special Resolution Regime (SRR) for problem banks. The bill stipulates that there are three necessary conditions for bankruptcy: an institution must already be unable to pay debts, that institution's bankruptcy must be in the public interest, and that bankruptcy must be in line with fairness. Meanwhile, bankruptcy applications can only be filed by the Bank of England, the FSA, and the British Treasury. During the process of dealing with the crisis, the Special Resolution Regime (SRR) had three ways to choose: one was private sector mergers and acquisitions; the second was the introduction of bridge banks; the third one was temporary nationalization. These three solutions helped the UK regulators to face and solve the financial crisis-related problems and emergence.

The current crisis extends well beyond the banking sector since almost every company is affected by the pandemic, and they are suffering from being unable to resume the work. Hence, the new financial regulator is pushing for loans and policies to help companies of all sizes. The FCA is making it easier for London-listed companies to raise emergency funds from their shareholders to help them through the coronavirus pandemic (Vincent 2020a). This time, regulators like FCA and PRA encourage more extensive use of simplified investment prospectuses, and the FCA has enabled investors to approve more share issuance without a meeting (Vincent 2020a). These new policies strongly support the operations and financing of these listed companies.

Furthermore, Christopher Woolard, a senior official in the FCA, said: 'The UK's capital markets will play a vital role in providing finance to businesses to help aid the recovery from this crisis' (Vincent 2020a). Since it is the first test of the business banking rules introduced after the 2008 financial crisis, the FCA tries its best to solve problems induced by the pandemic. The FCA monitors how banks handle the rollout of the government's bailout loan scheme after companies and politicians raised concerns (Vincent 2020b). In addition, this time the FCA is more worried about the impacts on consumers. The FCA said that there are four priorities for the future: ensuring safe payments and access to cash, avoiding unaffordable debt, protecting people from unsafe or unsatisfactory value products, and making sure prices and terms on online products are fair. Regulators are therefore making better decisions dealing with the COVID-19 lockdown crisis since they include both companies and consumers inside their regulatory plans.

The new regulatory system has proven to function well as the lockdown crisis unfolded, and businesses are slowly returning to normality. However, the aftermath of the COVID-19 pandemic will continue to test the choices of the regulators. Up to now, these two regulatory systems have been both robust and functional in both these two crises. Though the FCA and the PRA are new regulators, they have made the right choices since the start of the lockdown crisis, and the situation is under control.

How business and people's lifestyles have been impacted

Unlike the last crisis, which primarily affected the financial system, the effect of the COVID-19 pandemic on the UK is comprehensive, and almost all aspects of people's lives have been impacted by the lockdown rules. According to a survey on the economic impact of coronavirus by the Office for National Statistics in early April, more than 59 percent of the 4,600 businesses said they had no confidence in the financial resources they have for supporting their operations through the crisis. Among these companies, more than 65 percent of construction companies, food services, and heavy industries mentioned that they had more problems than other industries (Office for National Statistics 2020). Furthermore, businesses like retail and car sales have been impacted a lot, and their business model has been changed dramatically during the pandemic. Lastly, education institutions must also reform themselves since face-to-face education is not possible during this particular period.

Construction companies are impacted significantly by the COVID-19. According to IHS Markit/Cips purchasing managers' index, the UK construction index dropped from 52.6 in February to 8.2 in April and experienced an 84.4 percent decrease from one month to the next (Staton 2020). Even Rob Kent-Smith, head of national income accounting at the ONS, said that 'Construction saw a notable fall in February, as wet weather and flooding hampered housebuilding' (Rob 2020).

The terrible situation of the construction sector could expand to millions of Britons' families because the UK construction sector employs 2.4 million workers and produces about 6 percent of the country's total economic output (Romei 2020a). When the construction sector stops running, people's lives change a lot. Furthermore, The IHS Markit purchasing managers' index for UK construction dropped to 39.3 in March from 52.6 in February, making it the lowest recording in the last ten years. Construction involves high investment since infrastructure costs a lot and accounts for a large portion of the budget of governments and companies (Romei 2020b). Some of the largest housebuilders in the UK have furloughed more than 15 percent of their workforce and cut more than 20 percent of executive pay in March. Since many developers and investors have canceled or ceased their construction plans, land buying processes, and some other capital expenditures, construction companies had to stop their corresponding plans and businesses. Heads of the largest construction companies in the UK said their business would not restart until June and the construction sector will start to recover.

COVID-19 also has a large impact on the retail sector, since many workers must stay at home and wait for a recovery. The retail market had already started to decline before the COVID-19 lockdown, since the volume of UK retail sales dropped 0.3 percent in February over January, according to the ONS data. During the lockdown, Britons who work in the retail sector suffered because of the pandemic: nearly three million people who worked in the retail market were furloughed in the UK, and many have since then become unemployed. Moreover, the implications may become structural. Even though 43 percent of Britons would feel uncomfortable shopping outside supermarkets, according to the Ipsos Mori survey, the lockdown period could change people's habit of shopping permanently (Eley 2020).

The pandemic is also changing how retailers operate. First, retailers are more willing to open and invest in online shops and reduce the number of offline stores. According to data from the ONS, online grocery sales are 10 percent of the total sales, which has increased by more than 3 percent in a few weeks. Furthermore, several retailers are planning to work alongside e-commerce operations. Second, retailers are narrowing their supplies. During the lockdown period, supermarkets and stores were willing to supply more toilet rolls, pasta, and other essentials goods, and the number and kinds of goods like fruit and milk products decreased. Third, retailers want to develop and use new technologies in their businesses. The development of 5G and the internet of things (IoT) will change the supply chain of retailers. Retailers must evolve quickly and in a highly efficient manner to prepare for the next crisis.

The car industry, the representative of the manufacturing and production industry, is profoundly affected by the pandemic. The sales of cars have dropped significantly. According to Britain's motor industry trade association, the number of new cars registered in the country fell by 44.4 percent in March compared to the same month in 2019 (Partridge 2020), which is equivalent to a decline of 200,000 in vehicles purchased. The situation got even worse in April: UK new car registrations fell by 97.3 percent in April compared to the same month in 2019, with just 4321 cars sold (Attwood 2020).

The conditions in the car industry were worse than during the height of the financial crisis a decade ago since its supply chain has been severely disrupted. The car industry in the UK relies on parts coming from all around the world, especially the European continent and China. As long as these two areas suspend their supplies, the UK car industry cannot start to work either. Because of this, all major UK carmakers temporarily closed their production facilities, and more than ten thousand workers were furloughed. Furthermore, dealers had no choice but to close their showrooms and shut their stores. No one could enter their stores during the lockdown period.

The car industry cannot be suspended for a long time, and Rolls-Royce, as the first carmakers in the UK, slowly restarted production at its Goodwood facility on 4 May. Bentley also announced to restart its facility on 11 May as these luxury car companies are leading the way in warming up the UK car industry. Nevertheless, the UK car industry will not fully recover until the world supply chain can fully recover.

Education is another industry that has been massively affected. The pandemic has exposed every corner of society and has impacted every level of educational institutions. The higher institutions, especially universities, have been severely hit. The University of Oxford was forced to close its facilities for the first time since the Black Death, seven centuries ago. Other universities have had to close their doors as well, although instruction for most institutions continued online.

Two major problems were created by the lockdown. First, many new international students cannot come to the UK, and current students chose to leave the UK for safety reasons. Since the international students' tuition is higher than local students, universities stand to lose a large portion of their revenues if these international students cannot return to the UK. Second, the usual way of teaching in-person classes is no longer possible, and many universities turned to online classes instead. This leads to many new issues including a possible loss of quality in teaching and many students cannot focus that well in online classes. These developments are affecting every education institution in the UK and some schools have announced that they will not reopen until 2021.

Every corner of the British economy has felt the impact of the pandemic. exposed. Moreover, that impact has been social and political as well as economic. This is true elsewhere, of course. What distinguishes the United Kingdom is the fact that it is engaged in a unique experiment in leaving the European Union (EU). The pandemic also impacts the negotiations that are the final part of that process. That influence is the subject of the next section.

The interaction between this crisis and Brexit

On 30 January 2020, the European Parliament approved the official exit of the United Kingdom from the EU. The first round of negotiations about the new relationship between Britain and the European Union was held in Brussel in early March. The result was not optimistic. Suddenly, the pandemic changed the process of Brexit negotiations. The second round was postponed as EU chief negotiator Michel Barnier tested positive for the coronavirus. In addition to the logistical challenges of conducting sensitive discussions via virtual conference, neither the British government nor the European Commission considered finalizing Brexit as their priority. In the current situation, it is essential to find answers to the following questions: Will COVID-19 lead to a hard Brexit? Will the lockdown crisis's economic impacts function as an excuse for a hard Brexit to cover Britain's political concerns?

The COVID-19 pandemic seems likely to encourage a hard Brexit. First, the negotiation process is not smooth. Negotiation teams from both sides face tremendous pressure since they must determine the future relationship between the UK and the EU during the transition period ending in 2020. There are lots of agreements that should be made on topics such as scientific research, border controls, economic cooperation, free-trade, international security cooperation, fisheries, and transportations. A no-deal scenario is the worst outcome for both sides. Among all agreements, a free-trade agreement, aspiring to a zero-tariff, and zero-quota deal is the core and the most important deal of the negotiation process (Sloat 2020).

After the second round of talks concluded in April, however, the EU's chief negotiator, Michel Barnier, said he was disappointed and worried. Furthermore, Barnier accused the UK of denying joining thoughtfully on some issues and trying to slow down discussions (Parker and Brunsden 2020a). These words are unusual for negotiators like Barnier to use. He also mentioned that the whole process would not proceed any smoother in June's meeting unless the British changed their approach.

On 12 June the British government formally rejected an extension of the transition arrangements. According to Michael Gove, Cabinet Office minister: 'On 1 January 2021 we will take back control and regain our political and economic independence' (Brunsden and Payne 2020). Even though the legal deadline to request an extension of the transition period was 30 June, the UK government had already made its decision. Both sides accepted that the negotiations would have to conclude in 2020.

Many British politicians believe that a prolonged negotiation would only make the EU require Britain to pay more into the EU budget. Many Britons are full of complaints after three and a half years of Brexit stalemate. A more extended transition period would increase their anger and make the prime minister lose support from Brexiteers.

Initially, the EU held the opposite view. Trade agreement negotiations typically take years in Brussels, and now such time is not available, which means that the EU might find it helpful to extend the post-Brexit transition period. Besides, Brussels believed the transition period could be extended for two more years under the current Brexit terms of the agreement.

During the first summit held on 15 June, both the UK and the EU sides said, 'an intensive period of negotiations in July will be crucial to breaking the deadlock in the future-relationship talks over issues ranging from state aid to fish' (Parker and Brunsden 2020b). That both sides are willing to push for the speed for Brexit under current circumstances is a positive signal for the future of the UK–EU relationship and the negotiation process. However, 'an end-of-July deadline for sealing a UK–EU trade deal' was always unlikely.

Furthermore, the economic impact of the lockdown crisis functioned as an excuse for a hard Brexit to cover political concerns. Indeed, the pandemic has already created a massive economic crisis from which both the UK and the EU are suffering a lot, and both sides need a free-trade agreement to stimulate their economic development. Furthermore, trade unions would ask for an agreement that can benefit their businesses in their relations with Europe. The IMF also asked both sides to consider an extension to reduce the uncertainty brought by the COVID-19 pandemic.

The British government nevertheless worried that the rules governing the single market would complicate their economic response to the crisis. These rules are unacceptable for the UK to accept after Brexit partly because the EU failed to place the supranational institutions that would have made financial solidarity possible, leaving the single market and the euro vulnerable to inevitable shocks (Matthijs 2020). The influence of the European Court of Justice was another strong point of concern. The United Kingdom government and its citizens do not want to sacrifice their national sovereignty and national interests to a supranational entity. The political concerns overcome the economic interests of the UK side, and it makes it easier for the British government to argue that a hard Brexit would be better than an endless round of talks.

The COVID-19 pandemic has changed the form of Brexit negotiations, but it does not affect the core of why the Brexit negotiations are so hard to finalize. The lockdown has made the process slower than before, and the EU and the

UK disagree on whether to have an extension for the transition period. The economic pressure caused by the lockdown crisis on the UK economy could not help the EU to earn a comprehensive and more favorable Brexit deal since the British put their political reality before any economic factor.

Conclusion

This essay has discussed how the COVID-19 pandemic affects the United Kingdom in three specific areas. First, financial regulators in these two crises are different from each other due to the 2010 comprehensive reform of the UK's financial regulatory system. However, both regulators have reacted decisively to the severe problems caused by these two crises. Second, the economic life of businesses and individuals has been impacted significantly by the pandemic in many areas of the economy, such as construction, retail market, manufacturing industry, and education. Third, the negotiation process of Brexit between the EU and the UK has slowed down due to the pandemic. Nevertheless, both sides have now accepted that they will not extend the transition arrangements.

One more important thing to consider is how the UK will go through the current crisis. Because of the lockdown crisis, both supply and demand sides are affected negatively due to less production and consumption. This is an urgent problem for the UK government to solve since if the country would resume work swiftly and thereby stimulate consumption, the UK economy could bounce back much faster than other countries during the next few years. A lot will depend upon how effectively the government can respond. Although the scale of this crisis is unprecedented, the harmful consequences of the lockdown crisis could be fewer than the previous crisis.

11

THE NORWEGIAN OIL FUND AND THE CRISES OF 2020

Hayden Hubbard

The stated purpose of The Norwegian Government Pension Fund-Global, or 'the oil fund' as it is commonly called, is to 'ensure responsible and long-term management of revenue from Norway's oil and gas resources in the North Sea so that this wealth benefits both current and future generations (Norges Bank Investment Management 2020a). In this way, the fund has served as both a rainy-day fund and a savings mechanism. The fund carries with it a great deal of Norwegian national pride. In addition to being the largest in the world, the fund has been lauded for its transparency and governance as compared to other sovereign wealth funds of similar size. However, the fund's rigid investment strategy has inhibited its returns, and despite accumulating as much as $1.1 trillion in assets, its governance has remained in the hands of a small circle of politically appointed figures.

While the fund was able to provide some financial aid during the 2008 financial crisis, and experienced limited reforms following the crisis, its structure remained relatively rigid and there were trade-offs between improvements in the fund's investment strategy and the transparency of its governance. Furthermore, the fund has become increasingly politicized and there have been growing pressures to use the fund more generously. When the combined shocks of COVID-19 and the collapse of global oil prices created the country's 'worst economic contraction since WWII' (Holter 2020) the fund's ability to act as a rainy-day fund was brought to question. A scandal in the middle of these crises over the fund's new leadership added insult to injury by putting the fund's governance and transparency into further question.

Thanks to the oil fund, Norway should have been exceptionally prepared to respond to the crisis. However, even exceptional preparedness was not enough to overcome interdependencies in the Norwegian economy. This chapter explores the effectiveness of Norway's oil fund as a tool for responding to the crises of

2020 and examines how the fund can be reformed to maintain long-term sustainability and be better prepared as a rainy-day fund for future crises.

The origin of the fund and its shaping of current governance

In theory, almost all sovereign wealth funds are founded for one of three reasons: to hedge against commodity price volatilities in mineral rich nations, to diversify away from cash holdings or low-yielding U.S. treasury bills, or for long-term savings and a support system for crises (Alsweilem et al. 2015). In practice, sovereign wealth funds are known for their lack of transparency, risk of being swayed by private political interests, and ability to disrupt markets due to their size (Truman 2008). Furthermore, many countries that would have benefited from a fund, such as the UK and Canada, ended up using their natural resource revenues to reduce fiscal deficits and lower taxes instead – a move that many policymakers lament in hindsight (Gouett 2013). Despite efforts by the likes of the OECD to standardize best governance practice for sovereign wealth funds (often using Norway as a poster child), little has changed, and Norway's fund is extraordinary in its transparency, ethical standards, and disciplined governance.

Norway first began accumulating wealth upon the 1969 discovery of oil in the famous Ekofisk oil field 320 kilometers off the country's southeastern coast. The vast majority of this wealth passed through Norway's government through taxes, its controlling stake in Statoil (now Equinor), and a number of its own directly owned oil fields. However, it was not until 1990 that the Norwegian government took the opportunity to create a sovereign wealth fund out of its massive oil revenue stream (Norges Bank Investment Management 2020b). This intervening twenty-one years was vital to developing the fund's unique governance structure and investment strategy that shaped its decision making during the crises of 2020.

Norway's hesitancy in creating the fund was less due to the political unpopularity of large-scale government savings. Rather, it was because government ministries, especially the Ministry of Finance, worried that the fund would lack transparency, be misused politically, and result in unwarranted and destabilizing domestic investments. These concerns emerged from the poor performance of Norway's previous National Insurance Fund and the lack of transparency and stability in other emerging sovereign wealth funds at the time. When the Norwegian Parliament finally agreed to the fund in 1990 (though the first payment to the fund was not until 1996), they were prudent to create a careful organization structure and a number of rigid conditions governing the fund (Einar 2018).

The Government Pension Fund Act gave the Ministry of Finance responsibility for the fund which in turn gave management responsibilities to the Norges Bank Executive Board. The Executive Board is made up of twelve members appointed by the 'King in Council' (Norway's acting heads of government) who sets guidelines as to how the fund can be invested. The day-to-day operations of the fund are run by Norges Bank Investment Management and its CEO who reports back to the Executive Board and provides the board with advice on the fund's investment strategy. This structure aimed to ensure that the fund was not overly swayed by political interest and that it did not operate outside the government's fiscal objectives (Einar 2018). However, there have been concerns that those who manage the fund have not been as apolitical as originally hoped for. As fund assets have grown, the current structure has left a relatively small group of mostly non-finance experts running an increasingly large and complex investment portfolio. The CEO of Norges Bank Investment Management has an especially challenging task by singlehandedly operating the fund with his or her team, while trying to both follow and sway the guidelines of the Executive Board. The CEO also acts as the face of the fund and carries a great deal of public responsibility for the fund's performance.

The initial conditions of the fund established that it was only to be drawn down when the government had a fiscal deficit, while fiscal surpluses would be added to state oil revenues in contributing to the fund. The fund was also only allowed to make foreign investments (no investing in domestic infrastructure projects for instance) and these investments had to be listed stocks and bonds or real estate (real estate was included in 2010 and only makes up three to five percent of the fund). By 2004, the fund had added a framework of ethical guidelines for investment which disallowed investment in weapons manufacturers, coal producers, tobacco companies, and companies that do not respect workers' rights among others (Einar 2018). Lastly, the fund made its investments public and possible to view online by anyone. Despite all the recognition this framework has given the fund for its transparency (not to mention the way it conveys Norwegian values and serves as a source of national pride), it has also limited the fund in the way of performance and functionality.

Norway's original intention in creating the fund was to save for future generations and to hedge against commodity prices. As the fund has helped Norway to diversify its economy and become a finance center, however, its stated purpose has narrowed to focus on saving for future generations (Norges Bank Investment Management 2020a). Relatively few sovereign wealth funds have effectively made this transition. Norway's is one of the few large funds to have been established in a democracy. Its transparency, combined with its size, has also allowed it to have a much broader impact than its direct investments (The Economist 2016). Many institutions are influenced by the fund's investment decisions, as well as its ethical guidelines to not invest in certain firms. Such ethical guidelines are a true rarity compared to other funds and one of the hottest ongoing debates about the fund since its ethically justified disinvestments have at times seemed to have underlying political motives (Backer 2009).

Along with the fund's change in stated purpose, its policies have shifted over time. One of the main ways the fund has evolved is by allowing for domestic investments since 2001. Prior to the crises of 2020, the fund made up twenty percent of the government budget. The fund was allowed to contribute up to as much as the expected real return on the fund – four percent until 2017 when it was reduced to three percent (Norges Bank Investment Management 2020a). This change has been accompanied by growing political pressure to spend more from the fund (Miline 2020c), even though more has already been pulled from the fund in recent years. For instance, 2016 was the first time interest from the fund was used to fill a government budget shortfall. Still, this increase in expenditure was not due to any structural change in the policies governing how much the fund spends.

There has also been pressure from both finance experts and politicians for the fund to better diversify its investment portfolio. Though the fund's leadership has held that it operates independently from external pressure, it has gradually diversified its portfolio in recent years by investing in new sectors such as real estate. The fund has also increased its risk exposure by increasing its share of equity investment from forty percent to sixty percent in 2009 and then to seventy percent in 2017 (Einar 2018).

These policy shifts have resulted in trade-offs that have improved the fund's performance, but also garnered criticism for making the fund more political and possibly less transparent. Amidst international and domestic pressure to reduce inconsistencies and political biases in following its ethical guidelines, the fund adjusted its policies in 2014 so that the Council of Ethics began providing recommendations to Norges Bank (Norway's Central Bank) directly rather than through the Ministry of Finance (Norges Investment management 2020b). Despite this adjustment, and though investment returns make up well over half of the fund's revenues (more than oil revenues), the government announced that it would begin drilling for new oil fields in 2019. Additional oil revenues would allow for greater spending from the fund, appeasing political pressure, but the move garnered criticism of hypocrisy given the fund's eco-friendly ethical investment criteria.

Shifts in the fund's investment policy have been met with more mixed criticism. On the one hand, the fund's real estate investments have diversified its portfolio and a greater share of higher risk equity investments has allowed the fund to take advantage of its long-term investment horizon and increase returns. On the other hand, some experts argue that the fund's investment strategy shift did not emphasize diversification enough, incurring unnecessary risks while also making its assets less liquid, hindering the fund's ability to act as a rainy-day fund.

Despite these issues, the fund appeared to be in great shape going into 2020 with increasing returns and continued recognition for its transparency. Its performance had improved noticeably through 2019, surpassing $1 trillion in 2017 and increasing its yearly return from 4.2 percent during 2000–2009 to 8.1 percent during 2010–19. With a return of 19.9 percent in 2019, its best year ever, the fund surpassed $1.1 trillion and owned roughly 1.5 percent of all stocks globally (Norges Bank Investment Management 2020c). In light of the success, the fund's CEO of twelve years, Yngve Slyngstad, asked to step down at the end of 2019, agreeing to continue managing the fund until a new CEO was found. The oil fund was worth three times more than the country's GDP at the end of 2019 and oil revenues had declined to ten percent of GDP from twenty-four percent of GDP in 2008. However, with continued reliance on the oil industry for jobs and government revenue alongside the fund's increased exposure to market risk and the fund's decreased ability to liquidize assets (and thereby function as a rainy day fund), Norway's economy and the fund would prove much more vulnerable to the shocks of 2020 than anticipated.

The shocks of 2020 and Norway's response

The shocks of 2020 can be divided into three periods starting at the end of February and finishing at the end of May. The combined shocks of the oil price drop and the COVID-19 outbreak, alongside the political turmoil regarding the fund's leadership are so interconnected it is most feasible to analyze the issues and responses chronologically, rather than by subject. Between 26 February and 23 March the COVID-19 crisis emerged, and oil prices began to drop. From 26 March to 20 April the fund named its new CEO, a scandal over his appointment emerged and oil prices plummeted below zero for the first time ever. From 28 April to 19 June stocks and oil prices began their (albeit turbulent) recovery, interest rates fell to zero (their lowest ever) and the oil fund pulled from its principal for the first time in its history to address the economic crisis.

Late February to late March

Norway was one of the first European countries to experience its COVID-19 outbreak, recording its first case on 26 February. Oil prices and the Norwegian stock market had been falling gradually since mid-January, but stocks plummeted quickly at the end of February, hitting 13.3 percent of their January high on 27 February, parallel to an 11.4 percent fall in the Dow Jones by the same date. Oil prices collapsed shortly after, dropping 52 percent from their January high on 9 March and 68 percent from their January high on 18 March. Norway's stock market finally bottomed out to a 35 percent drop from the January high on 17 March, five days before the Dow Jones bottomed out with a similar decline. The massive oil price collapse and stock market decline slashed $114 billion (16.2 percent) from the oil fund by 26 March. Meanwhile, the exchange rate depreciated to its lowest rate ever on 19 March at 12.02 Norwegian Kroner (NOK) per $1 (a depreciation of 34 percent since the beginning of January). Because a large portion of the fund's assets are denominated in dollars, the sharp currency depreciation gave the fund close to its highest Kroner value in its history, reaching nearly NOK 10.5 trillion at the end of March (Milne 2020d).

Norway's response to the health crisis was immediate and effective. After rapidly deploying widespread testing and isolating the infected, the government announced an official lockdown on 12 March, preventing all events, closing all but essential business, and shutting its borders. The intensity of Norway's health response and lockdown, which was both expensive and economically disruptive, was compensated by comprehensive social and economic benefits made possible by the potential for increased expenditures from the sovereign wealth fund.

Economic measures were first announced 13 March with an interest rate cut from 1.5 percent to 1 percent and reductions in obliged employer payments to unemployed workers during temporary layoffs. A slew of tax benefits for affected businesses were also announced, including loss carry-backs to 2019 (which are normally not possible in Norway), the postponement of wealth tax payments, and many tax reductions specific to airlines. 15 May saw the creation of two new bond funds worth NOK 100 billion, providing ninety percent government-backed, three-year bonds, almost half of which were to be managed by Norway's domestic (and much smaller) sovereign wealth fund Government Pension Fund Norway (Fisen 2020). On 16 March employer, corporate, and VAT tax payments were delayed three to four months and VAT taxes for passenger transport, accommodation, and parts of the cultural sector were reduced from twelve percent to eight percent. Finally, interest rates were reduced further to 0.25 percent on 21 March and on 17 March the government announced a NOK 75 billion cash pay-out scheme aimed at closed businesses alongside social protection measures such as 100 percent unemployment compensation for the first twenty days of unemployment. Altogether, these measures weakened the government budget by NOK 200 billion (4.6 percent of GDP) by the beginning of April, creating an urgent need for support from the oil fund (Government of Norway 2020).

Although COVID-19 cases peaked by 27 March thanks to Norway's rapid healthcare response, unemployment shot to 10.9 percent by 24 March and the Oslo stock exchange had dropped as much as the U.S. stock indexes despite all the government's economic measures. This came as a surprise to many analysts given the comprehensiveness of the government's actions and the immense buoying force of the oil fund. There were some critiques of the response, such as only reducing VAT taxes on industries that had been virtually shut down (limiting their effect), but most critiques were addressed at underlying issues with the Norwegian tax system such as the lack of loss carry-backs and the complexity of its wealth tax (Bunn 2020). The sharp initial economic effects of the crisis speak less to the way the government responded and more to the vulnerability of the Norwegian economy to global shocks, due to its dependence on exports (38.44 percent of GDP as of 2018) including oil.

Late March to late April

On 26 March, the oil fund announced that Nicolai Tangen, founder of the London-based hedge fund AKO Capital, would take over from Yngve Slyngstad as CEO of Norway's sovereign wealth fund. By 6 April the Norwegian government announced that the pandemic was under control and the Oslo stock exchange had recovered 16.9 percent along with an uptick in oil prices. But then, on 19 April, news broke that just months before Tangen had been named the fund's new CEO, he invited Slyngstad to a $3 million closed seminar in the U.S featuring Sting, Jamie Oliver and others along with a private flight to and from Norway. The story dominated the Norwegian press in the weeks following as further anomalies in the recruitment of Tangen emerged. Under Norwegian law, candidates for senior government positions like the CEO of the fund should be made public prior to their appointment, but Tangen's name never was. Furthermore, there was still uncertainty regarding Tangen's relationship with his former hedge fund when he was appointed CEO. These inconsistencies put the greatest scrutiny on Oystein Olsen, Norway's central bank governor who led the recruitment process (Milne 2020b).

Tangen was only the third CEO appointed in the fund's 24-year history, but a scandal of this magnitude was unprecedented for the fund and had dangerous implications given its unfolding during such a critical period. Both Tangen and Slyngstad quickly apologized and swore to embrace transparency throughout the investigation, meanwhile Olsen ensured that Norges Bank paid Tangen back for all of Slyngstad's expenses during the closed seminar and tried to quickly dismiss the affair (Milne 2020a). By the end of April, public outrage over the scandal had quieted, but the scandal exposed potential weaknesses in the fund's governance which had previously been held with such high regard.

Late April to late May

After the 20 April scare when oil prices went negative for the first time ever (before quickly rebounding), the Norwegian economy made an unstable recovery and the fund became active in supporting Norway's long-term economic strategy. Even as schools reopened and lockdown measures were loosened on 11 May, the Norwegian economy experienced a number of unpleasant firsts. On 29 April oil production was reduced for the first time since 2002, with a cut of 250,000 barrels per day (bpd) in June (equal to 13 percent of total production), followed by a cut of 134,000 bpd for the rest of the year. This was coupled with delays in the start-up of several new oil fields such that by December oil production would be 300,000 bpd less than previously planned. Then on 7 May interest rates dropped even further to 0 percent, their lowest rate ever. Norges Bank projected that interest rates would stay at 0 percent until 2023 at the earliest, implicating the long-lasting effects of the crisis. Finally, on 12 May the Norwegian government proposed to pull $41 billion (419.6 billion NOK) from the oil fund in its revised 2020 budget. The withdrawal, worth 4.2 percent of the value of the fund at the time, would require a sale of the fund's assets for the first time in its history.

The Minister of Energy claimed that the cuts in oil production were in the best interest of Norway, though it was also a way of honoring their unofficial commitment with OPEC and helping to shore up oil prices. The fall in interest rates came as a surprise to many, but the Central Bank assured that they would not bring the rate below zero like other countries in Western Europe (Sheppard 2020). The selling of fund assets was perhaps the most dramatic measure, and though the fund's governance structure allows for such withdrawals in times of emergency, the government proposed a law in March that allowed it to pull from the fund without consulting parliament during the six months following the crisis. It was recognized at the time that the $ 41 billion taken from the fund would likely not be sufficient in light of persistently high unemployment rates (the country's highest since WWII) and having the worst currency depreciation against the Euro and the Dollar in the G-10. Even though the government threatened to intervene to save the Kroner's depreciation throughout the crisis, it had held back from any kind of direct intervention as of the end of June instead relying on increased spending from the fund to improve the currency situation.

The sharp market contraction required the fund to invest in new equities in order to follow its portfolio rules which required the fund to keep 70 percent of its investments in equity. In line with the fund's rigid investment strategy, the majority of these new acquisitions were in the U.S. and less opportunistic than purchases made by other sovereign wealth funds (Weiss and Holter 2020). The fund also sold $2.7 billion shares in twelve coal and oil companies in mid-May, citing violations of their ethical guidelines. One of the reasons the fund provided for the disinvestments were excessive carbon emissions from a number of the firms; it was the first time the fund had used this reasoning to drop shares. Some saw this as further evidence of the fund's politics and hypocrisy, since the fund kept shares in other energy companies with arguably worse environmental performance, and because the country had just ramped up it own oil production in 2019. Norway counteracted such criticism by claiming that its oil production was highly regulated, and its environmental standards were much higher than other countries.

Moving forward and implications of the crisis

Emerging from the crises of 2020, Norway's oil fund had two primary points of conflict. The first was determining how much more to spend to get the economy back on track, as well as determining long-term levels of expenditure in light of growing political pressure to spend more preceding the crises and a record amount of expenditure during the crises. The second was re-evaluating its investment strategy along with its governance structure after the unprecedented leadership scandal and investment losses.

By 19 June, currency depreciation was still 9.8 percent larger than 1 January while unemployment as of the end of May was 7.1 percent; this was down more than two percent from the peak in March (Federal Reserve Economic Data 2020), but if including 'partially unemployed persons' the unemployment rate was still much higher. Although the fund had climbed back to over $1.07 trillion by mid-June, from a trough of $930 billion in mid-March, these gains had slowed in the preceding two months and the $41 billion in spending wiped out much of the gains. According to the IMF's projections in early April, Norway's economy was projected to contract by 6.3 percent in 2020, less than the European average despite being especially vulnerable to the crisis, in large thanks to Norway's strong economic response. However, Norway's economy was projected to rebound only by 2.9 percent in 2021, the lowest projected rebound in Europe (International Monetary Fund 2020b). These estimates are also optimistic as oil prices declined further after the IMF released its projections, the IMF's more recent June projections for Europe were lower than their initial projections, and unemployment remained higher.

Given Norway's model of using the fund to substitute for fiscal spending deficits, and with increased fiscal spending likely throughout 2020, further strains on the fund's resources were almost guaranteed for some months after the crisis. Recent provisions providing the government with emergency powers to use the fund without parliament's approval made greater spending all the more likely. Jonas Gahr Store, the leader of the opposition party which is a slight favorite in the 2021 parliamentary election, openly called for the fund to be used politically. If he were to be named prime minister, greater spending in 2021 and beyond would be highly likely (Milne 2020c). In response, Olystein Olsen (the central bank governor) spoke harshly against the politicization of the fund in February, as did Erna Solberg, prime minister during the 2020 crises. However, some argued that Solberg's government had already used the fund politically, when deciding which companies to disinvest in for ethical violations.

A long-term increase in spending of Norway's sovereign wealth fund poses some major risks. Cross-country analysis of other sovereign wealth funds shows sustained increases in expenditure have negative results, such as increased inflation. The effects of such behavior in Norway would be especially dangerous given its aging population and the need for much greater future expenditure (Balding 2012). Stabilizing the fund's governance and improving its investment strategy is vital to alleviating the effects of forthcoming increases in expenditures.

For example, the fund's performance prior to 2008 was below its targets, and especially poor compared to other sovereign wealth funds (Kapoor 2017), however, the fund's leadership used the 2008 crises to propose greater diversification and increased equity investments as a share of the fund's portfolio. Considering its size and long-term investment horizon, the fund could have still performed much better between after 2008 with greater liberalization of its investment strategy.

The 2020 crises are a unique opportunity for the fund to evolve again. To maintain its goal of 70 percent equity investment, the government already made some portfolio adjustments during the 2020 crises, but this was accomplished primarily by acquiring U.S. stocks (which were relatively cheap following the market crash) rather than investing in higher-performing, long-term investments such as infrastructure and illiquid assets that are typical of sovereign wealth funds (Weiss and Holter 2020).

The fund's limits on investing in anything outside listed stocks, bonds, and some real estate lock it out from long-term, higher return investments and increases the fund's risks by skewing its investments towards primarily developed nations while reducing the diversity of its portfolio. Though improving the fund's investment strategy may constrain the fund's ability to act as a 'rainy day' fund (because it will hold less liquid assets), higher yearly returns on the fund can expand Norway's fiscal space every year. More importantly, it may make more sense for the fund to act solely as a savings instrument and take full advantage of its long-term investment potential, rather than being caught in-between being a savings instrument and a rainy-day fund. The fund already proved its limited ability to respond to the crises of 2020, and it may make more sense for Norway to create a separate 'rainy day' fund.

The fund's current sub-optimal investment strategy is linked to its governance. The fund's board is made up primarily of political figures and not finance experts. For all its recognition of transparency and good governance, the fund's management structure is not ideal for high performance (Kapoor 2017). This is in part why Tangen's appointment was so interesting. Not only has the scandal surrounding his appointment emphasized that the fund's governance is perhaps not as transparent as previously thought, his background as a hedge fund manager is novel for the fund and one would expect him to be in favor of diversifying the fund's investments. His opinion may be constrained by the political figures on the board, but his voice will be key to any post-crisis reforms.

Norway's outrage over the Tangen appointment scandal speaks to the country's values of equality and stability (Milne 2020b). The fund is viewed as the collective savings of Norway's people, and there is a great deal of risk aversion to expanding the fund's investments. The CEO of the fund is expected to act as a loyal public servant, not an ambitious financer – which is closer to Tangen's background. Improving the fund's investment strategy does not require increasing its risk profile however. Many funds have the same risk profile as Norway's fund and generate better returns because they do not have the same rigid bureaucratic limits on investment (Kapoor 2017). These limits can actually pose a greater threat to the fund, as was the case in 2008, when the fund contracted sharply without having reaped the rewards of its relatively high-risk profile (Qvigstad 2009).

Finally, what makes Norway's fund especially unique compared to other funds globally is its ethical standards such as committing to reduce carbon emissions. However, Norway has come under fire for increasing oil production preceding the 2020 crises even as it claimed to support emissions reductions and continued to disinvest in firms with high carbon emissions (SEI et al, 2019). Returns on the fund have outpaced oil revenues in recent years (which peaked in 2000) and increasing the fund's returns could allow Norway to become less reliant on oil revenues. Not only would this help Norway to put its money where its mouth is on helping the environment, but it would also help to reduce the effects of dual shocks like the combined oil price and stock market crash of 2020.

Conclusion

Norway's sovereign wealth fund is unique for its existence in a stable democracy, its commitment to ethical guidelines and its size relative to its population. The fund has benefitted from a tradition of transparency and stable governance which has helped it to become the largest sovereign wealth fund in the world and shaped its actions during the crises of 2020. However, the fund has become increasingly politicized prior to the 2020 crises and has faced growing demand for increased expenditure – which research has suggested to be dangerous for the country's long-term economic health. Despite the government's decisive health response and comprehensive economic measures during the 2020 crises, the Norwegian economy and the oil fund proved more vulnerable to the combined shocks of declining oil and stock prices than anticipated. The oil fund was strained by the crises and unable to prevent severe economic repercussions. Meanwhile, the scandal surrounding the fund's new CEO in the middle of the crisis threatened the fund's credibility and sowed doubt in the reality of the fund's lauded transparency and governance.

Like the 2008 crisis, the crises of 2020 are an opportunity for Norway's sovereign wealth fund to reevaluate its governance and investment strategy. The fund's performance has been relatively poor prior to the crisis, in part due to bureaucratic constraints on the fund's investment strategy, biasing it towards developed markets with lower returns. The fund's ethical investment standards are admirable, but somewhat hypocritical given Norway's recent plans for increased oil production. Increasing the fund's performance is more important than ever given the escalating constraints on its resources, the risks of future shocks, and increased pressure to reduce its dependency on oil for environmental reasons. Meanwhile, it may make more sense for the fund to create another means of rainy-day fund and take full advantage of the oil fund as a savings instrument. The fund's performance can be improved if its governance structure is made less bureaucratic and prioritizes performance similar to other sovereign wealth funds. Through improved performance, alongside the required changes in governance, the fund can recoup the losses of the 2020 crises, reduce its dependency on oil, and be prepared for the demands of its aging population and future crises.

CONCLUSION: INTERPRETING EUROPE'S RESPONSE TO THE CRISIS

Zoë Katharina Strauss and Erik Jones

Europe was not well prepared to face a crisis of this magnitude and with so many uncertainties attached to it. As shown throughout the book, navigating these uncharted waters has been a challenge for every European country during the first months as the crisis exposed the fragilities of an interconnected world. National leaders had to make decisions with imperfect information and European institutions seemed unsure about what role they should play. They did have one advantage, however. Europeans had been through the last crisis. That experience created lasting divisions, but it also underscored the importance of cooperation and decisive action. Those lessons turned out to be more important for Europe's future than any scars that remained from Europe's past.

Lessons learned

Despite the uncertainties, the exponential evolution of a virus rapidly made it clear that there was no time to waste as the coronavirus would have massive repercussions on the global economy. The integrated nature of Europe created a perfect place for the virus to infect thousands of people, to reveal the (political) vulnerabilities of the union, and to leave devastating economic damage behind. While policymakers were primarily focused on the health crisis during the initial phase, the economic impact of the lockdown was soon woven into the discussion as well. Especially with some European countries having the sovereign debt crisis still fresh in their memories, the outlook of yet another economic shock made people skeptical about the European Union's (EU) chances for survival.

While it is difficult to judge a response when the crisis is not even over yet, Europe has definitely made sure not to make the same mistakes twice. It has acted faster and more decisively during the COVID-19 pandemic, both on the national level and through its supranational institutions, compared to the financial and sovereign debt crises. Governments quickly announced lockdowns to slow down the spread of the virus and implemented comprehensive measures to preserve productive capacity and guarantee liquidity to individuals and firms. After an initial hesitance, European institutions leapt into the fray as well, starting with the European Central Bank and the European Commission, but also including the European Stability Mechanism and European Investment Bank. Lessons learned from the last crisis, such as how to use monetary policy instruments and financial regulation to strengthen the financial system and knit European markets together, faced their first stress test and showed positive results: sovereign debt markets have not disintegrated and the European banking sector is better equipped to deal with losses during the current crisis.

Despite these positive developments, the crisis revealed the deep divisions on whether the European response should be characterized by a more centralized or decentralized approach. Debates on debt mutualization through so-called coronabonds showed these opposing views at their extremes, resulting in provocative language from government officials, especially from the Netherlands. Many asked how the EU could call itself a union if it did not even show solidarity in a health emergency – a crisis that does not originate from fiscal irresponsibility or political malpractice.

But what might seem, at first sight, a lack of solidarity is largely a pragmatic choice driven by national politics. Such a national perspective is not necessarily bad: one has to take national developments into consideration when deciding on the role of the EU to avoid unintended consequences that could create political instability which would only worsen the crisis. The fact that all countries, including the 'frugal four', seem committed to finding a compromise that would help Europe's hardest-hit member states shows that there is some acknowledgment that the coronavirus-induced crisis is not the same as what Europe experienced in the Euro crisis. If not solidarity from the perspective of those most in need, there is at least a realistic understanding across the European Union of how the European recovery is dependent on all economies bouncing back, not just the Northern ones.

From policy to politics

Communicating this message and convincing citizens of the importance of the EU in this crisis nevertheless remains complicated. EU policymaking is too abstract and out of reach for many Europeans as they do not necessarily feel a direct link between decisions taken at the EU level and the impact of those decisions on their personal lives. From such a perspective, it is hard to explain how the technical monetary interventions or a potential increase in the budget of the Commission are helping Europeans in a personal sense. However, simply because it is a hard story to sell, does not mean that national politicians or the EU institutions themselves should not try to be better at it to enable people to draw their conclusions based on an informed opinion of the real merits of the EU.

For example, the ECB was arguably the most important actor in pulling Europe through the initial stages of the crisis – something that national politics did not stress enough. Despite tensions at the ECB already before the pandemic, its press conference on 12 March, and the ruling of the German Constitutional Court, the policies introduced by the Governing Council have stabilized financial markets and so made it possible for banks to lend to those who need credit. The ECB prevented a capital flight from Southern Europe, it secured the monetary transmission mechanism, provided much needed confidence to investors, and incentivized financial institutions to provide funding. Despite this vital support from the ECB, the overreliance on the ECB draws it into politically sensitive decisions and neglects the fact that the ECB by itself cannot solve the problems of governments, firms, and individuals. It is hard to explain the good the ECB does, but much easier to accuse it of doing bad.

Although the ECB has bought Europe much needed time, the crisis is far from over. A health crisis cannot simply be solved by bridge financing and regulatory forbearance. The many different properties and mutations of a virus make it an extremely difficult disease to eradicate or cure. So long as there are no vaccines or drugs, policymakers will have to continue to find a balance between medical concerns and economic damage resulting in an economy that does not operate at full capacity. The risk of more liquidity issues and insolvencies for individuals, companies, and even governments increases the longer the coronavirus lingers among us. Crucially, that risk is always going to be higher for the weaker and hardest-hit European countries.

Under these circumstances, Europe cannot continue to rely only on the ECB to solve these issues without pushing the ECB more and more into a politicized arena forcing the bank to make decisions a politically independent institution should not have to make. We can always question whether central bank independence is necessary and whether the role of the ECB has not already changed into an explicitly political one. What we cannot deny, however, is that the time has come for elected politicians to take responsibility for where Europe is headed.

The recovery phase and the prevention of insolvency problems come down to political decisions rather than economic or technical ones. Monetary policies can only do so much to incentivize the flow of money which means that ultimately fiscal measures are those that pull individuals and businesses through an economic shock. This implies yet another delicate balancing act that European leaders will have to make between centralizing fiscal responses through a European recovery plan with enough firepower while not exacerbating the political problems national governments have in their own countries.

Hanging together, not separately

As illustrated throughout the essays in this book, European countries each face their own unique political tensions despite all being faced with the same pandemic. Italy's sovereign debt and political instability continue to be extremely contentious issues. Spain has to cope with its weak health system, its fragile coalition, and its unemployment rate which is higher than anywhere else in Europe. France is trying to figure out what role it should play at the European level, combining self-interest with a conviction that fiscal integration would create a stronger European Union. And while the Netherlands strongly believes that loans and fiscal reform instead of grants and a bigger European budget should be the way forward, the Dutch government does want to help to bring the European economy back on track – keeping in the back of their head that whatever they will do will impact the outcome of the election in March 2021.

Accommodating all these various sentiments and interests at a European level has proven to be difficult. Finding a compromise that is fair and takes into account each other's concerns will demonstrate the extent to which the EU has become crisis-proof. It will also indicate whether Europe understands that the strength of the single market, with its free movement of goods, services, people and capital, depends on its members willing to commit to a level playing field and make up for the redistributive effects it has on different countries. Agreement on the recovery fund is a step in the right direction; successful ratification of that agreement will take the European Union even further; few should imagine, however, that this is the end of the story.

Countries less affected by the European response, such as the United Kingdom and Norway, have of course their own country-specific difficulties. However, analyzing these cases shows that fighting the coronacrisis alone is not easy for national governments either. For the UK, the economic fallout is expected to be just as bad or even worse than other European countries. On top of that, the economic impact of Brexit could soon make the situation even worse. The relatively late announcement of restrictive measures and unprepared health care services have also caused one of the highest death rates of the coronavirus in Europe.

Even Norway, a country which due to its sovereign wealth fund should be able to manage a crisis without too much difficulty proved to be vulnerable to the coronavirus. Although the oil fund provided means to finance fiscal policies, the fund was not able to prevent a severe economic shock to the Norwegian economy. Money alone is simply not enough to prevent the extensive repercussions of the pandemic.

For both countries inside and outside the European Union, muddling through, waiting, and hoping that the crisis will get better by itself, is unlikely ever to be a successful approach. Since no one can predict when the crisis will end, governments will have to be proactive. In the case of Europe, this means not only that governments will have to help individuals and companies which are more affected, but also that stronger governments will have to support the weaker ones to finance their way out of the crisis. Europe has made a first show of solidarity with the agreement on its recovery plan; hopefully there will be many more to follow.

REFERENCES

Acharya, Viral V., and Sascha Steffen (2015). 'The "greatest" carry trade ever? Understanding eurozone bank risks.' *Journal of Financial Economics* 115:2, pp. 215–236.

Acharya, Viral V., Tim Eisert, Christian Eufinger, and Christian Hirsch (2018). 'Real effects of the sovereign debt crisis in Europe: Evidence from syndicated loans.' *The Review of Financial Studies* 31:8, pp. 2855–2896.

Adema, Maaike (2008). 'Budgeting under expenditure rules in the Netherlands.' The Hague: Dutch Ministry of Finance, 10 July 2008.

AfD Kompakt (2020). 'Statt Corona-Bonds die Steuerzahler und Klein-/mittlere Unternehmen schützen.' (6 April 2020).

Agence France Trésor (2020). 'Une Prévision de Contraction du PIB De 8% en 2020.' Paris: Agence France Trésor, April.

Albertazzi, Ugo, Tiziano Ropele, Gabriele Sene, and Federico M. Signoretti (2014). 'The impact of the sovereign debt crisis on the activity of Italian banks.' *Journal of Banking & Finance* 46, pp. 387–402.

Allison, Graham (1971). *Essence of Decision: Explaining the Cuban Missile Crisis*. Boston: Little Brown, pp. 176.

Alsweilem, Khalid A., Angela Cummine, Malan Rietveld, Katherina Tweedie (2015). 'A comparative study of Sovereign investor models: Institutions and policies for managing sovereign wealth.' Discussion Paper, Belfer Center for Science and International Affairs and Center for International Development, Harvard Kennedy School.

Altavilla, Carlo, Lorenzo Burlon, Mariassunta Giannetti, and Sarah Holton (2019). 'Is there a zero lower bound? The effects of negative policy rates on banks and firms.' *Working Paper Series* No 2289 / June 2019. Frankfurt am Main: European Central Bank.

Al-Eyd, Ali, and Pelin Berkmen (2013). 'Fragmentation and monetary policy in the euro area.' *IMF Working Paper* 13:208. Washington D.C.: International Monetary Fund.

Alcidi, Cinzia, and Francesco Corti (2020). 'Will SURE shield EU workers from the corona crisis?' *Centre for European Policy Studies* (6 April 2020).

Amante, Angelo (2020). 'Italy's coronavirus epidemic began in January, study shows.' *Reuters* (24 April 2020).

AMECO (2020). 'Unemployment rate, total (percentage of civilian labour force); Member States: definition Eurostat (ZUTN).' *Unemployment Statistics*. Brussels: European Commission Economic and Financial Affairs.

Amnesty International (2018). 'Spain: Cruel austerity measures leave patients suffering.' *Amnesty News* (24 April 2018).

Anderson, Julia, Enrico Bergamini, Sybrand Brekelmans, Aliénor Cameron, Zsolt Darvas, Marta Domínguez Jíménez and Catarina Midões (2020). 'The fiscal response to the economic fallout from the coronavirus.' *Bruegel Datasets* (June 2020).

Andrade, Sandro C., and Vidhi Chhaochharia (2010). 'Information immobility and foreign portfolio investment.' *The Review of Financial Studies* 23:6, pp. 2429–2463.

Arnold, Martin (2019a). 'Lagarde hits out at Germany and Netherlands on public spending.' *Financial Times* (30 October 2019).

Arnold, Martin (2019b). 'Germany pulls back from recent overt criticism of ECB.' *Financial Times* (2 December 2019).

Arnold, Martin (2020). 'Eurozone banks warn of business lending crunch.' *Financial Times* (14 July 2020).

Arnold, Martin, and Javier Espinoza (2020). 'ECB pushes for eurozone bad bank to clean up soured loans.' *Financial Times* (19 April 2020).

Arrata, William, Benoît Nguyen, Imène Rahmouni-Rousseau, and Miklos Vari (2018). 'The Scarcity Effect of Quantitative Easing on Repo Rates: Evidence from the Euro Area.' *IMF Working Paper* 18:258. Washington D.C.: International Monetary Fund.

Attwood, James (2020). 'Coronavirus and the car world: Ferrari resumes production.' *Autocar* (5 May 2020).

Backer, Larry Catá (2009). 'Sovereign Wealth Funds as Regulatory Chameleons: The Norwegian Sovereign Wealth Funds and Public Global Governance Through Private Global Investment.' *Georgetown Journal of International Law* 41:2.

Badkar, Mamta, Philip Georgiadis, Myles McCormick, Sarah Provan, Georg Russell, Peter Wells, and Alice Woodhouse (2020). 'Coronavirus: 16 people test positive for coronavirus in Northern Italy – as it happened.' *Financial Times* (21 February 2020).

Baldo, Luca, Benoît Hallinger, Caspar Helmus, Niko Herrala, Débora Martins, Felix Mohing, Filippos Petroulakis, Marc Resinek, Olivier Vergote, Benoît Usciati, and Yizhou Wang (2017). 'The distribution of excess liquidity in the euro area.' *ECB Occasional Paper Series* No. 200 / November 2017. Frankfurt am Main: European Central Bank.

Balding, Christopher (2012). *Sovereign Wealth Funds: The New Intersection of Money and Politics.* Oxford: Oxford University Press.

Baldwin, Richard and Rebecca Freeman (2020). 'Supply chain contagion waves: Thinking ahead on manufacturing 'contagion and reinfection' from the COVID concussion.' *VoxEU Centre for Economic Policy Research* (1 April 2020).

Ballegeer, Daan and Joost van Kuppeveld (2020). 'Bankpresident Knot: politici moeten crisis aanpakken, niet achterom kijken.' *Het Financiële Dagblad* (March 2020).

Ballegeer, Daan and Han Dirk Hekking (2020). 'Een uitvinding van de duivel of manna voor het Zuiden?' *Het Financiële Dagblad* (April 2020).

Banca d'Italia (2020). 'The Italian Economy in brief.' *Number 2/2020.* Rome: Banca d'Italia, April 2020.

Bank of Spain (2017). 'Report on the financial and banking crisis in Spain, 2008–2014.' Madrid: Bank of Spain.

Battistini, Niccolò, Marco Pagano, and Saverio Simonelli (2014). 'Systemic risk, sovereign yields and bank exposures in the euro crisis.' *Economic Policy* 29:78, pp. 203–251.

Battistini, Niccolò and Grigor Stoevsky (2020) 'Alternative scenarios for the impact of the COVID-19 pandemic on economic activity in the euro area.' *ECB Economic Bulletin* Issue 3/2020. Frankfurt: European Central Bank, 1 May 2020.

Baudino, Patrizia, Jacopo Orlandi, and Raihan Zamil (2018). 'The identification and measurement of non-performing assets: a cross-country comparison.' *FSI Insights* No 7. Basel: Financial Stability Institute.

Bayer, Lili (2020). 'New factions emerge in EU recovery fund fight.' *Politico* (16 June 2020).

BBC (2020). "Hard Talk' with Sophie in 't Veld.' (May 2020).

Beblavy, Miroslav, and Ilaria Maselli (2014). 'An Unemployment Insurance Scheme for the Euro Area: A simulation exercise for two options.' *Centre for European Policy Studies Special Report 98*, pp. 1–70.

Beunderman, Mark (2017). 'Zuid-Europeanen vallen over 'drank en vrouwen'-uitspraak Dijsselbloem.' *NRC Handelsblad* (22 March 2017).

Bjork, Christopher, and David Roman (2012). 'Spanish Banks' Bad Omen.' *The Wall Street Journal* (18 April 2012).

Blanchard, Olivier J. and Lawrence H. Summers (2017). 'Rethinking Stabilization Policy: Evolution or Revolution?' *NBER Working Paper 24179.*

Blundell-Wignall, Adrian (2012). 'Solving the Financial and Sovereign Debt Crisis in Europe.' *OECD Journal: Financial Market Trends* 11:2.

Blyth, Mark (2013). *Austerity: The History of a Dangerous Idea.* New York: Oxford University Press.

Bouvet, Antoine, and Benjamin Schroeder (2020). 'ECB: Will it spend the 'envelope'?' ING (19 March 2020).

Brandolini, Andrea, Francesca Carta and Francesco D'Amuri (2016). 'A Feasible Unemployment-Based Shock Absorber for the Euro Area.' *Journal of Common Market Studies* 54:5, pp. 1123–1141.

Brouwers, Arnout (2020). Coalitie reageert verdeeld op Commissieplan, VVD wil 'solidaire leningen, verstandige hervormingen.' *De Volkskrant* (27 May 2020).

Brunsden, Jim and Sebastian Payne (2020). 'UK formally rejects Brexit transition extension.' *Financial Times* (13 June 2020).

Büchel, Konstantin (2013). 'Do words matter? The impact of communication on the PIIGS' CDS and bond yield spreads during Europe's sovereign debt crisis.' *European Journal of Political Economy* 32:C, pp. 412–431.

Bunn, Daniel (2020). 'Norway Opens the Fiscal Toolbox.' *Tax Foundation* (24 March 2020).

Buti, Marco, and Nicolas Carnot (2018). 'The case for a central fiscal capacity in EMU.' *VoxEU Centre for Economic Policy Research* (7 December 2018).

Canino, Iacopo, Gianluca Fanti, Ferigo Foscari, Leonardo Graffi, Michael Immordino, Andrea Novarese, Veronica Pinotti, Maria Cristina Storchi (2020). 'The "Cure Italy" and "Restore Liquidity" Decrees: Keeping Italian Companies Alive?' *White & Case* (10 April 2020).

Caracciolo, Giacomo , Federico Cingano, Valerio Ercolani, Giuseppe Ferrero, Fadi Hassan, Andrea Papetti, and Pietro Tommasino (2020). 'Covid-19 and Economic

Analysis: a Review of the Debate.' *Banca d'Italia Literature Review Issue no. 2.* Rome: Banca d'Italia.

Cardenas, Amalia (2013). 'The Spanish Savings Bank Crisis: History, Causes and Responses.' *IN3 Working Paper Series* 13:3. Barcelona: Universitat Oberta de Catalunya and Internet Interdisciplinary Institute.

Casert, Raf and Pan Pylas (2018). 'EU criticizes 'aggressive' tax practices of 7 member states.' *AP News* (7 March 2018).

Castaldi, Roberto (2020). 'Conte still 'cautious' on ESM but up to Italian parliament to decide activation.' (9 May 2020).

Carrión Álvarez, Miguel (2020). 'The ECB's response to the Covid-19 crisis.' *Funcas Europe.* (20 March 2020)

Centraal Bureau voor Statistiek (2013). 'Available household income 3.2 percent down in 2012.' Heerlen: CBS, 29 March 2013.

Centraal Bureau voor Statistiek (2015). 'Stand van zaken bezuinigingen bij CBS.' Heerlen: CBS.

Centraal Bureau voor Statistiek (2018). 'Dutch public debt now also below EMU target.' Heerlen: CBS, 28 March 2018.

Centraal Bureau voor Statistiek (2019). 'Nederland langs de Europese meetlat; 2019.' Heerlen: CBS, May 2019.

Centraal Bureau voor Statistiek (2020b). 'Grootste krimp consumptie huishoudens ooit gemeten.' *CBS Online News* (15 May 2020).

Centraal Bureau voor Statistiek (2020c). 'Consumptieradar; March–May 2020.' Heerlen: CBS, May.

Centraal Bureau voor Statistiek (2020d). 'Economie in laagconjunctuur.' Heerlen: CBS, May.

Centraal Bureau voor Statistiek (2020e). 'Exportradar.' March–May 2020.

Centraal Plan Bureau (2008). 'The Internal Market and the Dutch Economy: implications for trade and economic growth.' Den Haag: Centraal Plan Bureau, September 2008.

Chislett, William (2020). 'Spain in times of the coronavirus.' *El Cano Royal Institute* (27 March 2020).

Cingano, Federico, Francesco Manaresi, and Enrico Sette (2013). 'Does credit crunch investments down?' *The Review of Financial Studies* 29:10, pp. 2737–2773.

CNBC (2020). 'Italy supports coronavirus-hit economy, PM hails 'Italian model.' (16 March 2020).

Codogno, Lorenzo, Carlo Favero, and Alessandro Missale (2003). 'Yield spreads on EMU government bonds.' *Economic Policy* 18:37, pp. 503–532.

Collignon, Stefan (2004). 'Le fédéralisme budgétaire dans la zone euro.' In Maxime Lefebvre, ed. *Quel Budget européen à l'horizon 2013: Moyens et politiques d'une Union élargie.* Paris: Institut français des relations internationales, pp. 141–160.

Comfort, Nicholas, and Donal Griffin (2020). 'SocGen, Credit Agricole Boosted Risky Assets Before Crisis Hit.' *Bloomberg* (2 April 2020).

Cœuré, Benoît (2020). 'The effects of APP reinvestments on euro area bond markets.' Closing remarks at the ECB's Bond Market Contact Group meeting. Frankfurt am Main: European Central Bank, 12 Juni 2019.

Corradin, Stefano, and Angela Maddaloni (2017). 'The importance of being special: repo markets during the crisis.' *Working Paper Series* No. 2065. Frankfurt am Main: European Central Bank.

Corsetti, Giancarlo, and Aitor Erce (2019). 'Maturity, seniority and size: Make sure the ESM's pandemic crisis support is fit for purpose!' VoxEU Centre for Economic Policy Research (29 April 2020).

Council of the European Union (2020). 'COVID-19: Council adopts temporary support to mitigate unemployment risks in an emergency (SURE).' Brussels: Council of the European Union, 19 May 2020.

Cour-Thimann, Philippine, and Bernhard Winkler (2013). 'The ECB's non-standard monetary Policy measures, the role of institutional factors and financial structure.' *Working Paper Series* No. 1528. Frankfurt am Main: European Central Bank.

Creel, Jérôme, Fabien Labondance, and Sandrine Levasseur (2014). 'The French banking and financial system and the crisis.' Paris: Sciences Po, April.

Crofts, Dale (2020). 'Credit Agricole Sees Provision Surge as Bank Girds for Bad Loans.' *Bloomberg* (6 May 2020).

Daripa, Arup, Sandeep Kapur, and Stephen Wright (2013). 'Labour's Record on Financial Regulation.' *Oxford Review of Economic Policy* 29:1 (Spring), pp. 71–94.

Darvas, Zsolt, and David Pichler (2018). 'Excess Liquidity and Bank Lending Risks in the Euro Area.' *Monetary Dialogue September 2018. Policy Department for Economic, Scientific and Quality of Life Policies.* Brussels: European Parliament.

Darvas, Zsolt (2019). 'Who pays for the EU budget rebates and why?' *Bruegel* (4 December 2019).

Darvas, Zsolt (2020a). 'Having the cake, but slicing it differently: how is the grand EU recovery fund allocated?' *Bruegel* (23 July 2020).

Darvas, Zsolt (2020b). 'Three-quarters of Next Generation EU payments will have to wait until 2023.' *Bruegel* (10 June 2020).

Darvas, Zsolt (2020c). 'An uncompromising budget.' *Bruegel* (29 May 2020).

Davies, Pascale (2020). 'Coronavirus Threatens Spain with New Economic Crisis.' *Forbes* (5 April 2020).

De Cecco, Marcello (2007). 'Italy's dysfunctional political economy.' *West European Politics* 30:4, pp. 763–783.

De Guindos, Luis (2020). 'Europe's role in the global financial system.' Speech at the SUERF/De Nederlandsche Bank Conference 'Forging a new future between the UK and the EU' in Amsterdam, 8 January 2020.

De Guindos, Luis, and Isabel Schnabel (2020). 'Improving funding conditions for the real economy during the COVID-19 crisis: the ECB's collateral easing measures.' *The ECB Blog.* Frankfurt am Main: European Central Bank, 22 April 2020.

De Grauwe, Paul, and Wim Moesen (2009). 'Gains for All: A Proposal for a Common Euro Bond.' *Intereconomics* (May/June), pp. 132–135.

De Marco, Filippo (2019). 'Bank Lending and the European Sovereign Debt Crisis.' *Journal of Financial and Quantitative Analysis* 54:1, pp. 155–182.

De Miguel, Bernardo, Lluís Pellicer, and Carlos E. Cué (2020). 'El plan de choque europeo encalla por la resistencia de Alemania y Holanda.' *El País* (27 March 2020).

Demiralp, Selva, Jens Eisenschmidt, and Thomas Vlassopoulos (2019). 'Negative interest rates, excess liquidity and retail deposits: banks' reaction to unconventional monetary policy in the euro area.' *Working Paper Series* No 2283 / May 2019. Frankfurt am Main: European Central Bank.

Den Hartog, Tobias (2020). 'Rutte komt met eigen plan voor herstelfonds, hekelt plan van Merkel en Macron.' *Het Algemeen Dagblad* (20 May 2020).

De Hoon, Iven (2020). 'Is the Netherlands a tax haven?' *No More Tax.*

De Waard, Peter (2012). 'Als Nederland de EU verlaat.' *De Volkskrant* (26 May 2012).

Di Quirico, Roberto (2010). 'Italy and the Global Economic Crisis.', Bulletin of Italian Politics Vol. 2, University of Cagliari.

Doll, Mathias (2019). 'An Unemployment Re-Insurance Scheme for the Eurozone? Stabilizing and Redistributive Effects.' *EconPol Policy Report* 3:10, pp. 1–57.

Dombey, Daniel (2020a). 'Spain's economy set to suffer most from coronavirus crisis.' *Financial Times* (9 April 2020).

Dombey, Daniel (2020b). 'Political divisions deepen as Spain battles coronavirus.' *Financial Times* (2 April 2020).

Dombey, Daniel (2020c). 'Spain calls for €1.5tn EU recovery fund to "protect internal market".' *Financial Times* (21 April 2020).

Dombey, Daniel, Guy Chazan and Jim Brunsden (2020). 'Nine eurozone countries issue call for 'coronabonds'.' *Financial Times* (25 March 2020).

Dombret, Andreas (2013). 'The yin and yang of resolving the European sovereign debt crisis.' Speech presented at the Peterson Institute in Washington D.C., 17 October 2013.

Draghi, Mario (2012). 'Verbatim of the remarks made by Mario Draghi.' Speech presented at the Global Investment Conference in London, 26 July 2012.

Draghi, Mario (2019a). 'Press Conference.' Introductory Statement of the Press Conference on 12 September 2019. Frankfurt am Main: European Central Bank.

Draghi, Mario (2019b). 'Committee on Economic and Monetary Affairs.' Monetary dialogue with Mario Draghi. Brussels: European Central Bank, 23 September 2019.

Draghi, Mario (2019c). 'Press Conference.' Introductory Statement of the Press Conference on 24 November 2019. Frankfurt am Main: European Central Bank.

Drechsler, Itamar, Thomas Drechsel, David Marques-Ibanez, and Philipp Schnabl (2016). 'Who borrows from the lender of last resort?' *The Journal of Finance*, 71:5, pp. 1933–1974.

Dullien, Sebastian, and Daniela Schwarzer (2009). 'Bringing Macroeconomics into the EU Budget Debate: Why and How?' *Journal of Common Market Studies* 47:1, pp. 153–174.

Dullien, Sebastian, and Daniela Schwarzer (2011). 'Making Macroeconomic Stabilization Work: Lessons from the Crisis for the EU Budget Debate.' In Joachim Fritz-Vannahme and Armando García Schmidt, eds. *European Economic Governance: Impulses for Crisis Prevention and New Institutions.* Gütersloh: Bertelsmann Stiftung, pp. 93–118.

Dunford, Mick (1994). 'Winners and losers: The new map of economic inequality in the European Union.' *European Urban and Regional Studies* 1:2, pp. 95–114.

Dutch House of Representatives (2020). 'Antwoord op vragen van het lid Snels over de inzet van het ESM en Eurobonds.' The Hague: Tweede Kamer der Staten Generaal, 24 March 2020.

Economist Intelligence Unit (EIU) (2020). 'Industry Report: Financial Services, France.' London: The Economist Group, March.

Einar, Lie (2018). 'Learning by Failing.' *Scandinavian Journal of History* 43:2, pp. 284–299.

Eley, Jonathan (2020). 'Five ways coronavirus will change British retail.' *Financial Times* (1 May 2020).

Élysée Palace (2020). 'Initiative franco-allemande pour la relance européenne face à la crise du coronavirus.' 18 May 2020.

Encío, María (2018). 'European Money Markets.' Central Bank Seminar. Frankfurt am Main: European Central Bank, 12 July 2018.

Enderlein, Henrik, and Lucas Guttenberg (2020). 'Ausnahmeföderalismus als Dauerzustand.' *Wirtschaftsdienst* 100:6, pp. 400–404.

Erlanger, Steven (2020a). 'Coronavirus Has Lifted Leaders Everywhere. Don't Expect That to Last.' *The New York Times* (15 April 2020).

Erlanger, Steven (2020b). 'Merkel, Breaking German 'Taboo,' Backs Shared E.U. Debt to Tackle Virus.' *The New York Times* (18 May 2020).

European Banking Authority (2020). 'Guidelines on legislative and non-legislative moratoria on loan repayments applied in the light of the COVID-19 crisis.' Paris: European Banking Authority, 2 April 2020.

European Business Leaders' Convention (2020). 'EBLC Northern Light Online Summit 2020 – World Economy with Christine Lagarde.' European Business Leaders' Convention (26 June 2020).

European Central Bank (2013). 'Target Operations and Monetary Policy Operations.' *Monthly Bulletin*. Frankfurt am Main: European Central Bank, May 2013.

European Central Bank (2016). 'Recent developments in the composition and cost of bank funding in the euro area.' *Economic Bulletin* Issue 1 / 2016. pp. 26–45. Frankfurt am Main: European Central Bank.

European Central Bank (2017a). 'ECB (2017). 'The ECB's asset purchase programme and TARGET balances: monetary policy implementation and beyond.' *Economic Bulletin* Issue 5 / 2017. Frankfurt am Main: European Central Bank'. *Economic Bulletin* Issue 3 / 2017. Frankfurt am Main: European Central Bank.

European Central Bank (2017b). 'The ECB's asset purchase programme and TARGET balances: monetary policy implementation and beyond.' *Economic Bulletin* Issue 5 / 2017. Frankfurt am Main: European Central Bank.

European Central Bank (2019a). 'Macroeconomic projections for the euro area.' Frankfurt am Main: European Central Bank, 12 September 2019.

European Central Bank (2019b). 'Eurosystem staff macroeconomic projections for the euro area.' Frankfurt am Main: European Central Bank, 12 December 2019.

European Central Bank (2019c). 'ECB announces details of new targeted longer-term refinancing operations (TLTRO III).' *Press Release*. Frankfurt am Main: European Central Bank, 6 June 2019.

European Central Bank (2020a). 'ECB announces new pandemic emergency longer-term refinancing operations.' *Press Release*. Frankfurt: European Central Bank, 30 April 2020.

European Central Bank (2020b). 'ECB publishes supervisory banking statistics for the third quarter of 2019.' *Press Release.* Frankfurt: European Central Bank, 15 January 2020.

European Central Bank (2020c). 'ECB announces €750 billion Pandemic Emergency Purchase Programme (PEPP).' *Press Release.* Frankfurt: European Central Bank, 18 March 2020.

European Central Bank (2020d). 'Asset Purchase Programmes.' Frankfurt am Main: European Central Bank.

European Central Bank (2020e). 'Strategy Review.' Frankfurt am Main: European Central Bank.

European Central Bank (2020f). 'ECB Banking Supervision provides temporary capital and operational relief in response to coronavirus.' *Press Release.* Frankfurt am Main: ECB Banking Supervision, 12 March 2020.

European Central Bank (2020g). 'ECB provides further flexibility to banks in response to coronavirus.' *Press Release.* Frankfurt am Main: ECB Banking Supervision, 20 March 2020.

European Central Bank (2020h). 'ECB announces package of temporary collateral easing measures.' *Press Release.* Frankfurt am Main: European Central Bank, 07 April 2020.

European Central Bank (2020i). 'ECB provides temporary for capital requirements for market.' *Press Release.* Frankfurt am Main: ECB Banking Supervision, 16 April 2020.

European Central Bank (2020j). 'ECB takes steps to mitigate impact of possible rating downgrades on collateral availability.' *Press Release.* Frankfurt am Main: European Central Bank, 22 April 2020.

European Central Bank (2020k). 'Meeting of 11–12 March 2020 – Account of the monetary policy meeting of the Governing Council of the European Central Bank held in Frankfurt am Main on Wednesday and Thursday, 11–12 March 2020.' Monetary Policy Accounts, 09 April 2020.

European Central Bank (2020l). 'Meeting of 3–4 June 2020 – Account of the monetary policy meeting of the Governing Council of the European Central Bank held in Frankfurt am Main on Wednesday and Thursday, 3–4 June 2020.' Monetary Policy Accounts, 25 June 2020.

European Commission (2015). 'Proposal for a Regulation Of The European Parliament And Of The Council on the European Fund for Strategic Investments and amending Regulations (EU) No 1291/2013 and (EU) No 1316/2013.' Brussels: European Commission.

European Commission (2016). 'State of the Union 2016: Strengthening European Investments for jobs and growth.' Brussels: European Commission.

European Commission (2019). 'The EU budget at a glance.' Brussels: European Commission, May 2019.

European Commission (2020a). 'Spring 2020 Economic Forecast: A deep and uneven recession, an uncertain recovery.' Brussels: European Commission, 6 May 2020.

European Commission (2020b). 'Europe's moment: Repair and prepare for the Next Generation.' Press Release. Brussels: European Commission, 27 May 2020.

European Commission (2020c). 'The EU Budget Powering the Recovery Plan for Europe.' Brussels: European Commission, 27 May 2020.

European Commission (2020d). 'Country Report Spain 2020.' Brussels: European Commission, 26 February 2020.

European Commission (2020e). 'State aid: Commission approves French schemes to support economy in Coronavirus outbreak.' Brussels: European Commission, 21 March 2020.

European Commission (2020f). 'Commission Interpretative Communication on the application of the accounting and prudential frameworks to facilitate EU bank lending.' Brussels: European Commission, 28 April 2020.

European Commission (2020g). 'Proposal for a Council Regulation on the establishment of a European instrument for temporary support to mitigate unemployment risks in an emergency (SURE) following the COVID-19 outbreak.' Brussels: European Commission, 2 April 2020.

European Commission (2020h). 'Commission Work Programme 2020.' Brussels: European Commission, 29 January 2020.

European Commission (2020i). 'Coordinated economic response to the COVID-19 Outbreak.' Brussels: European Commission, 13 March 2020.

European Commission (2020j). 'Investor Presentation.' Brussels: European Commission, May 2020.

European Commission (n.d.-a). 'Stability and Growth Pact, the Preventive Arm.'

European Commission (n.d.-b). 'Medium-Term Budgetary Objectives (MTOs).' Brussels: European Commission.

European Council (2020a). 'COVID-19 coronavirus outbreak and the EU's response.'

European Council (2020b). 'Assessment of public debt sustainability and COVID-related financing needs of euro area Member States.' Brussels: Eurogroup, May.

European Council (2020c). 'Video conference of the members of the European Council, 26 March 2020.' Brussels: European Council.

European Council (2020d). 'Joint statement of the Members of the European Council.' Brussels: European Council, 26 March 2020.

European Council (2020e), 'Report on the comprehensive economic policy response to the COVID-19 pandemic.' Brussels: European Council, 9 April 2020.

European Investment Bank (2020a). 'Facts and figures.' Kirchberg: European Investment Bank.

European Investment Bank (2020b). 'EIB Group will rapidly mobilise up to EUR 40 billion to fight crisis caused by Covid-19 and calls on Member States to set up a further guarantee for SME and mid-cap support from EIB Group and national promotional banks.' Kirchberg: European Investment Bank.

European Investment Bank (2020c). 'EIB Group establishes EUR 25 billion guarantee fund to deploy new investments in response to COVID-19 crisis.' Kirchberg: European Investment Bank.

European Stability Mechanism (2019). 'Safeguarding the Euro in times of Crisis: The inside story of the ESM.' Luxembourg: Publications Office of the European Union. pp. 213–228.

European Stability Mechanism (2020a). 'Transcript of remarks by ESM Managing Director Klaus Regling video press conference after Eurogroup meeting 9 April 2020.' Luxembourg City: European Stability Mechanism.

European Stability Mechanism (2020b). 'Klaus Regling in interview with Corriere della Sera (Italy).' Interview with Federico Fubini published in Corriere della Sera on 19 April 2020. Luxembourg City: European Stability Mechanism.

European Union (2007). *Treaty of the Functioning of the European Union,* Part Six Institutional and Financial Provisions, Title I Institutional Provisions, Chapter 1 The Institutions, Section 6 The European Central Bank, Article 282.2, Consolidated versions of the *Treaty on European Union and the Treaty on the Functioning of the European Union,* 13 December 2007.

Europa Nu (2005). 'Referendum over EU-grondwet in Nederland.' (1 June 2005).

Europa Nu (2020a). 'De Nederlandse burger en de EU.'

Europa Nu (2020b). 'Forum voor Democratie.'

Europa Nu (2020c). 'Europees Herstelfonds uit de coronacrisis.'

Eurostat (2008). 'Euro area unemployment stable at 7.2%.' *Euroindicators 3/2008.* Luxembourg: Eurostat, 31 January 2008.

Eurostat (2014). 'Euro area unemployment at 11.5%.' *Euroindicators 180/2014.* Luxembourg: Eurostat, 24 November 2014.

Eurostat (2020a). 'Real GDP growth rate – volume.' *Eurostat Data Browser.* Luxembourg: Eurostat.

Eurostat (2020b). 'How usual is it to work from home?' Luxembourg: Eurostat, 24 April 2020.

Ewing, Jack (2020). 'Some Countries Are Better Armored for Epidemics Than Others.' *The New York Times* (19 March 2020).

Ferdinandusse, Marien, Maximilian Freier and Annukka Ristiniemi. (2020). 'Quantitative easing and the price-liquidity trade-off.' *Working Paper Series* No 2399 / May 2020. Frankfurt am Main: European Central Bank

Financial Times (2019). 'Backlash against the ECB stimulus is misplaced.' (17 September 2019).

Fitch Ratings (2020). 'Fitch Downgrades Italy to 'BBB-'; Outlook Stable.' (28 April 2020).

Fitch Solutions (2020). 'Covid-19 To Heavily Weigh On French Banking Sector Profits.' Country Risk & Industry Research. London: Fitch Solutions Group Ltd.

Fleming, Sam, and Mehreen Khan (2020a). 'A bluffer's guide to the EU's coronavirus response.' *Financial Times* (23 April 2020).

Fleming, Sam, and Mehreen Khan (2020b). 'EU fails to settle rifts over size and shape of "recovery fund".' *Financial Times* (24 April 2020).

Fonte, Giuseppe, and Angelo Amante (2020). 'UPDATE 1-EU bailout fund opens rift in Italy's coalition, PM calls for calm.' *Reuters* (April 14 2020).

Federal Reserve Economic Data (2020). 'Registered Unemployment Rate for Norway.' *Federal Reserve Bank of St. Louis* (12 June 2020).

Fredriksson, Olle, and Niklas Frykström (2019). '"Bad loans" and their effects on banks and financial stability.' Stockholm: Sveriges Riksbank.

Frijters, Serena, Xander and van Uffelen (2019). 'Hier komen de EU-euro's in Nederland terecht.' *De Volkskrant* (14 May 2019).

Furman, Jason (2016). 'The New View of fiscal policy and its application.' *VoxEU Centre for Economic Policy Research* (2 November 2016).

Gabor, Daniela (2012). 'The Power of Collateral: The ECB and Bank Funding Strategies in Crisis.' *SSRN* (19 May 2012).

Gade, Thomas, Marion Salines, Gabriel Glöckler, and Steffen Strodthoff (2013). 'Loose Lips Sinking Markets?: The Impact of Political Communication on Sovereign Bond Spreads.' *ECB Occasional Paper Series* No. 150. Frankfurt am Main: European Central Bank.

Giugliano, Ferdinando (2020a). 'Christine Lagarde Has a Troubling Ambition.' *Bloomberg* (19 February 2020).

Giugliano, Ferdinando (2020b). 'How the ECB Can Fight the Coronavirus Crisis.' *Bloomberg Opinion* (3 March 2020).

Gouett, Matt (2013). 'Sovereign Wealth Failure?' *OpenCanada* (4 December 2013).

Government of Norway (2020). 'The Government acts to mitigate effects of the COVID-19 pandemic on the economy.' Oslo: Government of Norway, 13 March 2020.

Grande, Giuseppe, Sergio Masciantonio, and Andrea Tiseno (2013). 'The elasticity of demand for sovereign debt. Evidence from OECD Countries (1995–2011)'. The sovereign debt crisis and the euro area. Rome: Banca d'Italia.

Griffin, Donal (2020). 'BNP Paribas Stock Trades Lost About $200 Million in Virus Rout.' *Bloomberg* (9 April 2020).

Gros, Daniel, and Stefano Micossi (2008). 'A Call for a European Financial Stability Fund.' *VoxEU Centre for Economic Policy Research* (30 October 2008).

Gros, Daniel, and Willem Pieter De Groen (2015). 'The Single Resolution Fund: How much is needed.' *VoxEU Centre for Economic Policy Research* (15 December 2015).

Gros, Daniel (2019). 'Who holds Italian government debt? A Primer.' *Centre for European Policy Studies (CEPS)* (June 2019).

Gros, Daniel (2020). 'EU solidarity in exceptional times: Corona transfers instead of Coronabonds.' *VoxEU Centre for Economic Policy Research* (5 April 2020).

Grüll, Philipp (2020). "Frugal Four' present counter-plan to Macron-Merkel EU recovery scheme.' *Euractiv* (24 May 2020).

Hackenbroich, Jonathan (2020). 'How Germany's Constitutional Court jump-started the Franco-German engine.' *European Council on Foreign Relations* (22 May 2020).

Hall, Ben, and Martin Arnold (2020).'Lagarde urges eurozone to launch joint fiscal stimulus.' *Financial Times* (8 May 2020).

Hallerberg, Mark (2013). 'Why is there Fiscal Capacity but Little Regulation in the US, but Regulation and Little Fiscal Capacity in the EU? The Global Financial Crisis as a Test Case.' In Philipp Genschel and Markus Jachtenfuchs, eds. *Beyond the Regulatory Polity?: The European Integration of Core State Powers.* Oxford: Oxford University Press, pp. 87–104.

Hernàndez-Morales, Aitor (2020). 'Spain goes into lockdown.' *Politico* (14 March 2020).

Herszenhorn, David, Jacopo Barigazzi, and Maïa de la Baume (2020). 'In budget summit, EU leaders live up to low expectations.' *Politico* (19 June 2020).

Hirsch, Cornelius (2020). Europe's coronavirus lockdown measures compared.' *Politico* (31 March 2020).

Hoekstra, Wopke and Stef Blok (June 2020). 'Kamerbrief over Kabinetsappreciatie Commissievoorstellen MFK 2021–27 en herstelstrategie COVID-19 uitbraak.' Letter to the Dutch Parliament, 9 June 2020.

Holter, Mikael (2020). 'Norway Delivers Shock Rate Cut to 0% Amid Worst Slump Since WWII.' *Bloomberg* (7 May 2020).

Horowitz, Jason (2020). 'Italy Announces Restrictions Over Entire Country in Attempt to Halt Coronavirus.' *The New York Times* (9 March 2020).

Horvath, Roman (2018). 'Financial market fragmentation and monetary transmission in the euro area: what do we know?' *Journal of Economic Policy Reform* 21:4, pp. 319–334.

Howarth, David, and Lucia Quaglia (2013). 'Banking Union as Holy Grail: Rebuilding the Single Market in Financial Services, Stabilizing Europe's Banks and 'Completing' Economic and Monetary Union.' *Journal of Common Market Studies* 2013 Vol 51 Annual Review, pp. 103–123.

Howarth, David (2013). 'State Intervention and Market-Based Banking in France.' In Iain Hardie and David Howarth, eds. *Market-Based Banking and the International Financial Crisis*. Oxford: Oxford University Press, pp. 128–150.

Hüther, Michael, Moritz Schularick, Jens Südekum, Christoph Trebesch, Gabriel Felbermayr, Sebastian Dullien, Peter Bofinger (2020). 'Europa muss jetzt finanziell zusammenstehen.' *Frankfurter Allgemeine* (21 March 2020).

Inman, Robert P., and Daniel L. Rubinfeld (1997). 'Rethinking Federalism.' *Journal of Economic Perspectives* 11:4, pp. 43–64.

International Capital Market Association (2020a). 'COVID-19 Market Updates: Monetary policy.' Zurich: International Capital Market Association.

International Capital Market Association (2020b). 'What happens to repo transactions when interest rates go negative?.' Zurich: International Capital Market Association.

International Monetary Fund (2019). 'France – Financial System Stability Assessment.' *IMF Country Report* 19:241. Washington D.C.: IMF, July.

International Monetary Fund (2020a). 'Fiscal Monitor, April 2020. Chapter 1 : Policies to Support People During the COVID-19 Pandemic.' Washington D.C.: The International Monetary Fund.

International Monetary Fund (2020b). 'World Economic Outlook, April 2020: The Great Lockdown.' Washington D.C.: The International Monetary Fund.

Istat (2020). 'Retail Trade.' Press Release. Rome: Istituto Nazionale di Statistica, 7 May.

INSEE (2020). 'Economic outlook – 23 April 2020.' Paris: Institut national de la statistique et des études économiques, April 2020.

Jabko, Nicolas (2015). 'The Elusive Economic Government and the Forgotten Fiscal Union.' In Matthias Matthijs and Mark Blyth, eds. *The Future of the Euro*. New York: Oxford University Press, pp. 70–89.

Janning, Josef (2019). 'Dutch courage: is the Netherlands overconfident in its EU influence?' *The European Council on Foreign Relations* (30 January 2019).

Janse, Kalin Anev (2020a). 'Funding health and stability.' European Stability Mechanism (28 April 2020).

Janse, Kalin Anev (2020b). 'Out of the Box: A new ESM for a new crisis.' European Stability Mechanism (03 June 2020).

Jones, Erik (2010). 'A Eurobond Proposal to Promote Stability and Liquidity while Preventing Moral Hazard.' *Istituto per gli studi di politica internazionale (ISPI) Policy Brief* No 180, March 2010.

Jones, Erik (2012). 'Italy's Sovereign Debt Crisis.' London: Survival: Global Politics and Strategy.

Jones, Erik, and Gregory W. Fuller (2015). 'European macroeconomic governance.' In Sonia Mazey and Jeremy Richardson, eds. *European Union: Power and Policy-Making.* London, New York: Routledge, pp. 327–349.

Jones, Erik (2017). 'The "eurobond" proposal: A challenging path towards integration.' *Funcas Spanish and International Economic & Financial Outlook (SEFO)* 6:5, (October 2017).

Jones, Erik (2019a). 'Christine Lagarde's Hardest Task Isn't In Her Job Description.' *Foreign Affairs* (5 November 2019).

Jones, Erik (2019b). 'Do central bankers dream of political union? From epistemic community to common identity.' *Comparative European Politics* 17:4, pp. 530–547.

Jones, Erik (2019c). 'A feasibility check on core elements needed for "orderly" sovereign debt restructuring and/or debt mutualisation in the Euro Area.' Brussels: European Parliament, May 2019.

Jones, Gavin (2020). 'Italy government wins Senate confidence vote on decree to help virus-hit economy.' *Reuters* (9 April 2020).

Kapoor, Sony (2017). 'How Not to Run a Sovereign Wealth Fund.' *Bloomberg* (3 December 2017).

Karnitschnig, Matthew (2020). 'What Merkel wants.' *Politico* (25 June 2020).

Kennedy, Simon, and Michelle Jamrisko (2020). 'V, L or 'Nike Swoosh'? Economists Debate Shape of Global Recovery.' *Bloomberg* (2 April 2020).

Khan, Mehreen, and Sam Fleming (2020). 'Brussels weighs up politics of suing Germany over Karlsruhe.' *Financial Times* (11 May 2020).

Knoema (2018). 'Contribution of travel and tourism to GDP as a share of GDP.' World Data Atlas, consulted for Italy, Spain and The Netherlands.

Krugman, Paul (2020). 'The Case for Permanent Stimulus (Wonkish).' *The New York Times* (7 March 2020).

Lagarde, Christine (2019a). 'Hearing at the Committee on Economic and Monetary Affairs of the European Parliament.' Introductory statement at the ECON committee of the European Parliament. Brussels: European Parliament, 2 December 2019.

Lagarde, Christine (2019b). 'Press Conference.' Introductory Statement of the Press Conference on 12 December 2019. Frankfurt am Main: European Central Bank.

Lagarde, Christine (2020). 'Press Conference.' Introductory Statement of the Press Conference on 23 January 2020. Frankfurt am Main: European Central Bank.

Lagarde, Christine, and Luis de Guindos (2020a). 'Press Conference.' Introductory Statement of the Press Conference on 12 March 2020. Frankfurt am Main: European Central Bank.

Lagarde, Christine, and Luis de Guindos (2020b). 'Press Conference.' Introductory Statement of the Press Conference on 30 April 2020. Frankfurt am Main: European Central Bank.

Lagarde, Christine, and Luis de Guindos (2020c). 'Press Conference.' Introductory Statement of the Press Conference on 04 June 2020. Frankfurt am Main: European Central Bank.

Landais, Camille, and Giulia Giupponi (2020). 'Building effective short-time work schemes for the COVID-19 crisis. *VoxEU Centre for Economic Policy Research* (1 April 2020).

Landauro, Inti, and Jesus Aguado, and Belen Carreno (2020). 'Spain approves 200 billion euro aid package for coronavirus crisis: PM.' *Reuters* (17 March 2020).

Lane, Philip R. (2020). 'The monetary policy response to the pandemic emergency.' *The ECB Blog*. Frankfurt am Main: European Central Bank, 1 May 2020.

Lachmann, Desmond (2020). 'The coronavirus could create a massive EU debt crisis (think Italy).' *American Enterprise Institute* (25 March 2020).

Ladurner, Ulrich (2020). 'Dann lieber ganz allein.' *Die Zeit* (13 May 2020).

Laurent, Lionel (2020). 'French Faith in Macron Hangs by a Mask Thread.' *Bloomberg* (20 April 2020).

Long, Katherine (2020). 'European banks likely to be hardest hit by pandemic are in Spain and Italy.' *Leasing Life* (20 April 2020)

Macron, Emmanuel (2017). 'Speech on New Initiative for Europe.' Paris: Élysée.

Mallet, Victor, and Miles Johnson (2012). 'The bank that broke Spain.' *Financial Times* (21 June 2012).

Mallet, Victor, and Roula Khalaf (2020). Macron warns EU unraveling unless it embraces financial solidarity.' *Financial Times* (16 April 2020).

Manceaux, Julien (2020). 'France: historic jump in unemployment claims.' *Economic and Financial Analysis THINK ING* (27 April 2020).

Marro, Enrico (2020). 'Mes, pronti 36 miliardi per la sanità. Ma serve il voto del Parlamento.' *Corriere della Sera* (8 May 2020).

Massoc, Elsa, Nicolas Jabko (2012). 'French capitalism under stress: How Nicolas Sarkozy rescued the banks.' *Review of International Political Economy* 19:4, pp. 562–585.

Matthijs, Matthias (2020). 'The Right Way to Fix the EU, Put Politics Before Economics.' *Foreign Affairs* (May/June 2020).

Mayordomo, Sergio, María Abascalb, Tatiana Alonsob, and Maria Rodriguez-Morenol (2015). 'Fragmentation in the European interbank market: Measures, determinants, and policy solutions.' *Journal of Financial Stability* 16, pp. 1–12.

McCaul, Elizabeth (2020). 'A pragmatic SREP delivers appropriate supervision for the crisis.' The Supervision Blog (12 May 2020). Frankfurt am Main: European Central Bank.

McMurtry, Alyssa (2020). 'Spain: Virus deaths, infections, job losses see uptick.' Anadolu Agency (5 May 2020).

Mercuri, Gianluca (2020). 'Perché Germania e Olanda sono contro i coronabond? Proviamo a capirlo (e a ricapitolare tutto).' *Corriere Della Sera* (8 April 2020).

Mertens, Daniel, and Matthias Thiemann (2019). 'Building a hidden investment state? The European Investment Bank, national development banks and European economic governance.' *Journal of European Public Policy* 26:1, pp. 23–43.

Messia, Hada, and Matthew Chance, Matthew (2011). 'Mario Monti nominated to replace Berlusconi.' *CNN* (14 November 2011).

Michel, Charles (2020). 'Conclusions of the President of the European Council.' Brussels: European Council, 23 April.

Milne, Richard (2020a). 'Norway's central bank risks undermining trust in $1tn oil fund.' *Financial Times* (11 May 2020).

Milne, Richard (2020b). 'Spotlight falls on top trio at Norway's oil fund.' *Financial Times* (26 April 2020).

Milne, Richard (2020c). 'Norway bank chief warns on politicising wealth fund.' *Financial Times* (13 February 2020).

Milne, Richard (2020d). 'Norway considers action to break 'extraordinary' krone slide.' *Financial Times* (13 February 2020).

Minder, Raphael (2020). 'Pedro Sánchez Will Lead Modern Spain's First Coalition Government.' *The New York Times* (7 January 2020).

Ministère du Travail (2020). 'Situation du chômage au premier trimestre 2020.' Press Release. Paris: Ministère du Travail, May.

Ministero dell'Economia e delle Finanze (2019). 'Update of the Economic and Financial Document 2019.' Rome: Ministero dell'economia e delle finanze

Ministero dell'Economia e delle Finanze (2020). 'La moratoria per microimprese e Pmi, cosa c'è da sapere.' (22 March 2020).

Momigliano, Anna, and Elisabetta Povoledo (2019). 'Italy's Leader Wins Confidence Vote After Denouncing Populist Rhetoric.' *The New York Times* (9 September 2019).

Misérus, Mark (2020). 'Waar haalt Nederland al die steunmiljarden vandaan?' *De Volkskrant* (18 March 2020).

Magyar Nemzeti Bank (2020). 'The moratorium on instalment payments of loans assists debtors, thereby maintaining financial stability.' Budapest: Magyar Nemzeti Bank.

Motta, Massimo, and Martin Peltz (2020). 'The EU recovery fund: An opportunity for change.' *VoxEU Centre for Economic Policy Research* (30 April 2020).

Müller, Klaus (2020). 'EU-27 support for national short-time work schemes.' European Parliament At a glance. Brussels: European Parliament, April 2020.

Nauta, Lize, and Nic Vrieselaar (2020). 'The Netherlands: Coronavirus to halve economic growth.' Economic Quarterly Report Rabobank (12 March 2020).

Nikolaeva, Maya (2020). 'Moody's says coronavirus is negative for credit ratings of French banks.' *Reuters* (19 March 2020).

Norges Bank Investment Management (2020a). 'About the Fund.' Oslo: Norges Bank Investment Management.

Norges Bank Investment Management (2020b). 'Fund History.' Oslo: Norges Bank Investment Management.

Norges Bank Investment Management (2020c). 'Annual Return by asset class' Oslo: Norges Bank Investment Management.

Nederlandse Omroep Stichting (2020).'Miljardenpakket voor corona-gedupeerden: wat zit erin voor mijn bedrijf?' *NOS Nieuws* (17 March 2020).

Oates, Wallace E. (1999). 'An Essay on Fiscal Federalism.' *Journal of Economic Literature* 37:3, pp. 1120–1149.

Obstfeld, Maurice, and Kenneth Rogoff (2009). 'Global Imbalances and the Financial Crisis: Products of Common Causes.' Paper presented at the 2009 Federal Reserve Bank of San Francisco Asia Economic Policy Conference.

OECD (2019a). 'OECD Economic Surveys Italy.' Paris: Organization for Economic Co-operation and Development, April 2019.

OECD (2019b). 'Value added by activity.' *OECD National Accounts Statistics: National Accounts at a Glance.* Paris: Organization for Economic Cooperation and Development.

OECD (2019c). 'OECD SME and Entrepreneurship Outlook 2019.' *OECD Policy Highlights.* Paris: Organization for Economic Cooperation and Development, 20 May 2019.

OECD (2020a). 'OECD Economic Outlook.' Paris: Organization for Economic Cooperation and Development, 10 June 2020.

OECD (2020b). 'OECD Tourism Trends and Policies 2020.' Paris: Organization for Economic Cooperation and Development.

Office for National Statistics (2020). 'Output in the Construction Industry.' Newport: Office for National Statistics, April.

Oomkes, Lex (2004). 'Euroscepsis onder Nederlandse kiezers.' *Trouw* (11 June 2004).

Oxfam International (2013). 'The true cost of austerity and inequality. The Netherlands case study.' (September 2013).

Oxfam International (2020). 'Once again, the EU lets tax havens off the hook.' (18 February 2020).

Paqué, Karl-Heinz (2020). 'Italy's insistence on Eurobonds is dividing Europe.' *Alliance of Liberals and Democrats for Europe* (20 April 2020).

Parker, George, and Jim Brunsden (2020a). 'Britain and the EU revisit familiar misunderstandings on Brexit.' *Financial Times* (27 April 2020).

Parker, George, and Jim Brunsden (2020b) 'Boris Johnson and EU pledge renewed vigour in trade talks.' *Financial Times* (15 June 2020).

Partridge, Joanna (2020). 'New car sales in UK plunge by 44% as coronavirus bites.' *The Guardian* (6 April 2020).

Paternoster, Dario, and Dražen Rakić (2019). 'The European Investment Bank.' Brussels: European Parliament, May 2019.

Patrick, Margot, and Pietro Lombardi (2020). 'Société Générale Posts Surprise Loss as Bad-Loan Charges Surge.' *The Wall Street Journal* (30 April 2020).

Perrone, Manuela, and Gianni Trovato (2020). 'Scontro Conte-Pd-M5S sul Mes, governo diviso. Il premier: all'Italia non serve.' *Il Sole 24 Ore* (11 April 2020).

Picketty, Thomas (2020). *Capital and Ideology* (trans. Arthur Goldhammer). Cambridge, MA: Harvard, 2020.

Peilingwijzer (2020). Op basis van peilingen I&O Research, Ipsos en Kantar. June 2020

Pisano, Gary. P, Raffaellla Sadun, and Michele Zanini (2020). 'Lessons from Italy's Response to Coronavirus.' *Harvard Business Review* (27 March 2020).

Politico (2020). 'Poll of Polls.'
Pope, Stephen (2020). 'The ECB Wants To Hear From The Public; Will Lagarde Listen?' *Forbes* (24 February 2020).
Posanar, Joshua (2020). 'Germany offers unlimited help to keep coronavirus-battered economy afloat.' *Politico* (13 March 2020).
Powell, Jerome H. (2020). 'Speech: Current Economic Issues.' Washington D.C.: Peterson Institute for International Economics, 13 April 2020.
Presse- und Informationsamt der Bundesregierung (2020). 'A French-German Initiative for the European Recovery from the Coronavirus Crisis.' *Pressemitteilung 173/20.* Berling: Presse- und Informationsamt der Bundesregierung, 18 May 2020.
Prins, Carlijn, and Ester Barendregt (2020). 'Nederland: krimp in eerste kwartaal, maar minder sterk dan in buurlanden.' *RaboResearch – Economisch Onderzoe*k (15 May 2020).
Purps, Kornelius (2017). 'The best way to track ECB rate-hike expectations.' *Economics & FI/FX Research. Rates Perspectives* No. 26. Milan: UniCredit, 27 April 2017.
Quatremer, Jean (2020). 'L'Union rhabillé de la dette aux pieds.' *Libération* (30 Mai 2020).
Qvigstad, Jan F. (2009). 'Jan F Qvigstad: The global economic crisis and its impact on Sovereign Wealth Funds – the example of Norway.' Speech by Mr Jan F Qvigstad, Deputy Governor of Norges Bank (Central Bank of Norway), at a meeting for financial sector representatives in Geneva hosted by the Royal Norwegian Embassy, Geneva (11 May 2009).
Ramos, Ana B., and Christina Castro (2020). 'Madrid suspende las clases en centros públicos y privados y el Gobierno recomienda el teletrabajo.' *El Independiente* (9 March 2020).
Ranasinghe, Dhara (2020). 'Italian bond yields pull back from highs after report of Bank of Italy buying BTPs.' *Reuters* (18 March 2020).
Randow, Jana (2020). 'ECB's Jens Weidmann Signals Openness to Tweaking Inflation Goal.' *Bloomberg* (3 February 2020).
Rankin, Jennifer (2020). 'EU leaders clash over economic response to coronavirus crisis.' *The Guardian* (26 March 2020).
Redeker, Nils, and Natascha Hainbach (2020). 'Flattening the Recession Curve Comparing: Initial Fiscal Responses to the Corona Crisis Across the EU.' Hertie School Jacques Delors Centre Policy Paper, 9 April 2020.
Regan, Aidan et al. (2020). 'Letter: It is time for Brussels to launch a eurobond.' *Financial Times* (23 March 2020).
Rijksoverheid (2012). 'Wetsvoorstel Wet verhoging AOW- en pensioenrichtleeftijd.' 5 June 2012.
Rijksoverheid (2020a). 'Kabinet zet financiële steun klaar voor KLM.' 24 April 2020.
Rijksoverheid (2020b). 'Steunmaatregelen kabinet helpen ruim 2 miljoen mensen.' 1 May 2020.
Rijksoverheid (2020c). 'Coronavirus: verruimde BMKB-regeling voor ondernemers versneld open.' 15 March 2020.
Rijksoverheid (2020d). 'Coronavirus: kabinet neemt pakket nieuwe maatregelen voor banen en economie.' 17 March 2020.
Rijksoverheid (2020e). 'Coronavirus: financiële maatregelen.' March 2020.

Rijksoverheid (2020f). 'Coronavirus: pakket nieuwe maatregelen voor banen en economie.' March 2020.

Rijksoverheid (2020g). 'Coronavirus: verlenging en uitbreiding noodpakket banen en economie.' Bijlage 1: Overzicht Noodmaatregelen. Rijksoverheid, 20 May 2020.

Ritz, Robert A., and Ansgar Walther (2015). 'How do banks respond to increased funding uncertainty?' *Journal of Financial Intermediation* 24:3, pp. 386–410.

Romei, Valentina (2020a). 'Most UK businesses unsure they can survive coronavirus, survey shows.' *Financial Times* (9 April 2020).

Romei, Valentina (2020b). 'Coronavirus pandemic deals heavy blow to UK construction activity.' *Financial Times* (6 April 2020).

Rooijers, Eva, and Marcel de Boer (2020). 'Banken krijgen EURO 200 mrd extra kredietruimte van DNB vanwege coronavirus.' *Het Financiële Dagblad* (2020).

Rottinghuis, Kees (2020). 'Drie maanden corona in Nederland, een overzicht van de maatregelen.' *NRC Handelsblad* (22 April 2020).

Royo, Sebastian (2013a). Lessons from the Economic Crisis in Spain. Basingstoke: Palgrave. Chapter 6.

Royo, Sebastian (2013b). 'A "Ship in Trouble": The Spanish Banking System and the International Financial Crisis.' In Iain Hardie and David Howarth, eds. *Market-Based Banking and the International Financial Crisis*. Oxford: Oxford University Press, pp. 151–178.

Ruscher, Eric, and Borek Vašíček (2016). 'Revisiting the real interest rate mechanism.' *Quarterly Report on the Euro Area* (QREA) 14:4, pp. 33–48.

Salzano, Giovanni, Demetrios Pogkas, and Ben Sills (2019). 'Why Italy's Debts Are Europe's Big Problem.' *Bloomberg* (4 February 2019).

Sánchez Nicolás, Elena (2020a). 'Italy and Spain: worst – or just first?' *euobserver* (31 March 2020).

Sánchez Nicolás, Elena (2020b). 'Spain poised for first coalition since Franco' *euobserver* (7 January 2020).

Scazzieri, Luigi (2020). 'Trouble for the EU is brewing in coronavirus-hit Italy.' *Centre for European Reform* (2 April 2020).

Schelkle, Waltraud (2013). 'Fiscal Integration by Default.' In Philipp Genschel and Markus Jachtenfuchs, eds. *Beyond the Regulatory Polity?: The European Integration of Core State Powers*. Oxford: Oxford University Press, pp. 105–123.

Schuknecht, Ludger, Jürgen Von Hagen, and Guido Wolswijk (2009). 'Government risk premiums in the bond market: EMU and Canada.' *European Journal of Political Economy* 25:3, pp. 371–384.

Segreti, Giulia (2020). 'ECB ready to do more for coronavirus emergency if needed, Visco tells paper.' *Reuters* (23 March 2020).

SEI, IISD, ODI, Climate Analytics, CICERO, and UNEP (2019). 'The Production Gap: The discrepancy between countries' planned fossil fuel production and global production levels consistent with limiting warming to 1.5°C or 2°C.'

Sheppard, David (2020). 'Norway to cut oil production by 13%.' *Financial Times* (29 April 2020).

Sloat, Amanda (2020). 'Brexit is not immune to coronavirus.' *Brookings Institutions* (26 March 2020).

Spilimbergo, Antonio, Steve Symansky, Olivier Blanchard, and Carlo Cottarelli (2008). 'Fiscal Policy for the Crisis.' *IMF Staff Position Note of the Fiscal Affairs and Research Departments.* Washington D.C.: The International Monetary Fund, 29 December 2008.

Statista (2019). 'Share of total contributions to the European Union budget in 2018, by Member State.'

Statista (2020a). 'Cumulative number of Coronavirus (COVID-19) cases in Italy since February 2020.' (14 May 2020).

Statista (2020b). 'Number of new Coronavirus (COVID-19) cases in Italy since February 2020 (as of May 14, 2020), by date of report.' (14 May 2020).

Statista (2020c). 'Monthly unemployment rate in Italy from January 2018 to March 2020.' (May 2020).

Statistical Data Warehouse (2020). 'GDP Growth – Euro Area.' Frankfurt am Main: European Central Bank.

Staton, Bethan (2020). 'UK construction activity collapses in April.' *Financial Times* (6 May 2020).

Stevis-Gridneff, Martina (2020). 'E.U. Moves to Shore Up Economies Reeling from the Virus.' *The New York Times* (23 April 2020).

Stubbington, Tommy (2019). 'Italian bonds under pressure in wake of political volatility.' *Financial Times* (9 August 2019).

Stubbington, Tommy (2020a). 'Italy bonds reprieved as S&P downgrade avoided.' *Financial Times* (24 April 2020).

Stubbington, Tommy (2020b). 'Rise in Italian yields has echoes of eurozone debt crisis.' *Financial Times* (17 March 2020).

Stubbington, Tommy, and Miles Johnson (2020). 'Fitch cuts Italy's credit rating to one notch above junk.' *Financial Times* (29 April 2020).

Svimez (2020). 'L'impatto economic e sociale del Covid-19: Mezzogiorno e Centro-Nord.' (9 April 2020).

Taylor, Paul (2020). 'Hey, big spender! EU prepares to splash the cash.' *Politico* (24 June 2020).

The Economist (2016). 'How Not to Spend It.' (24 September 2016).

The Economist (2020a).'The Dutch grumble over Europe's coronavirus cheque.' (18 April 2020).

The Economist (2020b). 'European finance ministers ponder coronabonds.' (9 April 2020).

The Local (2020). 'The 25-billion-euro plan to rescue Italy's economy from coronavirus crisis.' (16 March 2020).

Thomas, Leigh (2020). 'Lockdown pushes French unemployment to 11-year low in first quarter.' *Reuters* (14 May 2020).

Tooze, Adam (2018). *Crashed: How a Decade of Financial Crises Changed the World.* New York: Viking, 2018.

Trading Economics (2018). 'Netherlands GDP per capita.'

Trading Economics (2020). 'The Netherlands Government Spending to GDP.'

Treaty of Rome (1957). Treaty establishing the European Economic Community (EEC Treaty).

Tremlett, Giles (2020). 'How did Spain get its coronavirus so wrong.' *The Guardian* (26 March 2020).

Truman, Edwin M. (2008). 'A Blueprint for Sovereign Wealth Fund Best Practices.' *Peterson Institute for International Economics* (April 2008).

Valero, Jorge (2020). 'Leaders pledge to agree on recovery package next month.' *Euractiv* (19 June 2020).

Vallée, Shahin (2020). 'Options for a European Recovery Fund.' *German Council on Foreign Relations* (11 May 2020).

Van Rompuy, Hermann (2012). 'Towards a Genuine Economic and Monetary Union.' Brussels: European Council, December 2012.

Verschuren, Etienne (2017). 'Dijsselbloem verweert zich na kritiek op 'drank en vrouwen' uitspraak.' *NRC Handelsblad* (22 March 2017).

Vincent, Matthew (2020a). 'FCA makes emergency fundraisings easier for UK-listed companies.' *Financial Times* (8 April 2020).

Vincent, Matthew (2020b). 'UK regulator says coronavirus is first test of post-2008 banking rules.' *Financial Times* (20 April 2020).

Walker, Ali, and Eline Schaart (2020). 'How Wopke Hoekstra became Europe's bond villain.' *Politico* (19 April 2020).

Weiss, Miles, Michael and Holter (2020). 'Norway's $1 Trillion Wealth Fund Expands U.S. Stakes Amid Rout.' *Bloomberg* (1 May 2020).

Werner, Erica (2020). 'House Democrats pass $3 trillion coronavirus relief bill despite Trump's veto threat.' *The Washington Post* (16 May 2020).

World Bank (2018). 'GDP (constant 2010 US$) – France.' World Bank national accounts data.

Wolff, Guntram B., Rebecca Christie (2019). 'Politics, not policy will help Lagarde save the eurozone.' *Politico* (29 October 2019).

Woudt, Job. (2020) 'Rijk maakt overuren om bedrijven van noodgeld te voorzien.' *Het Financiële Dagblad* (March 2020).

Wyplosz, Charles (2020). 'The European Commission budget: Old show with new twists.' *VoxEU Centre for Economic Policy Research* (14 February 2020).

Za, Valentina, Gareth Jones, and Helen Popper (2020). 'Italy's Di Maio Says 'Pragmatism' Comment Referred to EU, Not ESM.' *Reuters* (25 April 2020).

Zondag met Lubach (2020). 'Italië is boos.' Season 11, 5 April 2020.

Zunzunegui, Fernando (2020). 'The Spanish loan debt moratorium due to COVID-19, a minimal measure.' *Regulación Financiera: Revista de Derecho del Mercado Financiero* (21 April 2020).

Made in the USA
Monee, IL
04 November 2026

67380392R00105